Insight Guide

New Orleans

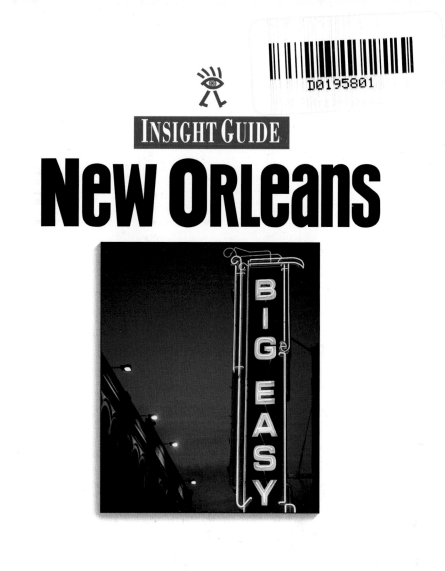

Discovery CHANNEL

APA PUBLICATIONS
Part of the Langenscheidt Publishing Group
L

D0195801

ABOUT THIS BOOK

Editorial

Project Editor
Martha Ellen Zenfell
Editorial Director
Brian Bell

Distribution

UK & Ireland
GeoCenter International Ltd
The Viables Centre , Harrow Way
Basingstoke, Hants RG22 4BJ
Fax: (44) 1256-817988

United States
Langenscheidt Publishers, Inc.
46–35 54th Road, Maspeth, NY 11378
Fax: (718) 784-0640

Worldwide
Apa Publications GmbH & Co.
Verlag KG (Singapore branch)
38 Joo Koon Road, Singapore 628990
Tel: (65) 865-1600. Fax: (65) 861-6438

Printing

Insight Print Services (Pte) Ltd
38 Joo Koon Road, Singapore 628990
Tel: (65) 865-1600. Fax: (65) 861-6438

© 2000 Apa Publications GmbH & Co.
Verlag KG (Singapore branch)
All Rights Reserved
First Edition 1992
Third Edition 1999
Reprinted 2000

This guidebook combines the
interests and enthusiasms of
two of the world's best known
information providers: Insight
Guides, whose titles have set the
standard for visual travel guides
since 1970, and Discovery Channel, the world's premier source of
nonfiction television programming.
Insight Guides' editors provide
practical advice and general
understanding about a
place's history, culture
and people. Discovery
Channel and its
extensive web site,
www. discovery.com,
help millions of viewers
explore their world from the comfort of their home and also encourage them to explore it firsthand.

How to use this book
The book is carefully structured
to convey an understanding of
New Orleans and its culture and
to guide readers through its
sights and attractions:

◆ The book begins with
History and **Features**,
topped with a yellow
color bar. They cover
the city's origins
and culture in lively
essays written by on-
the-spot specialists.

◆ The **Places** section, with a blue bar, provides full details of all the sights and all the areas surrounding the city worth seeing. The major places of interest are coordinated by number with specially drawn maps.

◆ The **Travel Tips** section, with an orange bar, at the back of the book, offers a convenient point of reference for information on travel, accommodation, places to drink and to eat, and other practical aspects of the city. Information may be located using the index printed on the back cover flap, which also serves as a handy bookmark.

The contributors

This new edition builds on the earlier edition also project edited by Southern-girl-turned-Londoner **Martha Ellen Zenfell**, a journalist and editor who has been in charge of many American-based Insight Guides. Zenfell had the ideas for the book, then found the writers and sought out the photographers. First on the list, then as now, was **Honey Naylor**, long-term French Quarter resident who now lives in the Louisiana house in which she was born. Not only is she this book's main writer, but she's also our woman on-the-spot who keeps London informed of any changes to the area. Our specialists are local, talented and varied: historian **Clive Hardy**; newspaper woman **Iris T. Kelso**; editor and publisher **Errol Laborde**; editor and novelist **Susan Larson**; music producer **Kalamu ya Salaam**; and broadcaster **Tom Fitzmorris**. Other local tidbits came from **Arthur Hardy, Patti Nickell, Mel Leavitt**, and **Gaspar J. "Buddy" Stall**. The photographs came from a variety of sources, but the overall tone and feel can be put down to the images of **Ping Amranand** and Big Easy snappers **Syndey Byrd, Alex Demyan** and **Brian Gauvin**, who also penned a couple of pieces for us. Thanks, too to **Tim Harper; Lisa** and **David Shroyer; Beverly Gianna** of the Nola Metropolitan Convention and Visitors Bureau; **Bruce Morgan** of the Louisiana State Office of Tourism; and in London **Emily Hatchwell; Jeff Evans** and **Tim Harrison**.

Map Legend

-----	State Boundary
-----	National Park/Reserve
-----	Ferry Route
✈ ✈	Airport: International/Regional
🚌	Bus Station
P	Parking
❶	Tourist Information
✉	Post Office
† ✝	Church/Ruins
†	Monastery
☪	Mosque
✡	Synagogue
🏰	Castle/Ruins
∴	Archeological Site
∩	Cave
⚱	Statue/Monument
★	Place of Interest

The main places of interest in the Places section are coordinated by number with a full-color map (e.g. ❶), and a symbol at the top of every right-hand page tells you where to find the map.

CONTENTS

The living is easy around Jackson Square.

Travel Tips

Insight on ...

Information panels

Places

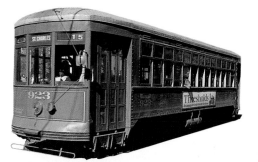

THE CITY THAT CARE FORGOT

A mix of cultures, a history as hot and spicy as its food, and an easy-going

attitude to life have given New Orleans a character unlike anywhere else

As a matter of geography and politics, New Orleans is very much an American city. But to understand the place properly, it is important to realize that, in terms of character and personality, it is much more than just American and much more than just a city.

In many ways New Orleans is an island, with the river curving around one side, Lake Pontchartrain and its marshes on another, and located along the nation's southern rim by the Gulf of Mexico. Like an island it tends to have a style of its own, including its own dialect. Its celebrations, though influenced by places near its borders as well as by the ships passing through, are also distinctive.

In some ways, New Orleans might even be considered to be the northern-most isle of the Caribbean, a crescent-shaped piece of territory that seems as though it were pushed from the sea into the womb of Louisiana by some ancient hurricane. As in most Caribbean spots, there is a black majority in New Orleans, though a European heritage and white economic power.

A culture of celebration

Like the Caribbean, New Orleans also has a native music form, a tradition of Carnival celebrations, poverty, yet a wealthy social class, voodoo, and a form of cooking that is as hot and spicy as the passions of both the islands and the city. See New Orleans and, in some ways, you see the world.

See New Orleans and you're also likely to see some type of celebration, many of which reflect different parts of the world. Festivals reign all year long in New Orleans. Next to Mardi Gras, the biggest festival is the New Orleans Jazz Fest, which is spread over two weekends in late April and early May. But sometimes it is the smaller celebrations that can be the most charming.

PRECEDING PAGES: Mardi Gras merry-makers; deli men and muffulettas; well-heeled residents of the French Quarter; a secure home entrance.
LEFT: wedding bells.
RIGHT: belle and bow on Bourbon Street.

New Orleans, being a port city, has a substantial ethnic heritage. St Patrick's Day is celebrated by the Irish here; the only difference is that the local version has a Mardi Gras touch, including floats. And whereas in Mardi Gras trinkets are thrown from the floats, the St Patrick's revelers also throw cabbage and potatoes.

Two days later the local Sicilians celebrate St Joseph's Day by building altars to their patron saint. Many of the altars are built in homes as repayment for favors granted to those who prayed to St Joseph for help. St Joseph is also honored by the city's black community. By tradition, the Mardi Gras Indians – "tribes" of blacks who wear glittery American Indian costumes on Mardi Gras – make one appearance outside Carnival, and that is usually on a weekend near to St Joseph's Day. Some black families also build altars to the saint.

New Orleans, of course, is a living altar to the god Music and on weekends during the fall, you will find various black marching groups enlivening their neighborhoods with spontaneous brass-band parades. By reputation, however, if not by fact, the groups of people with which New Orleans is most identified are the "Creoles" and the "Cajuns," both terms that are frequently misused. New Orleans, by its heritage, is a Creole city, but, despite what some natives think and what some brochures may suggest, it is not strictly Cajun.

A "Creole," as the term was originally used in the city, was any native-born person whose family was directly linked to either France

or Spain. During the next two and a half centuries that term would blur and become less relevant as the population of New Orleans increasingly comprised American hybrids rather than first-generation Europeans. The word "Creole" would come to describe just about anything that had some link, albeit a distant link, to New Orleans itself. Thus a locally grown species of tomato is known as the "Creole tomato," a version of the popular soup, gumbo, is called "Creole gumbo."

When applied to people in modern New Orleans, the term is most often given to those within the black community whose ancestry traces back to the union of slave women who served as mistresses to French gentlemen. They

> ### LAZY LIVING
> The leisured pace helped preserve the city's unique architecture during a period when many other towns were brutally modernized.

constitute an important part of the city and its culture, now as well as then.

The so-called "black Creoles" tend to have fairer skin than most other American blacks. They generally have French names, and their families tend to have more wealth than the rest of the black community. They have been the business leaders within black New Orleans and, in recent years, an increasing number of the city's leadership has been from that group of people. New Orleans, once a Creole city, is becoming a Creole city again – only the definition has changed.

The Cajun heritage

"Cajun" is a little less complex, although the word seems to be equally misused. The original Cajuns were French who had settled in Nova Scotia on the northeastern Canadian shore. During the 1700s, they were displaced by the British and moved to France, but, failing to settle, they headed back to North America. The largest group of them settled in southern Louisiana. As the section of Nova Scotia from which they originally came was known as "Acadia," the word "Cajun" evolved to describe them. If there is a Louisiana town that can truly be called "Cajun" it is Lafayette – about 120 miles west, as the crow flies, from New Orleans.

The Cajuns are known as a fun-loving people who have their own music and dance form. Cajun cooking is known for its spiciness. New Orleans' prominence in modern Cajun history lies in being the home of Paul Prudhomme, the rotund Cajun chef who has created a new era of Cajun dishes and popularized them around the world. Prudhomme's version of blackened redfish became such a rage that the Gulf of Mexico was almost depleted of the fish.

Adding to the confusion are the many residents of Louisiana whose ancestry is French and who think they are "Cajun," but who in fact are not. They are the descendants of early settlers who came directly from France and who were part of no particular great migration other than the movement west. They are technically not Cajuns, at least not according to blood and history, although they are by spirit and personality.

When people of different types share one island, they develop some similarities. New Orleanians are, for the most part, united in:

- thinking that they are a unique people and that nobody else really understands them;
- being overwhelmed by snow or cold weather, which they seldom experience;
- expecting their food to be spicy;
- celebrating Mardi Gras (even if that means leaving town for the holiday);
- being fascinated by politics;
- rooting for their frequently beleaguered professional football team, the Saints.

Like the inhabitants of tropical islands, New Orleanians tend toward life at a leisurely pace, and it is that pace that is one of the most endearing characteristics of the city. It is a town that

impressive aquarium draw both to the waterfront.

Water continues to nourish the city. New Orleans' port may not what it was in the days before railroading, when steamships lined the waterfront; nevertheless, it is still one of the busiest ports in the world.

The survival instinct

But if shipping is in the middle of an economic struggle, another industry, tourism, has increased dramatically. Paddle wheelers that once carried bales of cotton along the Mississippi now carry groups of visitors instead. Nearby, the European architecture of the French Quarter has been

has never been in a hurry. Sometimes that has worked to its advantage. New Orleans, for example, was not in a hurry to modernize at a time when other cities were tearing down old buildings and plowing across their waterfronts to make way for expressways.

Because of that, New Orleans preserved its French Quarter and maintained its river's edge, which today is the center of recreational and leisure development. The city is discovering that, when done correctly, what serves the tourist can serve locals as well. Developments such as the

LEFT AND ABOVE: New Orleanians feel they are a unique people and that nobody else understands them.

preserved, but behind the walls there is still a living, working neighborhood.

The city itself is also showing signs of life, although it is troubled by the maladies of modern cities everywhere. In a sense, New Orleans might be compared to Venice and other grand old romantic cities of the world that sometimes suffer by comparison to the economic and political roles they held in previous centuries, but that survive fairly well intact all the same.

Great cities are immortal because there is so much to them worth preserving. If New Orleans ceased to exist there would be a need to create something to take its place. Most people, after all, yearn for an island.   ❑

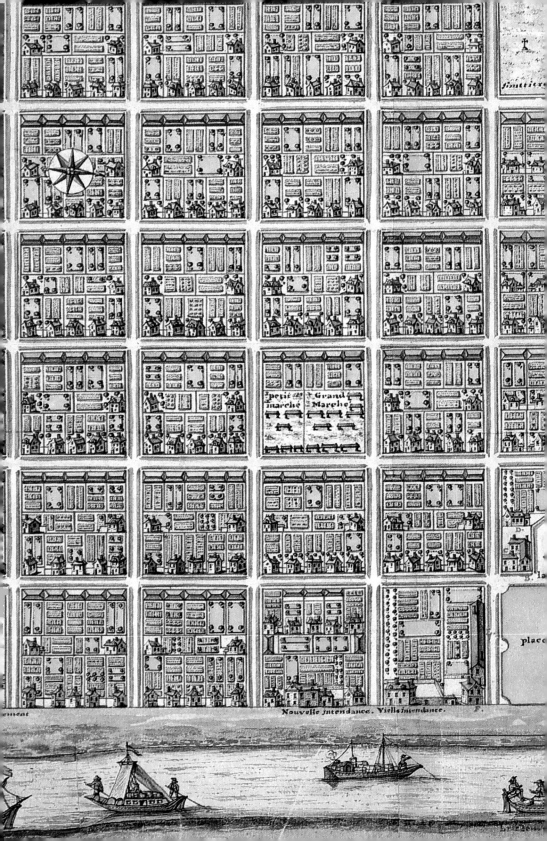

simitiere

petit marché   Grand Marché

Nouvelle intendance. Vielle intendance.

place

Eglise des Religieuse.

fleuve S. louis
à 400 pieds de profondeur

Decisive Dates

1541 Spanish explorer Hernando de Soto, traveling across-country from present-day Florida, becomes the first European to see the Mississippi River.

1682 Rene Robert Cavalier, Sieur de La Salle, follows the Mississippi all the way from Canada to the Gulf, where he plants the French fleur-de-lis, erects a wooden cross, and claims the territory for France. He names it *Louisiane*, after his king, Louis XIV.

1699 Pierre Le Moyne, Sieur d'Iberville, leads an exploratory party north from the mouth of the Mississippi. On March 2, they make camp south of New Orleans, which they christen *Pointe du Mardi Gras*. On May 4, Iberville sails for France to raise money and recruit colonists, leaving his brother Bienville in command.

1704 The *Pelican* arrives from France, bringing soldiers, workers, and 23 girls as brides for colonists. Thirty-five people die in a yellow fever epidemic.

1717 The French government grants an exclusive charter to John Law's Company of the West (later called The Company of the Indies) for control of Louisiana.

1718 On Law's instructions, Bienville selects the site for a colony on the Mississippi River and christens it *La Nouvelle Orleans*, after Philippe, Duc d'Orléans, regent to the child-king Louis XV. The colony has a total population of 68.

1720 The population of the colony, including about 600 black slaves, is estimated at around 6,000 people.

1722 Bienville establishes his official residence in New Orleans, which is officially designated the capital of the colony.

1723 A hurricane destroys most of the homes and many of the crops in New Orleans.

1728 The first *filles à la cassette* (casket girls) arrive in New Orleans, sent by the French government to become brides for the settlers.

1729 Natchez Indians attack Fort Rosalie, killing 250 colonists and slaves and taking more than 450 captive. Political and religious discord in the colony accelerates.

1731 The Company of the Indies relinquishes its charter, and Louisiana becomes a French Crown Colony.

1736 Peace is made with local Indians.

1740 Two hurricanes devastate crops and create near-famine conditions in the colony.

1762 By the secret treaty of Fontainbleau, Louis XV gives the troublesome Louisiana colony, including New Orleans, to Spain.

1769 Alejandro O'Reilly, an Irishman in the service of Spain, arrives in New Orleans with 2000 troops to restore order after a rebellion against the previous Spanish governor, Don Antonio de Ulloa. "Bloody O'Reilly" executes five leaders of the revolt, and forces leading Creoles to swear allegiance to Spain.

1785 A Spanish census puts the population of New Orleans at 4,980, and the entire colony at more than 32,000.

1788 Four-fifths of New Orleans is destroyed by a raging fire.

1794 A second great fire in New Orleans destroys more than 200 buildings.
Louisiana's first newspaper – *Le Moniteur de la Louisiane* – is published in New Orleans.

1796 Spanish Governor Carondelet establishes the first police force in New Orleans.

1800 Napoleon Bonaparte of France and Charles IV of Spain sign the secret Treaty of Ildefonso, which provides for the recession of Louisiana to France.

1803 In March, the transfer of Louisiana from Spain to France is announced. In April,

President Thomas Jefferson's $15 million purchase of Louisiana is concluded. On December 20, Commissioners W.C.C. Claiborne and General James Wilkinson accept Louisiana from France in the name of the United States. The population of Louisiana is estimated at 49,473, and of New Orleans at 8,056.

1805 New Orleans is incorporated as a city.

1812 Louisiana is admitted to the Union as the 18th state, and the first state constitution is adopted.

1815 The Battle of New Orleans.

1831 The Pontchartrain Railroad – the first railroad west of the Alleghenies – begins both passenger and freight service.

1838 New Orleans' first Mardi Gras parade takes place on Fat Tuesday.

1840 With a population of 102,193, New Orleans becomes the fourth largest city in the country.

1853 Over 11,000 New Orleanians die in the worst yellow fever epidemic in history.

1857 New Orleans' first Carnival organization – the Mystick Krewe of Comus – is formed.

1861 On March 21, Louisiana formally joins the Confederacy.

1862 On April 16, a Yankee fleet begins a five-day bombardment of Forts Jackson and St Philip at the mouth of the Mississippi. Ten days later New Orleans falls, and Gen. Benjamin Butler begins military rule of New Orleans.

1865 The war ends, and Reconstruction of the South begins.

1868 Under Radical Republican Governor Benjamin F. Flanders, a new state constitution is adopted. Louisiana is readmitted to the Union.

1872 Rex, King of Carnival, parades for the first time in New Orleans.

1884 The World's Industrial and Cotton Centennial Exposition opens in New Orleans,

1900 Louis Armstrong is born in the slums.

1915 New Orleans music is introduced to Chicago. It is called "jazz."

1928 Huey Pierce Long is inaugurated as Governor of Louisiana.

1933 After four years of construction, the $2 million Harvey Locks are completed, linking the

Mississippi and the Intracoastal Waterway.

1948 Tennessee Williams is awarded the Pulitzer Prize for *A Streetcar Named Desire*.

1957 The 24-mile-long Lake Pontchartrain Causeway – the world's longest overwater highway bridge – is dedicated.

1963 For the first time in the school's history, five blacks are accepted at Tulane University.

1975 The Louisiana Superdome opens.

1977 Ernest N. ("Dutch") Morial becomes the first black mayor of New Orleans.

1979 As a result of a police strike, Mardi Gras in New Orleans is canceled.

1987 Pope John Paul II visits New Orleans on a tour of the US. The plaza in front of St Louis Cathedral is christened Place Jean Paul Deux.

1991 The state legislature legalizes riverboat gambling on the Mississippi River and state waterways.

1993 A license is awarded to Harrah's Jazz Co. permitting them a land-based casino. It opens several years later.

1998 The New Orleans Center for Creative Artists opens a multimillion dollar facility below the French Quarter. NOCCA graduates include Harry Connick, Jr. and Wynton Marsalis.

2000 New Orleans celebrates the new millennium in customary big-party style.   ❑

PRECEDING PAGES: Plan de la Ville de la Nouvelle Orleans, 1755.
LEFT: General Pierre Gustave Toutant Beauregard, an early Confederate leader of the Civil War.
RIGHT: playwright Tennessee Williams.

COLONIAL BEGINNINGS

In its early years, New Orleans was a political pawn shuttling between
France and Spain – a hotbed of crooked speculation and unease

On April 9, 1682, at a site on the Mississippi River about 90 miles below present-day New Orleans, the French explorer Robert Cavalier, Sieur de la Salle, and 53 followers erected a cross and a column and proclaimed the region drained by the great river a possession of Louis XIV. Spanish adventurers had skirted and even passed through what is today Louisiana since the early 16th century, but they had come seeking only the quick wealth of gold and silver. Finding none, they had moved on, leaving nothing to mark their passage. La Salle, however, and the other French explorers who shortly followed in his lead, were mainly intent on establishing a colonial empire for the greater glory of their king.

Two years after he first sailed down the Mississippi and claimed the vast heartland of North America for his sovereign, La Salle returned to the region to establish a settlement at the mouth of the great river. But sailing into the Gulf of Mexico, his small flotilla missed the river's mouth and ended in Matagorda Bay, Texas. La Salle spent the next two years in a futile search for the river. His quest ended only when he was murdered by his own men.

War and financial problems prevented further French efforts to establish control over the lower Mississippi Valley until 1697, when the Treaty of Ryswick brought France a respite from war and permitted Louis XIV to once more consider his North American empire. He commissioned an expedition under the command of the Canadian, Pierre le Moyne, Sieur d'Iberville, to establish a colony on the Mississippi and secure French interests in the region.

Consisting of two warships and two small coastal vessels called *traversiers*, Iberville's expedition sailed from Brest in late October 1698. Following stops at Santo Domingo and Pensacola Bay, the small flotilla finally dropped anchor in early February at Ship Island, about 12 miles off the Mississippi Gulf Coast. In the months that followed, Iberville established a headquarters for the colony on Biloxi Bay, at the site of present-day Ocean Springs, Mississippi. During the following spring, he established a second fort, this time on the Mississippi River near the present town of Phoenix. Named for de

la Boulaye, it was the first French settlement in present-day Louisiana. Progress in securing the region for France was slow, however. Wars and Louis XIV's profligacy consumed French energies for the better part of the next decade and a half, and Louisiana remained on the periphery of French concerns.

Mississippi Bubble

Then, in 1715, with the death of the king, Philippe, Duke of Orleans came to power as Regent for Louis XV, the five-year-old great-grandson of the deceased Sun King. For Louisiana this changing of the guard at Versailles would be important. Included in the

---

LEFT: Robert Cavalier proclaims the region a possession of France in 1682.
RIGHT: Philippe, Duke of Orleans, in whose honor the new town was named.

Regent's coterie of friends was the then up-and-coming Scottish financial wizard and bon vivant, John Law. Under the Regent's sponsorship, Law devised a get-rich-quick scheme that included the extravagant promotion of Louisiana as a source of great riches for the easy taking. Later dubbed the Mississippi Bubble, the scheme eventually contributed to the virtual bankruptcy of France, but not before it had two important consequences for Louisiana.

> **LAW'S LANDSCAM**
>
> John Law's landscheme promised settlers "fabulous wealth". All they found once they got to Louisiana were mosquito-infested swamps.

The first to happen was a dramatic increase in the population of the colony, from about

400 in 1717 to about 8,000 in 1721. The second significant consequence was the founding of the city of New Orleans. In 1717, Law's Company of the West determined that a town named in honor of the Regent, the Duke of Orleans, should be established 30 leagues above the entrance to the river at a spot which could be reached by the Mississippi and by Lake Pontchartrain. The town was founded and later governed by Jean Baptiste le Moyne, Sieur de Bienville, Iberville's younger brother and his natural successor when the explorer died, having previously accompanied Iberville on his frontier expeditions.

Work to clear the forest and dense cane breaks that covered the area began in the early spring of 1718, but progress was slow, and when a great flood caused havoc with these initial efforts there was some consideration given to a different location. The project had produced little more than a small clearing and some 35 or 40 haphazardly situated huts and cabins when Adrien de Pauger, an engineer, arrived in late March of 1721 with a plan. Working under the burdens of bureaucratic impediments and natural obstructions, Pauger and 10 soldiers managed in a few weeks to clear a sizable swath close to the river and lay out a grid pattern of streets in the clearing. Much of the building that occurred over the next year and a half was destroyed when the area suffered its first recorded hurricane on September 11, 1722. However, the basic plan of the city had been established, and it dictated the configuration of the rebuilding that quickly followed.

Slavery in the colony

Black slavery had existed in Louisiana from the colony's earliest years, but it was only in 1719 and 1720 that large numbers of black slaves began to arrive. By 1724, these slaves had become so numerous that Bienville felt compelled to promulgate the *Code Noir* for their regulation. Originally drawn up at Versailles for the care and governing of the large slave population in Santo Domingo, the *Code Noir* was designed not only to regulate slave conduct, but to protect slaves from injustice and other ill-treatment. Thus, while it prescribed such harsh penalties as branding and mutilation and even death for stealing or running away or striking a white, it required that masters properly feed and clothe their slaves and allow them respite from work on Sundays and Holy Days.

Other important provisions stipulated that slaves be instructed in Catholicism; that concubinage with slaves and marriage between blacks and whites were forbidden; and that slaves were prohibited from carrying weapons, owning property, and congregating. It also decreed Catholicism the state religion and ordered the expulsion of Jews from the colony. Perhaps most interesting of the Code's numerous provisions was one that granted freed slaves the same rights, privileges and immunities as those enjoyed by the freeborn.

Bienville, for all his long service and considerable accomplishments in establishing French control in the lower Mississippi Valley, seemed always to be at odds with other administrators in the colony. By 1724, it was concluded that criticism of his administration was sufficiently serious to warrant a full investigation. Bienville was recalled to France, but the political and religious discord that plagued the colony was not resolved by his removal. In fact, the respect of the Indians for the French, which Bienville had established and skillfully managed over many years, deteriorated rapidly following his departure. The situation finally boiled over on

by 1733, conditions in New Orleans were precipitous. Money and provisions were in short supply, and morale among administrators and colonists had sunk to a new low.

New hope, old woes

Fortunately, at least two events gave some promise of a brighter future. A small contingent of Ursuline nuns arrived in New Orleans in August, 1727, to establish a school for girls and to care for the sick. The period also witnessed the arrival of several shiploads of young marriageable women of good character. Because the government supplied each of these

November 28, 1729, when Natchez Indians surprised Fort Rosalie on the bluff at Natchez, killing about 250 colonists and slaves, and taking captive perhaps another 450 women, children, and slaves.

Political and religious discord in the colony accelerated. Men of influence decided that Louisiana was a poor investment and petitioned Louis XV to accept its retrocession. The king agreed, and Louisiana was returned to the Crown. Bienville was summoned from retirement to once more govern the colony. But

LEFT: Sieur de Bienville, founder of New Orleans.
ABOVE: trading with the Indians, *circa* 1720.

girls with a chest of clothing and linens, they were called *les filles à la cassette*. Dubbed "casket girls" by later generations, their presence, like that of the Ursulines, added an element of social stability to what was then a raw frontier community. This benign influence would have its effect only after time, however, and, for Bienville, faced with such immediate problems as the growing hostility among the Indians, the ladies were scant comfort.

In an attempt to subdue the openly belligerent Chickasaws, and no doubt intimidate and bolster French prestige among tribes that might be wavering, Bienville mounted two campaigns. In the first of these in 1736, miscalculation and delay turned the operation into a bloody French defeat and withdrawal, leaving French prestige among the Indians even further diminished. Four years later, another move was made against the Chickasaws, but sickness, heavy rains and delays intervened, and in the end, Bienville decided to call off the campaign and offer a negotiated peace. For once, happenstance favored the French. The Chickasaws misinterpreted Bienville's intentions and sued for peace themselves. The end result, however, was less than a French triumph.

For Bienville this failure decisively to defeat and subjugate the Chickasaws climaxed years

DON ALESSANDRO O'REILLY

of frustrations. Aging and depressed by what he viewed as his personal failure, Bienville tendered his resignation and in 1743 left Louisiana for France, never to return.

As it happened, events were already taking place in Canada and Europe that would drastically alter the future course of Louisiana's history. In the 80 years since La Salle had claimed the vast region for Louis XIV, the colony had never shown a profit. Entrepreneurs, joint-stock companies, and two French monarchs had all lost fortunes in attempting to develop it. With the loss of Canada by 1760, Louis XV and his ministers were determined to be rid of the troublesome colony of Louisiana so that they might concentrate their efforts on saving France's West Indian islands.

Spanish cousin

By the secret Treaty of Fountainbleau signed in 1762, Louis XV gave New Orleans and the portion of Louisiana lying to the west of the Mississippi River to his cousin, Carlos III of Spain. This news was received with dismay, particularly in New Orleans, where a mass meeting was held and several of the city's prominent citizens harangued the crowd with inflammatory speeches. A petition urging the king to rescind the colony's transfer was approved, and a wealthy merchant, Jean Milhet, was appointed to carry it to Louis XV at Versailles. But to no avail.

Word of the French Crown's refusal to reclaim Louisiana provoked much huffing and puffing in the streets and taverns of New Orleans, but the bluster of the populace soon subsided. For a small group of the colony's elite, however, the prospect of Spanish rule remained anathema. The merchants and public officials who had prospered under the lax and often corrupt administration of French rule, felt threatened by any change in the status quo, and Spain had a reputation for strictly administering colonies.

On March 5, 1766, Don Antonio de Ulloa, accompanied by a few officials and some 80 soldiers, landed at New Orleans during a driving rainstorm. His reception by the colony's senior officer, Captain Aubry, and other local officials was formal, courteous, and – at least superficially – friendly. A small and not very attractive man with a grating voice and a nervous manner, Governor Ulloa, then aged 50, was regarded as one of Europe's leading scientists. A conscientious and industrious man, he was, unfortunately, also singularly lacking in diplomacy and any form of social grace.

While most of his efforts to improve the condition of the colony and its inhabitants were largely successful, at least some of his actions further antagonized the small clique of malcontents. The growing disaffection of the citizenry for Governor Ulloa and his administration finally turned into open rebellion on October 27, 1768, when the Spanish cannons in New Orleans were spiked during the night. On the following day a number of the city's merchants and planters drafted a petition calling for the expulsion of Governor Ulloa and other Spanish authorities, while a mob of several hundred roamed through the streets shouting obscenities and threats against the Spanish authorities. On October 29 the Superior Council met and issued a decree ordering Ulloa and his troops to leave the colony. Apparently realizing the futility of remaining in New Orleans, Ulloa sailed for Cuba.

Some nine months would pass before Spain reasserted its authority over the colony. As the principal official on the scene during the interim, Captain Aubry forwarded reports

THE BIG SECRET

The secret Treaty of Fountainbleu, transferring Louisiana from France to Spain, was signed in 1762. But the news didn't reach New Orleans for nearly four years.

of 24 ships had entered the river and dropped anchor. The large size of the Spanish fleet left no doubt that the Spanish Crown meant to assert its sovereignty in Louisiana. The next day at a large public gathering in the Place d'Armes, Captain Aubry announced the impending arrival of General Alejandro O'Reilly and his forces. He advised the citizenry that immediate and complete acquiescence to Spanish authority was imperative and warned that any defiance of that authority risked severe consequences.

on local conditions to his own government at Versailles and to the Spanish authorities in Havana. Conditions of turmoil and instances of near violence were common themes in these communications, with the onus for such conditions falling on Ulloa in Aubry's reports to Versailles, and on local French officials in his separate reports to Havana.

The torpor that envelops New Orleans during the hot summer months was suddenly broken on July 24 by word that a Spanish armada

LEFT: Nouvelle Orleans became a Spanish city under General O'Reilly.
ABOVE: a pre-renovation Place d'Armes.

Down with the French

Three weeks later, all 24 vessels of O'Reilly's fleet had completed the tedious upriver voyage to New Orleans and lay moored opposite the Place d'Armes. At five in the afternoon, the loud bang of a signal cannon startled the curious who had thronged the levee and muddy streets since early morning. A cadence of snare drums followed, interspersed with barked commands in Spanish, as some 2,600 Spanish troops marched in close precision down gangplanks across the low levee and into the Place d'Armes.

A brief ceremony ensued during which the flag of Bourbon France came down and that of Bourbon Spain went up. The ceremonies concluded with shouts of *Viva el Rey* from sailors high in the fleet's riggings and the thunderous reverberations of a salute from the ships' cannon. The provincial populace of New Orleans had witnessed a spectacle that none would forget. Three days later, after reviewing reports by Ulloa and others, and interviewing several local officials, O'Reilly ordered the arrest and trial of 12 leaders in the revolt against Don Antonio de Ulloa. Six were condemned, and five of these – one having previously died in a scuffle with his jailers – were ordered to be hanged. When no hangman could be found, O'Reilly ordered the shooting of the condemned men. The exe-

cutions were carried out the next day in the courtyard of a barracks located near the present site of the Old Mint Building.

Over a period of a few months, O'Reilly instituted a wide range of reforms. For the colony as a whole, he substituted Spanish laws for the French laws that had previously governed, while in New Orleans he replaced the old French Superior Council with a Spanish *Cabildo*, or municipal council. He organized a competent militia and improved the city's fortifications and public structures. To better the social and economic condition of the citizenry, he set prices for food and essential commodities to prevent profiteering and abolished import and export duties to encourage trade. He also ordered a census, which revealed that New Orleans had a population of almost 3,200 persons of all conditions and backgrounds. Perhaps most important of all, O'Reilly wisely left the customs of the local populace undisturbed, a practice which his followers would continue and build upon.

Growing prosperity

Realizing the importance of trade as a basis for any future prosperity, officials often turned a blind eye to the colony's illicit commerce with the British in West Florida and towards smuggling in general. The incipient prosperity that resulted from this benign oversight was further advanced when the governor lowered duties on imports and exports, and initiated regulations that permitted trade with France and the French West Indies, and the duty-free purchase of slaves for a period of 10 years. These actions fostered a general improvement in the economy, which, in turn no doubt, contributed to the lessening of the initial tensions between the local populace and the new Spanish authorities. In addition, any resentment the city's elite bore towards the Spanish for O'Reilly's punishment of the rebellion's leaders soon subsided, as successive and successful leaders married into prominent local families.

The nascent commerce that had been nurtured under previous administrations blossomed during that of General Don Esteban Rodriguez Miro. Great quantities of goods came down the river from the American settlers in the Ohio country and the Northwest Territory. As the transshipment port for these goods, New Orleans in the late 1780s was on the verge of an economic cycle of prosperity that would con-

THIS ALLEY IS NAMED IN MEMORY OF THE SPANIARD ANTONIO DE SEDELLA ALSO LOCALLY KNOWN AS P. ANTOINE WHO WAS RECTOR OF THE CATHE-DRAL FROM 1785 TO 1790 AND FROM 1795 TO 1829.

SPANISH TYRANT – OR BENEFACTOR?

While generations of New Orleans schoolchildren have been instilled with the notion that General O'Reilly was a cruel tyrant and have been taught to refer to him as Bloody O'Reilly, the evidence does not support such harsh reprobation. In fact, O'Reilly's firm handling of the revolutionaries and the changes which he inaugurated laid the foundation for a greater degree of well-being than ever previously enjoyed by Louisiana or its capital, New Orleans. During half a century of French rule, New Orleans and the majority of its people had managed to do little more than survive. Under the Spanish, New Orleans and its people prospered as never before.

tinue and expand, with only minor setbacks, for the next three-quarters of a century.

A census published during Miro's first year as governor revealed that the colony's population had almost doubled under the Spanish and that New Orleans had a population of about 5,000. To govern this burgeoning population, Miro issued a series of regulations entitled *Bando de Buen Gobierno*, or Proclamation of Good Government. Viewed from today's perspective, perhaps the most interesting of the Proclamation's strictures was one that

NEW-LOOK ORLEANS

Governor Miro's new building regulations were intended merely to protect New Orleans from fire. But they also transformed it.

a candle on the altar of a private chapel in a home on Chartres Street fell against some drapery. Because of a strong wind and the refusal of religious authorities to permit the ringing of church bells on Good Friday, fire fighters were not alerted quickly, and the fire was soon out of control. By evening, between 800 and 900 structures had been consumed, with only a few buildings still standing along the river and on the western fringe of the town. Of these remaining structures, the Ursuline Convent on Chartres Street was the most notable.

forbade the wearing of finery by women of color and required that they cover their heads with a *tignon*, a local form of madras turban.

Disaster strikes

In 1788, New Orleans suffered the first of two catastrophic fires that taken together would destroy virtually all of the city that had been built by the French. The 1788 fire began in the early afternoon of Good Friday, March 21, when

LEFT: the rebuilding of New Orleans after the 1788 fire saw a strong Spanish influence asserting itself.
ABOVE: the Ursuline Convent on Chartres Street was one of the few buildings to survive the fire.

Under Miro's direction, a program of rebuilding was begun, and within months, public and private structures were rising from squares of charred desolation. Where formerly there had been a provincial French town, there arose a powerful Spanish town. Where there had been separate residences, there now arose buildings joined by a common wall so that the appearance from the street was one of a continuous façade. Masonry rather than wood became more common as the principal building material and ceramic tile replaced shingles as a roofing material. Perhaps the most notable change was the introduction of an inner courtyard or patio.

The change in the city's appearance, which

began with the rebuilding after the fire of 1788, continued under Miro's successor, François Louis Hector, Baron de Carondelet, who took office on January 1, 1792.

Under Carondelet's administration, the economy of New Orleans continued to expand and the city saw a number of innovations and improvements that altered its appearance and its social environment. Among the most important of these initiatives were the establishment of a corps of armed and uniformed night watchmen to patrol the streets from dusk to dawn; the instal-

> ### CITY OF CULTURE
>
> As well as establishing and editing the colony's first newspaper, the *Moniteur de la Louisiana*, Carondelet inaugurated its first theater in 1792.

lation of oil lamps at street corners to facilitate night traffic; and the digging of a drainage canal from the rear of the city to Bayou St John. Later improvements soon converted the canal, which followed the roadbed of present-day Lafitte Street, to a major waterway for commercial traffic between the city, Lake Pontchartrain, and the eastern Gulf of Mexico. It would remain an important means of transportation and commerce until well into the 20th century.

The revolutionary spirit that swept over France in the early 1790s not surprisingly evoked a sympathetic response in the French Creoles (i.e. persons descended from the original settlers) of New Orleans. These feelings finally boiled over in 1793 with the execution of Louis XVI and the declaration of war between Spain and France. In New Orleans, the singing of the *Marseillaise* and other revolutionary songs and animated talk of republicanism became commonplace. Fearing the worst, Carondelet issued a proclamation that forbade the singing of such songs, the reading or distribution of any printed materials about events in France, and even conversation on the subject.

Architectural shift

For a time Carondelet was successful in suppressing anti-royalist and republican sentiments, but early in 1795 these feelings flared anew. Mobs roamed through the streets destroying property and shouting threats against Spanish officials. By forming an alliance with the local landowning and wealthier classes, Carondelet once more managed to dampen the revolutionary fervor. He also worked to enlarge these conservative classes by encouraging the nobility fleeing France to settle in the colony.

In 1794, on the Feast of the Immaculate Conception, December 8, New Orleans experienced a second major conflagration when children playing in a courtyard on Royal Street accidentally ignited some hay. A strong wind fanned the fire, and in a little over three hours, more than 200 buildings were destroyed.

While fewer structures were lost than in the 1788 fire, the monetary loss was far greater. Determined to prevent such fires in the future, Carondelet instituted a building code with the strict requirement that all structures of more than one story in the built-up part of the city be constructed of adobe or brick and also that they would have tile roofs. These provisions hastened the changing appearance of New Orleans, which increasingly took on a Spanish flavor. The imposing Cabildo and Presbytère, which flank the St Louis Cathedral in what is now Jackson Square, are prominent examples of Spanish-influenced buildings that were begun after the fire of 1794.

It would not be long, however, before time began to run out for the Spanish in Louisiana. ❏

LEFT: New Orleans enjoyed a period of rapid growth under the leadership of Baron de Carondelet.
RIGHT: a Creole courtyard in stained glass.

VIEUX CARRE AND CARNIVAL

*In just four decades, New Orleans was transformed from a loss-making backwater
into an economic boomtown. The steamboat was coming*

The rise of Napoleon Bonaparte to First Consul of France was the impetus for the decline of the Spanish in Louisiana. Having consolidated his power at home, Napoleon turned his attention to the acquisition of an overseas empire. To this end he pressured Spain to cede Louisiana back to France.

While the retrocession was accomplished by the Treaty of San Ildefonso, which was signed on October 1, 1800, the actual transfer of control over the colony was postponed until the insurrection then raging in the French colony of Saint-Domingue could be quelled. The revolutionary ideas that Carondelet had so feared as potentially dangerous to the well-being and stability of Louisiana had, indeed, ignited a blood bath on the West Indian island that Napoleon regarded as essential to his plans for an overseas empire.

Word of the retrocession reached President Thomas Jefferson, who viewed French control of New Orleans as a threat to the essential egress of American goods produced in the upper valley. In an effort to avoid the necessity of having to seize the city, which some influential members of Congress increasingly favored, Jefferson sent Secretary of State James Monroe to approach the French about the purchase of New Orleans.

American transfer

Even before Monroe arrived in Paris, Napoleon had determined that the colony could not be held and that it was in his best interest to sell not only New Orleans but all of Louisiana to the United States. Negotiations took a little over two weeks. In the end, a price equivalent to $15 million was agreed upon and official documents for the transactions, dated April 30, 1803, were signed during the first days of May.

Word of Louisiana's sale to the United States

LEFT: the transfer of Louisiana to American rule took place in Jackson Square on December 20, 1803.
RIGHT: de Ulloa, the first Spanish governor. The rise of Napoleon brought the decline of the Spanish.

reached New Orleans in mid-August. The city's populace, already bewildered and more than a little anxious in the contemplation of the colony's transfer to France, received the news with less than enthusiasm. The arrival of Napoleon's emissary, Pierre Clement de Laussat, in late March had stirred considerable anxiety.

In addition to the general apprehension which any citizenry might feel if faced with the prospect of such change, there were the more specific concerns of at least two important groups in the local community. The religious were fearful that Laussat might introduce the anti-Catholic measures then prevalent in France; indeed, the Ursulines were so panicked by the prospect that they left for Havana. Another group made uneasy by Laussat's arrival were the émigrés from the French Revolution who feared the imposition of republicanism, which they considered evil incarnate.

If New Orleanians felt little or no enthusiasm for the idea of being governed by the

United States, the new status at least relieved their foreboding over Laussat and a return to French rule. For his part, Laussat was chagrined. As the newly appointed Colonial Prefect of Louisiana, he had come to New Orleans to build an empire for France, and now, only months later, he learned that his assignment had been changed to that of liquidator for a major part of the empire.

In accord with his new role, however, Laussat formally received the colony from Spain on November 30 and three weeks later transferred

ownership of the land to the United States.

At the time of Louisiana's transfer to the United States, New Orleans was a small, provincial town of just over 8,000 people with blacks accounting for slightly more than half of the population. More than half of the latter were slaves, but the number of free blacks was substantial. Creoles of French, African, and Spanish descent were in the majority, but there was also a significant element with other origins. Physically, the town consisted of about 1,300 structures situated almost entirely in the area that is today called the *Vieux Carré* – or, more commonly, the French Quarter.

At the heart of the old town, facing the river

PIRATES ON PAY

The notorious privateers Jean and Pierre Lafitte were offered full pardons in return for fighting in the Battle of New Orleans.

across a large, unkempt square (then called the Place d'Armes) stood a twin-towered St Louis Cathedral flanked by a two-storied Cabildo and a partially constructed Presbytère. In addition to perhaps 10 commission houses, two or three small banks, and a half dozen general stores, there were taverns, gambling houses and billiard rooms.

The streets were unpaved, and what few sidewalks there were, were mainly of cypress planking. Open ditches flanking the street served as drains, but all too often they were clogged with garbage and unspeakable waste. Hard rains were the principal agent for flushing these ditches, but more often than not, they only inundated the streets and distributed the waste more widely. In dry weather clouds of dust coated everything and everyone with a layer of grime. When the stench became unbearable, and then only occasionally, slaves were put to work flushing the ditches.

The Battle of New Orleans

On June 19, 1812, just seven weeks after Louisiana's admission to the Union, the United States declared war on Great Britain. For the next two and a half years the war would go badly for the United States, with even its capital being sacked and burned in the fierce summer of 1814. However, except for a British blockade at the mouth of the Mississippi, Louisiana and New Orleans remained largely unaffected. Then, in the final weeks of the war, New Orleans became the scene of the only major American victory of the entire conflict.

Aware that the British were assembling a large force in Jamaica for a probable campaign against Louisiana, the Federal government in November, 1814, ordered General Andrew Jackson to proceed to New Orleans. Jackson arrived in the city with a small force on December 1, just nine days before a massive British fleet from Jamaica dropped anchor close to the entrance to Lake Borgne. Consisting of 50 vessels and an army of 10,000 troops under the command of General Sir Edward Pakenham, it was a force sufficient to give pause to even so undauntable a general as Jackson.

Since his arrival in the city, Jackson had worked feverishly to prepare a proper defense. He had ordered the immediate redeployment to

New Orleans of troops in Baton Rouge, Natchez and Mobile; ordered the positioning of artillery at strategic approaches to the city; and ordered old fortifications strengthened and new ones to be constructed.

On the morning of December 28, General Pakenham ordered a reconnaissance in force to test Jackson's defenses, but after suffering heavy casualties and making no gains, it retreated. Then on New Year's Day, the Americans decided to celebrate the occasion with a full military review on the field behind their

WASTED LIVES

A peace treaty between Britain and the US had been signed in Belgium on December 24 – two weeks before the Battle of New Orleans.

ragtag ranks broke and everyone raced helter-skelter back to the breastworks. The Americans regrouped and returned fire, and an artillery duel commenced. It inflicted very little damage on the American line and broke off about one o'clock when the British guns finally went silent.

At about six o'clock on the morning of January 8, British units in tight formation began a steady-paced advance on the American lines. American artillery firing grapeshot and ball cut large swaths through the close ranks that continued

line. As bands played, various units of what may have been the strangest looking army ever assembled marched up and down, with banners flying. Consisting of general citizenry of all conditions and classes, regular army troops, ill-trained militiamen, free men of color of various shades, rough-hewn privateers, and a few Indian warriors, it was a true panoply of American frontier democracy. In the middle of the ceremonies British cannon suddenly commenced a bombardment, and all turned to confusion as the

LEFT: the Battle of New Orleans commenced on January 8, 1815, and became a significant victory.
ABOVE: duels were fought in New Orleans' City Park.

without flinching to press forward. Finally, Jackson's riflemen opened a continuous fire that riddled the British ranks. Units dropped back and reformed and then moved forward once more. Suddenly, however, units began to break up as men turned and ran. Reportedly, Pakenham was riding forward to rally the troops when he was shot from his horse. It was at this point that British General John Lambert ordered a retreat that marked the end of the Battle of New Orleans.

Widely differing casualty figures have been given for the battle of January 8. A participant on the American side put American casualties at 71, including 13 dead. The British placed their dead at 858 and wounded at 2,468, with many missing. While authorities differ on specific figures, all have agreed that American losses were very small and British losses horrifically large.

Under United States sovereignty, New Orleans entered upon an era of extraordinary prosperity that would last, with only brief setbacks, for some 57 years. This prosperity and the expansion that it fueled were the result of several factors, the most important of which was the city's location on the Mississippi River. Because the Mis-

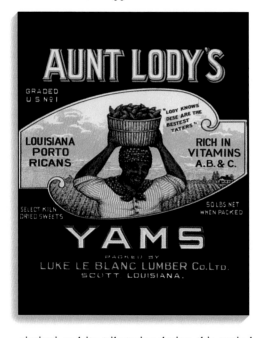

AUNT LODY'S

GRADED
U S Nº I

LOUISIANA
PORTO
RICANS

"LODY KNOWS
DESE ARE THE
BESTEST
TATERS"

RICH IN
VITAMINS
A.B.& C.

SELECT KILN
DRIED SWEETS

50 LBS NET
WHEN PACKED

YAMS

PACKED BY
LUKE LE BLANC LUMBER Co.Ltd.
SCOTT LOUISIANA.

sissippi and its tributaries during this period served as the primary means of commercial transportation for the vast Mississippi valley, and because virtually all goods entering or leaving had to pass through New Orleans, the city became a sort of tollhouse for the region. Arriving from upriver, the products of the valleys were reloaded at New Orleans to oceangoing vessels for shipment to the East Coast and Europe. Handling this transshipment required an army of factors, insurers, shippers, stevedores, and the like, with each extracting a toll.

A second factor which contributed to the city's burgeoning economy was the advent of the steamboat. Up to 1812, shipping on the

river was by keelboat and *radeau*, a form of flatboat, with propulsion by sail, oar, and pole. Such craft worked reasonably well when moving with the current, but were less than satisfactory when moving against it. The problem was solved by the coming of the steamboat, which converted the great river from a one-way to a two-way artery of commerce. Although the steamboat failed to make New Orleans a major entry point for imports, it played a significant role in the city's becoming a port of entry for some half-million immigrants in the period before 1860.

Major port

Ships carrying cotton, sugar, and other goods from New Orleans to such ports as Liverpool, Le Havre, and Hamburg quickly found a profitable return cargo in the Irish, French, and German immigrants seeking cheap passage to the promise of the New World. Only a few of these immigrants would remain in the city, the great majority journeying upriver in quest of cheap land and a new life. In doing so, they provided a profitable passenger market for steamboats returning upriver after depositing their cargoes in New Orleans.

While the number of European immigrants settling in the city remained relatively small in comparison to the number who passed through, it was sufficient, when coupled with the large influx of Anglo-Americans and their slaves, to quickly balloon the local population. Thus, the city's population grew from just over 8,000 in 1803 to 41,000 by 1820, and better than double again by 1840 to make the city the fourth largest in the nation. This growth in population would continue unabated up to the outbreak of the Civil War, with the 1860 census recording a populace of just over 168,000. Blacks by then no longer outnumbered whites as they had until 1830, but still remained a large segment of the total population that included about 11,000 slaves.

Prior to the Louisiana Purchase, most New Orleans Creoles had had little contact with Anglo-Americans except for the rustics who arrived in the city by keel and flatboat. Having sold their cargoes, these rough-hewn men often spent at least a few days in rowdy carousing along the riverfront, before departing for their upriver farms and communities. Not surprisingly, such individuals and their behavior left a not very flattering impression on the Creoles.

The Anglo-Americans who arrived in New Orleans after 1803 were, in the main, a very different lot. Businessmen, lawyers, doctors, bookkeepers, and such, they were the newly emerging American middle class, better educated and, of course, far more polished than their frontier countrymen. Almost to a man they had come to make their fortunes in what was fast becoming the El Dorado of the American West. In brief, they were more given to industry and hustle than to drunken brawling.

Even so, for the Creoles these newcomers resentment, and occasional hostility. Conversely, courtesy and friendliness on the part of an individual American usually elicited a like response from the average Creole.

French disdain

The French immigrants from the continent and Saint-Domingue regarded the local Creoles with as much or even more disdain than the Americans. To these Frenchmen the city's French Creoles were bumpkins. But the Americans were the real threat to the city's Gallic culture, and the recognition of this fact by the two French-speaking groups quickly led to their

and especially their rapidly growing numbers posed a threat. To begin with, they didn't speak French or show the slightest inclination to learn how. *Mon Dieu*, on occasion they even voiced the opinion that it was a backward impediment! Nor did their inability to speak French impede their fulsome capacity to communicate their disdain for the locals and their ways. For their part the Creoles responded to real or fancied slights by the Americans much as any indigenous people might: with trepidation, diffidence,

---

LEFT: yams were one of the state's many exports.
ABOVE: Louisiana's burgeoning economy was influenced by the invention of the steamboat.

BOOM TOWN

Anglo-Americans from across the South and East Coast made up the majority of the great influx of the early 1800s. But there were other sizable groups, most notably the Irish, the Germans and, not least, the French. In all, the city was a port of entry for some half-million immigrants from Europe in the period before 1860.

Room had to be found for all these new arrivals, and New Orleans quickly grew in size. Where only a few years before there had been woods and bogs and plantation fields, roadways were now being cut, lots cleared, and buildings erected as landowners subdivided their properties which bordered on the original city.

alliance against the common enemy. Because the foreign French were generally better educated and more worldly than the "country" Creoles, they became the leaders of this particular alliance.

With this leadership the coalition soon became a political force in the city and state and for many years successfully promoted legislation favorable to its constituencies, while simultaneously thwarting American interests and ambitions. But time and circumstance were not on the Creoles' side. With each passing year more Americans came into the city and state, and as their number increased their power grew.

THE HIGH PRICE OF PROGRESS

In the early 1830s, Samuel J. Peters, a native of Canada, and some fellow entrepreneurs formed the New Orleans Canal and Banking Company to construct a canal from the rear of the newly emerging American enclave, centered around the suburb Faubourg Ste Marie, to Lake Pontchartrain. Just as the Carondelet Canal served the commercial interests of the Vieux Carré, the new canal would serve as a quick route to the American sector.

The work of digging the canal, which had to traverse a vast cypress swamp, fell to Irish immigrants desperate for work. In the process many thousands of them died of cholera, yellow fever, and malaria.

Signs of New Orleans' expanding prosperity were everywhere. In 1833, American businessmen incorporated three small hamlets to form the city of Lafayette. Here, those who made fortunes by brokering and shipping and otherwise handling the cotton, sugar, and other products that passed through the port, built palatial homes surrounded by lush gardens. Here, also, many of the poor Irish who worked on the new canal would live with their families of four and five and even more to a room in small cottages or tenements close by the river. For many years, Magazine Street served as the town's principal thoroughfare separating the Irish section, now called the Irish Channel, from the wealthier area which was eventually dubbed the Garden District, an appelation still used today.

Three cities in one

By the mid-1830s, American influence had grown to a point where it seriously challenged the power wielded by the coalition of foreign French and Creoles. An indication of this growing American power came in 1836 following a court case in which a Creole charged with killing an American in a duel was acquitted. Angered by the court's verdict and determined to break the coalition's control of the city council, the Americans persuaded the state legislature to withdraw the existing city charter and issue a new one dividing the city into three municipalities, each governed by its own board of aldermen and a recorder.

The new charter still provided for a single mayor and a city-wide board of aldermen composed of representatives from the three municipalities, but this fourth board was only authorized to regulate matters of interest to all three municipalities. Under this 1836 charter the old Vieux Carré became the First Municipality, the new American sector above Canal Street became the Second Municipality, while the Third Municipality was composed of all other areas of the city not included in the others.

A large and conspicuous segment of the local population that had no voice in the government of the city were the free people of color. They could not vote or hold office or serve on juries or in the militia. In general, however, they had more legal rights than free blacks in most other Southern states or even some Northern states. They did have access to the courts for redress, and they could own and bequeath property, including slaves. While most were small trades-men, more than a few were capable entrepreneurs and some amassed considerable fortunes.

While the laws were generally restrictive of the rights and privileges granted to free blacks, they were often not enforced. The famous quadroon balls that openly controverted a law prohibiting blacks from intermingling with whites in public places were an example of such permissiveness. (A quadroon is a person of mixed blood, one-quarter black.)

Laws governing slaves were if anything even

FREE PEOPLE OF COLOR

Despite its reliance on slavery, by 1840 New Orleans had the largest number of free people of color of any Southern city.

Perhaps the most poignant reminder of how central this peculiar institution was to the city's commerce and culture were the slave auctions held annually during the late winter and early spring. The most famous of these were held in the great halls of the St Louis and St Charles hotels. Here dealers, speculators, merchants, and planters gathered to bid for slaves brought in from the various showrooms and holding barracks throughout the business district. In addition to these large annual auctions, by 1860 there were some two

more restrictive, but these, too, were seldom enforced. Thus, while the law prohibited slaves from owning or carrying guns, many did so with the full knowledge of their masters. There is also considerable evidence that, at least in New Orleans, free blacks and even many slaves were anything but obsequious or particularly submissive in their dealings with white people. More than one visitor to the city remarked on the sight of "impudent" slaves lolling in groups on street corners.

LEFT: plantation slaves.
ABOVE: New Orleans had stores that specialized in domestic servants.

dozen slave markets in the city, which catered throughout the year to the needs of planters and other buyers.

Cobble and flagstone

By the mid-1840s, New Orleans had become one of the nation's great cities. Indeed, if taken with the several communities that were then closely linked to it by rail and were soon to be annexed, it was one of the nation's first great metropolitan centers. Its streets and sidewalks were paved with cobble and flagstone, and illuminated by gas light, the latter having been introduced in 1834 by James Caldwell, an English actor, entrepreneur, and political leader in the American Second Municipality. Caldwell was also a leader in establishing the English-language theater in New Orleans with the erection of his American Theater in the Second Municipality. Illuminated by gas and seating 1,100, it easily rivaled the already well-established St Philips and Orleans theaters which catered to a primarily French-language audience in the First Municipality.

Further evidence of the Americans' growing leadership and dominance in the city came with the establishment in the Second Municipality

DEADLY RECORD

In 1853 yellow fever wiped out 11,000 citizens – the most virulent epidemic in American history.

meanwhile, a number of small private schools continued to educate children of the free blacks, and in 1847 a group of free blacks established a school for that community's indigent orphans. Shortly after its founding, the school received some state funding, which was probably the first instance of support for black education by any state in the southern region.

Perhaps the most conspicuous monuments to the city's affluence in the last two decades before the Civil War were its palatial hotels, which featured accommodations the equal of

of a public school system. Until then education of the city's young had been pretty much hit-and-miss, with a handful of small private and parochial schools or individual tutors providing instruction for children of the well-to-do. Based on a Massachusetts model, then considered the best in the nation, the system was quickly adopted by the other municipalities.

Education for all

Children of slaves and free people of color were excluded from the system and would have to wait another 25 years before war and Union occupation finally initiated the beginnings of public education for the city's blacks. In the

any in the world. Of the city's six or seven major hotels, the most famous was the St Charles, which stood on the site of the present Place St Charles office building in the American Second Municipality. Built at the same time as the St Louis Exchange Hotel, it was regarded by contemporaries as an American response in the rivalry between the Anglo-Americans and the alliance of Creoles and foreign French.

That the Americans had gained the upper hand in this rivalry became obvious in 1852 when the city's three municipalities were reunited under a single board of aldermen and mayor. The newly built Second Municipality Hall (today called Gallier Hall) on Lafayette

Square was chosen as the seat of the new city government. As if to cap their economic and political dominance, the Americans, in 1857, captured the public's imagination with a Carnival parade that would serve as the model for all of the city's future pre-Lenten celebrations.

Carnival coup

Carnival had, of course, been celebrated in New Orleans since its earliest days by masked balls and public cavorting in the streets. During the Spanish period and the early years of American rule it had been discouraged because of rowdy behavior caused by prohibitions against

Even as Anglo-American eminence was asserting itself, the city was treated to a final, but very grand, effervescence by its old French heritage. Between 1847 and 1851 the *tout en somme* that centered on the old Place d'Armes in the Vieux Carré was completely refurbished and given the formal Second-Empire appearance that it retains today. The Cathedral was rebuilt, the Cabildo and Presbytère were heightened by the addition of mansard roofs, and the Pontalba apartment buildings were constructed on the up and down river sides of the square, which itself was enclosed with a fence and laid out as a formal garden. This magnificent recon-

Grand Ball of his Royal Highness, Rex, King of the Carnival, at Exposition Hall, February 25th.

masking. But these laws, like laws prohibiting rain, were not particularly effective. By the early 1850s the celebration had become increasingly disorderly, and many were calling for it to be outlawed. Then on Mardi Gras night in 1857, a group of Americans calling themselves the Mistick Krewe of Comus put on a torchlight parade that recast Carnival in the mode that it still follows today. The Americans had won not only the political and economic contest but the cultural contest as well.

LEFT: invitation to the ball. As the card states, costume was *de rigueur*.
ABOVE: society celebrated Carnival in style.

struction was given the name Jackson Square.

But even as the city reached its zenith in the 1850s, the foundation of its prosperity and eminence had already been eroded for some two decades as a result of factors over which it had no control or, indeed, of which it was not even aware. This reversal of fortune had begun in the 1830s when the Erie Canal began to divert the commerce of the upper Midwest to the East and New York, but the loss was not at first noticeable. By the early 1850s, however, the railroads reached Chicago and the rate of such diversion to the East accelerated. New Orleans had lost its exclusive patent as the tollhouse of the great Mississippi Valley. ❑

DIXIE BLOSSOMS

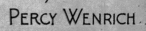

MARCH-TWO-STEP
BY
PERCY WENRICH

EROME H. REMICK & CO
DETROIT 5
NEW YORK

CIVIL WAR AND SHADY LADIES

By the 1850s, New Orleans ranked among the wealthest cities in America.

But war was on the horizon, and with it came an uncertain future

Historians and others initially blamed the Civil War for New Orleans' economic decline in the postwar years. In truth, the Civil War had little to do with this reversal of fortune. New Orleans, in fact, weathered the War Between the States far better than most Southern cities.

Many New Orleanians had little or no initial enthusiasm for the idea of secession from the United States of America. The city's merchants and bankers had strong economic and social ties to the North and were cool to the idea, as were the city's many German immigrants who certainly had more affection for their newly adopted country than for any theoretical Southern nation, especially one with slavery, which was anathema to them.

With Abraham Lincoln's selection as president, however, public sentiment began to shift. Urged on by such pro-secession leaders as Benjamin Morgan Palmer, firebrand pastor of the city's First Presbyterian Church, and the state's two senators, Judah P. Benjamin and John Slidell, the public quickly succumbed to secession fever, and on January 26, 1861, the state legislature adopted an Ordinance of Secession taking Louisiana out of the Union.

Sartorial rebels

In the weeks that followed, the city was alive with the talk of war and frenetic preparations for soldiering. Units were formed and open fields became parade grounds. Because there were no regulations governing uniforms at the time, the style, color, and cut of such garments usually reflected the taste of the well-to-do gentlemen who had decided to raise and lead the unit. The sartorial result was occasionally incongruous and often startling. The war's hostilities commenced on April 12 when a New

Orleans Creole, General Pierre Gustave Toutant Beauregard, ordered the bombardment of Fort Sumter in Charleston Harbor. New Orleans, however, would only begin to experience the war's effects six weeks later, when federal naval forces blockaded the mouth of the Mississippi. Inflation set in, and economic chaos followed as prices soared and the value of money plummeted. But no further federal action against the city occurred for almost 11 months.

Chaos and confusion

Finally, toward the middle of April 1862, word reached the city that a large Federal fleet had been sighted approaching forts Jackson and St Philip, some 66 miles below the city. News that an artillery duel had begun between the forts and the fleet kept the city in a state of near panic until April 24 when word came that the Federal fleet had run the gauntlet between the forts and was approaching the city. Pandemonium ruled. Realizing that the city could not be defended, local Confederate forces abandoned it, and with their departure chaos took over: warehouses were burned, boats were sunk at their moorings, and mobs roamed the streets looting and terrorizing the law-abiding citizens.

With his fleet arrayed in the river in front of the city, local Flag Officer David G. Farragut demanded that the city be surrendered to the Yankees. To Farragut's surprise and probably chagrin, the mayor of New Orleans refused, and for the next several days there was a standoff. Farragut threatened to bombard the city, but relented after meeting with a delegation of the city's foreign consuls. This *opéra bouffe* was finally resolved on May 1 when a Federal force under the command of Major General Benjamin F. Butler landed and promptly arrested Mayor John F. Monroe.

In the days that followed, Federal troops were subjected to numerous insults by the women of New Orleans. By May 15, the situation had become intolerable and Butler issued his famous Order No. 28, which warned that any woman insulting a Federal officer or sol-

---

PRECEDING PAGES: French Market and the Red Store, *circa* 1829–50.
LEFT: the word "Dixie" originated in New Orleans. It came from the French word for "ten" (*dix*) on $10 bank notes. The notes were called "dixies".

dier could expect "to be treated as a woman of the town plying her vocation." The order apparently had the desired effect, but proved to be a public-relations blunder with politicians, preachers, and other social arbiters in Europe and the South, who called it despotic and an affront to Southern womanhood. Three weeks later, Butler again came under a storm of criticism when he had William Mumford hanged from the portico of the US Mint in the Vieux Carré for tearing down a United States flag from the same building.

These incidents, and the fact that some of his officers profited from the sale of Confederate property seized under the Federal Confiscation Act, unleashed a storm of criticism of Butler. While Butler is still regarded by many New Orleanians as having been a thoroughgoing scoundrel and ogre, historical evidence does not support such a judgment. There is evidence that Butler profited from some illicit dealings in hot cotton, but not that he stole any silver, a popular local legend which gave rise to the nickname "Silver Spoons" Butler.

In truth, Butler kept a tight rein on his men, and there is no record of serious looting by his troops, such as occurred elsewhere in Louisiana

Under Siege

During the Civil War, New Orleans was the American city occupied longest by enemy troops of the Union Army (1862-65).

under Generals Nathaniel P. Banks and Ulysses S. Grant. If anything, Butler's administration was honest, efficient and – when judged as a military occupation of an enemy city – mild.

On July 23, 1864, a state constitution was adopted which abolished slavery; established a public school system for all children regardless of race; and authorized the legislature to grant suffrage to individuals who paid taxes, had served in the military, or were intellectually qualified. This, in effect, permitted the enfranchisement of blacks. The convention also adopted a resolution that allowed for its reconvening in the future. The first legislature to meet under the new constitution unanimously ratified the Thirteenth Amendment, which abolished slavery, but failed to enfranchise blacks.

Lieutenant Governor J. Madison Wells initially appeared to gain some favor with white people by his friendly attitude toward ex-Confederates. This attempt to curry favor with former soldiers backfired on Wells, however, when radical white Republicans and the Union Radical Association of mainly French-speaking Creole blacks refused to recognize his administration.

Feat of Clay

Asserting that Louisiana by its act of secession had lost its statehood and become a territory, these dissidents held a convention of their own and nominated Henry Clay Warmoth, a young man from Illinois, for territorial delegate to Congress. In the election that followed, blacks voted for the first time and to no one's surprise Warmoth, who ran unopposed, was elected. To almost everyone's surprise, however, Congress refused to recognize him. In the meantime, ex-Confederates grew increasingly bold in their drive to regain power and exclude Radical Republicans, blacks, and former Unionists such as Wells from any role in either city or state governance. Alarmed by this growing assertiveness of the former Confederates and unhappy with Governor Wells, the Radicals called for the reconvening of the 1864 convention to revise the constitution. If the legislature would not enfranchise the blacks, the Radicals would do it by constitutional emendation. Called for July 30, 1866, at the Mechanics Institute, which stood where the Fairmont Hotel stands today on University Place, the convention itself was poorly attended, but attracted large, uneasy throngs which milled about in the nearby streets.

The meeting began quietly enough at about 1pm, but almost immediately was adjourned for an hour so that absent members could be rounded up. The first trouble began during the adjournment when a parade of blacks with an American flag and a band heading for the Mechanics Institute attempted to cross Canal Street.

FREETOWN

On July 23, 1864, a state constitution was adopted which abolished slavery and established a public school system for all.

mob, were quickly run down and either shot or beaten senseless.

Federal troops from Jackson Barracks arrived to restore order shortly after 3 o'clock, but by then the riot was over. Casualty figures vary slightly but an army report placed the number of wounded at 146 and the dead at 38, with blacks totaling 34 of the latter tally. Following an extensive and formal investigation, General Sheridan placed the blame for the riot and killings on Mayor Monroe and Chief of Police Thomas E. Adams. Some

Hecklers in the crowd shouted taunts and cat-calls, and large rowdies jostled several of the marchers. Suddenly two shots were fired and pandemonium followed; police and hooligans from the crowd charged the black marchers, who fled to the Mechanics Institute. For a time those in the building held the mob in the street at bay, but suddenly the barricaded doors were breached. Those inside were shot or clubbed even as they attempted to surrender. Other people, jumping from tall windows to escape the

LEFT: notorious Civil War-time Yankee and administrator, Major General Benjamin F. Butler.
ABOVE: a funeral in the woods, 1860.

months later a Congressional investigation came to much the same conclusion.

Military rule

The rioters won the battle in New Orleans, but lost the war in Washington. Their actions furnished much of the impetus for the Reconstruction Acts, which Congress passed over President Andrew Johnson's veto in March, 1867. By these acts, Louisiana and other states of the former Confederacy were placed under military rule until new state constitutions could be fashioned to meet with Congressional approval. In New Orleans, General Sheridan, acting under this new authority, removed a number of senior public officials including Mayor Monroe. He also replaced the governor and called for elections to authorize a constitutional convention and, if so authorized, to then select delegates.

The vote for a constitutional convention was overwhelmingly favorable, and on November 23, 1867, the elected delegates were called to order at noon in the Mechanics Institute. Three and a half months later, on March 9, 1868, the assembled convention adjourned after adopting a constitution that not only enfranchised the blacks, but contained

PUBLIC CORRUPTION

Bribes and swindles thrived under Governor Warmoth's tenure. As Warmoth himself said, such things were "the fashion."

police. The idea for such an agency was regarded at the time as progressive and was popular all across the country during the second half of the century. Under Warmoth's authority, however, it served mainly as an armed extension of the governor's office, assuring Warmoth's control over the body politic and his own perpetuation in office.

Two governors

Infighting over the spoils of office, and to a lesser extent philosophical differences, eventu-

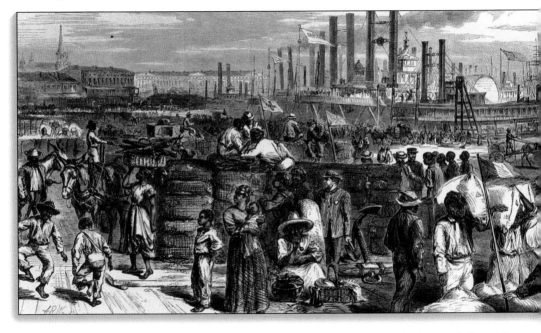

civil rights clauses designed to prevent discrimination in a wide range of public activities. It also disenfranchised many of who had been active in the Confederacy.

Realizing that the state's white Democrats would not willingly submit to rule by Radical Republicans and their black allies, Warmoth, now the new governor, got the legislature to create a police force that would be under his control. To do this the legislature combined the parishes (counties) of Orleans, Jefferson, and St Bernard into a Metropolitan Police District with a constabulary administered by a board appointed by the governor.

It was, in effect, the origin of today's state

ally led to an open split in the state's Republican party that pitted Warmoth and his followers against the Radical Republicans, both black and white. This resulted in numerous ugly disputes that came to a head during the election of 1872. Following a vicious campaign in which both sides committed all manner of election fraud, returning boards on each side claimed victory.

The impasse remained, and on January 13, 1873, New Orleanians witnessed inaugurations for two governors. William Pitt Kellogg's inaugural ceremonies for the Radical Republicans began a little before noon in the Mechanics Institute, while John McEnery's commenced for the Democrat and Liberal Republicans about an hour later in Lafayette Square. *The Daily Picayune* covered both events, but its reportage left no doubt about its partiality. Under the banner headline "LEGAL GOVERNMENT IN LOUISIANA," it described McEnery's inauguration as a "great and propitious event" before "large and enthusiastic crowds." The Kellogg ceremonies, on the other hand, were reported as taking place in a "bayonet citadel on Dryades Street... surrounded by a dusky mob." Finally, on May 22, President Grant recognized Kellogg's government as the legal authority of Louisiana. Presidential recognition and the force that it represented, gave Governor Kellogg's regime a degree of stability.

March his government was little more than a paper entity. The final end of the Packard government came on April 24, when Federal troops guarding his statehouse were removed and Nicholls' government took possession of the building. Reconstruction in Louisiana had at long last ended.

Politically at least, the state was back on track but financially all was not well. The erosion of the city's economic base, which began in the 1840s and 1850s with the diversion of upper valley commerce via the Erie Canal and railroads, was accelerated by the war and the postwar boom in Northern rail-

Two years later, Louisiana was once more treated to the spectacle of two inaugurations for the governorship, with Stephen B. Packard taking the honored oath at the St Louis Hotel and Francis T. Nicholls at St Patrick's Hall on Lafayette Square.

Nicholls immediately commissioned General Ogden's White League as the state's militia. These actions, as well as President Grant's refusal to intervene, resulted in a general desertion among Packard's followers and by late

LEFT AND ABOVE: the first and last port of call. But by the end of the Civil War railroads were making an impact, and the city was losing its economic power.

KNOWING NO BOUNDS

While the closing years of Reconstruction were marked by civic acrimony and bloody clashes, they also witnessed an extraordinary physical expansion of New Orleans, in part at least, as a direct result of such strife.

An example of this last was the 1870 annexation of Jefferson City, an incorporated town above New Orleans. When the town's officials refused to recognize the authority of Governor Warmoth and his Metropolitan Police, the governor had the legislature enact a bill that redrew the boundaries of New Orleans to include the upriver community. This permitted Warmoth to appoint any officials necessitated by the incorporation.

road building. By the end of Reconstruction the impact of this economic realignment was painfully apparent throughout much of New Orleans, where business was at a standstill and much of the population was unemployed and in utter despair.

Foreign trade

During the 1880s, however, the city began to experience a quickening in its commercial life. This upturn resulted from several factors, the most important being the growth of foreign trade through the port and the emergence of the city as a major distribution center for the South.

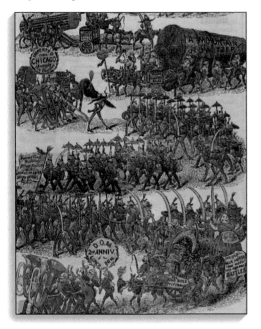

The growth in foreign trade, was made possible by the construction of jetties at the river's mouth during the late 1870s. A few years later in the early 1880s, railroads linked New Orleans with the rest of the nation, and the economic synergism that resulted from these two forces gave the city a greater prosperity than it had experienced in almost a quarter of a century of reasonably big industry.

The local economy was further buoyed during these years by a steady growth in the cotton and sugar industries. As the leading center throughout the nation for the distribution of these commodities, the city took a hefty percentage of the value from every bale of cotton and hogshead of sugar that its pressers, refiners, factors, shippers, and huge army of laborers handled. Further sustaining this economy were the city's numerous foundries, mills, machine shops and cooperages that created and maintained much of the equipage that was used by these industries.

The route to riches

Not surprisingly, this quickening of commercial activity stimulated a degree of optimism in the business community that hadn't been felt since the halcyon years of the late 1850s. New Orleans was not alone in this new found buoyancy which, under the catchphrase the "New South" was then enjoying much currency in the counting rooms of the region.

In New Orleans, its leading exponent was Major E. A. Burke, railroad executive, state treasurer, and flamboyant editor of the city's *Times-Democrat* newspaper. More than anything else, Burke's remarkable gift of the gab persuaded the city's business and political leadership that their financial salvation – indeed, their prosperity – lay in a world's fair. With such assurances Burke managed to garner about $2 million in loans and gifts from federal, state, and city governments, and corporate sponsors.

The World's Industrial and Cotton Centennial Exposition opened on on December 17, 1884. While initially successful, the whole project had been poorly managed and severely underfunded. The fair attracted just a fraction of the crowds previously anticipated and, like so many grandiose schemes before and since, the New Orleans exposition of 1884–85 ended as a dismal failure.

A DISASTROUS EXPOSITION

Chronic overspending meant that, although much heralded, The World's Industrial and Cotton Centennial Exposition was all but bankrupt when it opened belatedly and largely unfinished on December 17, 1884.

The opening day's ceremonies attracted a crowd of about 14,000, but thereafter attendances plummeted. Bad press about the fair's numerous shortcomings certainly didn't help, but overly optimistic projections had created expectations beyond any possible fulfillment. It finally closed on June 1, 1885, with only about one quarter of the originally projected attendance and a $500,000 debt.

Above and beyond its large debt, it accomplished none of the goals promised by its promoters. It brought no significant new industry to the city and stimulated no noticeable increase in port activity. Nor is the popular assertion that it stimulated residential development in the upriver path to its site persuasive. In a city where high and dry land was scarce and mainly in the natural levee adjacent to the river, a growing population made such development inevitable.

The exposition did have a legacy, however, but it was one which its promoters did not anticipate, and which nobody would recognize at the time. Indeed, it would only become truly apparent many years after the exposition had long since been forgotten by most of the citizenry of the city.

This other America

That legacy was tourism, or more specifically, the tourist industry. The city had attracted a steady trickle of visitors since the 18th century, but these had been mostly wealthy individuals in search of the exotic, and their fleeting presence had no impact on the city. The exposition would mark the beginning of middle-class or mass tourism, a phenomenon that would eventually, in our own time, profoundly affect the city and its unique culture.

Actually, the inception of mass tourism in New Orleans evolved from a combination of factors, with the exposition as a catalyst. Bored by a fair that promised much but delivered little, journalists sent to cover the event turned instead to writing about the city itself and its notably different culture. A spate of articles describing the quaint old city and its unusual ways soon appeared in Northern newspapers and national journals where they aroused the curiosity of a burgeoning middle class just then beginning to enjoy paid vacations and the pleasure of travel.

New Orleans would experience no immediate surge of tourists as a result, but the message had gone out about "this other America," a strange,

LEFT AND ABOVE: trade expositions in the 1880s, although largely unsuccessful in financial terms, did introduce New Orleans to early tourists who read in newspapers about its exotic qualities.

exotic place, unlike anywhere else in the country, and what had been a trickle of visitors increased to a steady flow that grew substantially with each passing year.

The city still had problems, however. The establishment in Louisiana of legalized racial segregation in the last decade of the century had great consequences for New Orleans and, indeed, the nation over the long term. Throughout most of the 1870s and '80s, political parties and factions of all stripe courted the black vote, but in 1890 the political winds in Louisiana shifted when the

> ### LEGAL FOUNDATIONS
> Louisiana is the only state to base its civil law on Roman law, rather than Anglo-Saxon law, practicing the Napoleonic code.

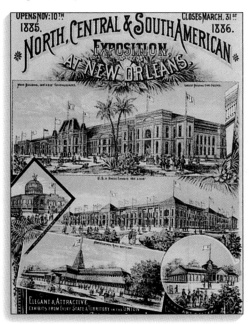

state legislature passed an act requiring separate accommodations for blacks and whites on railroads operating within the state. It was this law that Homer Adolph Plessy, the New Orleans Creole of color, deliberately challenged when he took a seat in a "whites only" car of an excursion train in the early summer of 1892. Plessy was arrested, tried, and convicted of violating the state's separate accommodations law.

Four years later, on appeal to the United States Supreme Court, Plessy's conviction was sustained in a ruling that came to be known as the "separate but equal" doctrine.

It was this doctrine that would serve as the legal foundation for segregation in New

Orleans and the rest of the South for the next 60 years. It would also serve as a stimulus for the disenfranchisement and the all but complete removal of blacks from any part in the political process. This was fully accomplished by the state Constitutional Convention of 1898, which included property and educational qualifications that effectively removed or barred most blacks from the voter registration rolls.

The cruel irony is that these reforms were the work of genuine reformers who believed they were acting in the best interest of both the city and the state. Many of the same individuals responsible for these reforms had been promi-

Storyville

In an attempt to control prostitution, which was then boisterously unrestrained and city-wide, the Flower administration in 1897 decided to enact an ordinance that restricted such activity to a relatively small area of about 20 city blocks located just beyond the city's old French Quarter and not far from what is today known as Armstrong Park.

The district was soon being referred to by the affectionate nickname, Storyville, much to the chagrin of Sidney Story, the silk-stocking councilman who had been the author of the restrictive ordinance. The area flourished for

nent leaders in the Citizens League, a group that had been the driving force behind the 1896 election of Mayor Walter C. Flower, a politician and wealthy Louisiana cotton broker.

Flower's major and not inconsiderable accomplishment in office was the reorganization of city government under a brand new charter and the establishment of a civil service system. While these and many of the other civic and government reforms enacted by Mayor Flower have long since been forgotten, at least one reform of the Flower administration resulted in considerable notoriety at the time and is today very much remembered by the more romantic citizens of New Orleans.

some two decades, during which time its fame became worldwide. Indeed, in an attempt to satisfy the erotic inclinations of visiting men who flocked to the district, special directories known generically as "Blue Books," were issued, containing the names and addresses of individual prostitutes and illustrated advertisements with none too subtle texts for the more fashionable establishments. These are much prized by collectors today, whose passion for such items often approaches the veneration accorded relics during the Middle Ages. ❏

ABOVE: some of the ladies who earned their living in New Orleans' Storyville district.

Absinthe

O scar Wilde supposedly said of it: "After the first glass, you see things as you wish they were; after the second, you see things as they are not; finally, you see things as they really are, and that is the most horrible thing in the world."

The liquid to which Wilde was referring was absinthe, the fashionable yellow-green, dangerously potent liqueur whose hallucinogenic qualities produced some of the most influential art of our time. Manet's *Absinthe Drinker* and Degas's *L'Absinth* are testaments to its intensity while Van Gogh, Toulouse-Lautrec and Gauguin were all regular drinkers. Picasso was highly influenced by absinthe during "the Blue Period" and later produced his sculpture *The Glass of Absinthe*. Absinthe was a bitter drink, with an alcoholic strength of about 19 over proof, made of herbs that grew in the Swiss Alps, such as aniseed, liquorice, coriander, and fennel. Its essential component was the herb wormwood, which induced a curious, dreamy state of intoxication appreciated by artists and fashionable society. Absinthe's commercial appeal was recognized by Henri Louis Pernod, who, in 1805, built a factory in France and began to export it.

The drink soon caught on in New Orleans, the "Paris of North America." Its appeal was confirmed when the Juncadella mansion on Bourbon Street was turned into a coffeehouse. The bartender hired was Cayetano Ferrér, who had already achieved recognition among the *bon ton* of local society for his skills in the bar of the old French Opera House. In 1874, when Ferrér became the leaseholder, the name of the coffeehouse was changed to the "Absinthe Room," and then to "The Old Absinthe House" in honor of his most popular drink.

The establishment's centerpiece was a long bar, with a fountain that slowly dripped water into the spirit glasses. This approximated the French method of serving the liqueur, which was to pour, drop by drop, about two ounces of water into every ounce glass of absinthe. Water added slowly turned the green liquid the desired shade of yellow; water added quickly produced an inferior, less dry, taste. As a sweetener, water was

RIGHT: detail from the painting, *The Absinthe House*.

dripped over a lump of sugar before mixing with the spirit. The sugar was placed on a special perforated spoon that rested on the rim of the glass. These "absinthe spoons," are now in vogue as collectors' items.

Despite its popularity, the drink's notoriety grew. Wormwood was addictive, and the drink's image suffered due to its proximity to drug-related crimes. In 1905, a Swiss farmer named Jean Lanfray shot his two daughters, his wife, and then attempted to shoot himself. It was heard at his trial that Lanfray had earlier drunk six quarters of wine, six brandies, and two absinthes. The judge ruled that the farmer was

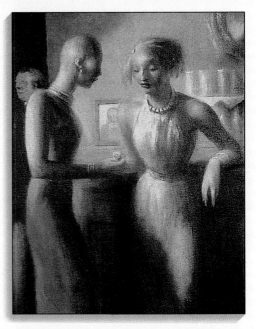

suffering from "absinthe-induced delirium." Lanfray subsequently hanged himself in jail.

This scandal was the turning point. The drink was banned – in Switzerland in 1905 and by ruling of the US Senate in 1912. To counter the attack, outraged members of the New Orleans Absinthe Association devised a legal alternative, which they produced for 22 years after the ban. Today, pernod and pastis are recognized as weaker substitutes to absinthe. The Old Absinthe House on Bourbon Street is still a popular watering hole, but the original bar, its marble pitted by water marks from the dripping faucet, is located in another tavern farther down Bourbon Street. ❑

NEW ORLEANS TODAY

Like the river that defines its borders, New Orleans keeps on rolling along: by inventing jazz, preserving the French Quarter, and luring waves of new visitors

New Orleans in the early years of the 20th century saw changes that would forever affect its future. The emergence of jazz as the city's distinctive contribution to American culture, the construction of a drainage system that converted a swamp to reasonably dry ground, and an end to the only legalized prostitution district in the nation were landmark events. The drive to save historic buildings in the French Quarter also began.

Jazz came of age during the era of Storyville, the prostitution district created by city ordinance in 1897. For another 20 years, New Orleans-born musicians like King Oliver, Louis Armstrong, and Jelly Roll Morton would play in the taverns around the city and in some of the bawdy houses that made up this rough and rowdy area around Basin Street. Storyville came to an end during World War I, closed down by the Secretary of the Navy when military authorities complained. But by that time jazz had already made its way upriver to St Louis and Chicago. Prostitution, though illegal, survived in houses run by well-known madams into the 1950s, but open prostitution was no longer the best-known characteristic of the city.

In the swim

In the early 1900s, New Orleans, which is below sea level, was still a swamp. It suffered constant flooding, even in the French Quarter, which is on relatively high ground. Famous restaurants in the French Quarter frequently had to close their doors because of water in the dining rooms. But in 1913, a young engineer and authentic genius, A. Baldwin Hood, invented the pumps that lifted the city out of the mud. Defying the existing laws of hydraulics, these miraculous machines were christened Wood Screw Pumps. Using these, the city's Sewerage and Water Board constructed an underground drainage system with more than 120 miles of canals carrying the

PRECEDING PAGES: Canal Street crowds.
LEFT: the original streetcar named Desire.
ABOVE RIGHT: the Saint Charles Hotel.

water to Lake Pontchartrain. It became the world's largest draining system and was copied by the Dutch, who bought Hood's pumps to drain their Zuider Zee. Today, New Orleans has possibly more miles of canals than Venice.

Local projects were put on hold in New Orleans as elsewhere in the country after April

16, 1917, when the United States declared war on Germany. World War I had begun. American involvement in the war, however, was so brief that, even though American troops were trained at local military institutions and war materials were shipped through the port, the war had little impact on the city.

The 141st Field Artillery of New Orleans, one of the country's oldest and most famous artillery units, sailed for France on August 26, 1918, but never saw action. The regiment was in Brittany when, less than three months later, the troops got word that the Armistice had been signed.

It was after World War I, in the 1920s, that private citizens began their efforts to save the

French Quarter. By the 1920s, the Vieux Carré had become a slum. The old Creole families, descendants of the early French and Spanish settlers, had long since moved out. Poor Italian immigrants crowded into the 18th-century townhouses and cottages that formed the historic district. The famous Pontalba Buildings on Jackson Square were decaying apartment blocks. Iron grillework was being pulled off historic buildings and sold, and the centuries-old architectural heritage of the city was being bulldozed for parking lots.

RULE WITH A VIEUX

In 1936, the Vieux Carré Commission was founded to protect buildings of architectural value, the first of its kind.

Even the city's businessman-mayor, Robert Maestri, backed the preservation movement. He had little formal education, and wasn't impressed by history, but he did love the French Quarter. Maestri was of Italian descent, and by that time the Quarter had become known as "Little Italy." Besides, New Orleanians badly needed the jobs the WPA projects provided.

Roosevelt poured federal money into New Orleans after Louisiana's best-known governor, Huey P. Long, was assassinated in September, 1935. Long, elected governor as the Depression

Stopping the rot

A fledgling preservation movement began in the 1920s as private citizens sought some way to halt the destruction. Finally, in 1936, a state constitutional amendment created the Vieux Carré Commission and granted it broad police powers to protect buildings of architectural and historic value. It was the first commission of its kind in the United States.

The Works Progress Administration, a federal agency President Franklin D. Roosevelt created to provide jobs during the nation's Depression, contributed to the reclamation of the Vieux Carré. It restored the Pontalba Buildings and the French Market in the late 1930s.

ACCENT ON BROOKLYN

Mayor Robert Maestri was a rough-cut diamond. President Franklin D. Roosevelt visited in 1937 and was honored at a luncheon at Antoine's restaurant. As the president feasted on Oysters Rockefeller, Maestri turned to the leader and asked, "How ya like dem ersters?" Many older New Orleanians still pronounce "oysters" as "ersters" and "oil" as "erl."

Although tourists and Yankees associate the city with the Deep South and that region's drawled, honey-coated accent, the real Crescent City dialect is one that is rapid and brusque, more often associated with Brooklyn, New York, than with any of the states in the South.

loomed in 1928, was a savior to some and a tyrant to others. He became a threat to Roosevelt after becoming a US senator, attacking the President and advocating his own "Share The Wealth" program. Many thought he would run for President. New Orleans was a center of anti-Long sentiment, but the family cast a long shadow over local politics for years to come.

World War II galvanized the city from December 7, 1941, the day the Japanese attacked Pearl Harbor, to V-J Day, when the Japanese signed surrender documents on September 2, 1945. Because of New Orleans' exposed position as a port city, army troops were moved in to protect high-

war, ended Mayor Maestri's 10-year reign. He returned just in time to become the reform candidate for mayor. With a group of women spearheading the reform movement, Morrison was elected mayor in an upset victory in 1946. He would remain in office until 1961, when President John Kennedy appointed him Ambassador to the Organization of American States.

A modern city

In those 16 years, New Orleans became a modern city. With construction funds up during World War II, Morrison consolidated railroad lines to bring them into one terminal and con-

ways, water purification plants, and other vital facilities on the Sunday the Japanese struck Pearl Harbor. German submarines operating in the Gulf of Mexico, south of New Orleans in 1942, sank 12 allied ships in one month.

Rationing, war work, and air raid drills became a way of life in the city. Over 5,000 servicemen from Louisiana died or were killed in action during the war.

Mardi Gras and Louisiana-style politics resumed with the war's end. A dashing young Army colonel, Chep Morrison, home from the

LEFT: decorating graves on All Saints' Day, 1900.
ABOVE: St Charles Avenue's palms are now gone.

structed overpasses and underpasses to move traffic over the remaining tracks. He introduced modern planning methods to city government, launched a youth recreation program that became a model for the nation, and built a new City Hall as part of a governmental complex on Loyola Avenue.

Morrison was not a die-hard reformer. His police department was corrupt. Illegal lotteries, houses of prostitution, and racehorse handbook operations continued into the 1950s. Lavish gambling houses flourished in adjacent parishes. Another scar on Morrison's record was his failure to provide protection for the handful of black children who integrated two New Orleans public schools under court order in 1960. Unruly racist crowds gathered and harassed federal marshals as they marched the children into the schools. Nevertheless, Morrison managed to change the face and outlook of New Orleans. He brought the city into the 20th century.

Morrison died in a plane crash in 1964. Victor H. Schiro, the city's second mayor of Italian descent, had been named to succeed Morrison in 1961, and later was elected to two terms in office. He distinguished his first year in office by providing police protection for children

> ### SUPERDOME
>
> The Superdome, the city's mushroom-shaped sports arena, was conceived as a gimmick for Mayor Schiro's election in 1966.

tourism industry has grown to replace oil and gas as a major source of city, and state, revenue.

New Orleans saw another preservation movement around this time that benefited the French Quarter. Again, it was private citizens who led the movement. With court suits and protests, they blocked construction of an elevated expressway that would have run along the riverfront in the Quarter. Even its advocates now agree the expressway would have damaged the historic district irreparably. Visitors to New Orleans unknowingly

entering integrated public schools. It was also Schiro who first put forward the idea for the Superdome sports arena, the impressive home to New Orleans' major sporting events.

It's a gas

It was during the Schiro administration that Poydras Street, now the city's main business thoroughfare, was widened and paved. The street is now lined with the city's major skyscrapers. Most of these newer buildings went up during the boom years of the oil and gas industry in Louisiana in the late 1970s and early 1980s. When oil prices plummeted, the entire oil industry became depressed. As it has evolved, the

benefit from that decision and honor Schiro's successor, Maurice Landrieu, when they visit the Moonwalk on the Mississippi River just across from Jackson Square. Landrieu changed his name legally to his nickname "Moon," when he entered the political arena. Landrieu succeeded Schiro in 1970.

The Moonwalk was the first project of the young administration. The walk, giving visitors and local citizens access to the river, was first of all just a dirt pathway with a few street lights. With federal money, the present imposing stairway was built, the walkway was improved, and the Moonwalk became a New Orleans landmark. Landrieu also established the pedestrian mall around Jackson Square. He was also the first mayor to fully realize the potential of the tourist industry – an industry that is predicted by the year 2000, to not only put $2 billion into New Orleans' coffers, but also expected to be the number one industry worldwide.

Black power

Landrieu's other enduring legacy was bringing black citizens into full participation in city government. He had been elected with a solid black vote. He brought blacks into decision-making jobs in City Hall for the first time.

With the growing black population and voter

He also emphasized tourism and the French Quarter. Brass plaques on the sidewalks of the Quarter bear Ernest Morial's name. They commemorate a large paving and sidewalk-construction campaign done to prepare the Quarter for the expected influx of visitors during the New Orleans World's Fair in 1984. The fair, held at the site now occupied by the Riverwalk marketplace on the Mississippi River, failed to attract large numbers of visitors nationwide. It was a financial flop, but an enormous success with local citizens, who bought tickets and visited it repeatedly for its jazz music, its Cajun dancing, and its Italian Village.

registration in the city, blacks elected one of their own with the help of a segment of the white business establishment in May 1978; Ernest N. "Dutch" Morial became the city's first black mayor. An appeals court judge and a leader in New Orleans' civil rights movement, Morial was the first mayor to have to confront the city's declining revenue base. One of his attempts to diversify the city's economy was the establishment of an industrial district that is now developing in eastern New Orleans.

LEFT: movies like *The Big Easy* raised the profile of the city.
ABOVE: even GIs go for Dixie beer.

Besides fond memories for local citizens, the fair is credited with initiating the boom in tourism. During the year prior to the official opening of the fair, a fever of enthusiasm swept through the city, and many improvements were made. Among them are some luxury hotels, including the world-class Windsor Court, the Riverwalk market, the attractive pedestrian malls leading to the riverfront fair site, and the extremely successful Convention Center, which in 1999 expanded to include more than a million square feet of exhibit space. The expansion of the Convention Center has created further demand for hotel rooms, a demand being met by numerous new hotels in the Central Business District and the Garden District. The luxury Ritz Carlton occupies the old Maison Blanche building on Canal Street; the Jockey Club all-suites hotel will be on the site of Kolb's Restaurant on St Charles Street; and there are plans to convert several office buildings into luxury hotels. Among the buildings mentioned are the Pere Marquette Building, the Lykes Buildings, and the World Trade Center.

Dutch Morial died suddenly and dramatically on Christmas Eve, 1989, when, after watching a football game at a friend's house, he suffered a heart attack brought on by an asthma attack.

A councilman and former state senator, Sidney

Barthelemy, became the city's second black mayor with a landslide vote in 1986. He won a second term in 1990. He promoted the city's riverfront developments, including the Aquarium of the Americas and the adjacent Woldenberg Park on the riverfront. And after years of lawsuits, controversy, and Keystone Cop-like machinations, Barthelemy's dream of a gambling casino at the foot of Canal Street has been realized with the $840 million, 50,000 sq ft Harrah's Casino.

In May 1994, Dutch Morial's son, Marc, was elected mayor of the city. A former State senator, Marc Morial campaigned on cleaning up the city, both literally and figuratively. Almost immedi-

ately after taking office, he renegotiated a contract to bring more casino dollars into the city.

Among major new attractions, the city can look to the National D-Day Museum, opening in the year 2000, and the Ogden Museum of Southern Art, both in the Lee Circle area. The Sports Arena, adjacent to the Louisiana Superdome will be home to the New Orleans Brass minor league ice hockey team, and, local sports boosters hope, a professional basketball team. Plans are also underway for a $77 million theme park called Jazzland in east New Orleans, possibly to open in 2000, which will feature live entertainment, amusement rides, regional food and fun for the whole family.

Movie mystique

The tourist and convention industry helped sustain the city through the economic slump that resulting from the near collapse of the state's oil and gas industry. Movies like *The Big Easy*, which deals with police corruption, and *Blaze*, the story of former Louisiana Governor Earl Long's affair with a strip-tease artist starring Paul Newman as Long, created a new mystique for the state and its largest city. Part of the Oliver Stone movie *JFK*, telling the story of a New Orleans district attorney's investigation into the assassination of President Kennedy, was filmed in New Orleans, while recent movies tend to be based on the books of local or Southern writers, like *Interview with the Vampire* and *The Pelican Brief*. The Oscar-winning *Dead Man Walking* was also filmed here.

New Orleans today suffers from the problems that plague most American cities, along with its own unique difficulties. But its crime rate has dropped dramatically – some sources say by as much as 20 percent – and it remains a city that tourists enjoy and local residents love. Dedicated New Orleanians often say New Orleans is a good city to visit, but it's even better to live here. In its 12th Annual Best Places to Live issue, *Money Magazine* ranked New Orleans among the Top 20 American cities.

It is this distinct blend of tourist and local support that the people of New Orleans believe will protect their city through its hard times – and perhaps for another 200 years. ❏

LEFT: casinos did a great deal to change the face of the city's entertainment industry.
RIGHT: fit as a fiddle – contemporary New Orleans.

GOVERNORS AND OTHER GRIEVANCES

With some of the sneakiest politicians in recent history, New Orleanians are pretty skeptical of government. That doesn't stop them being fascinated

As a Carnival town, New Orleans is often called the City that Care Forgot. Politically, it might be characterized as the City that Forgot to Care. But that's not quite true. This is a city that cares, but in its own way.

Food, football, and politics are the major topics of conversation in New Orleans, though not necessarily in that order. Locals tend to regard all three as popular sports, though food is usually the only one they participate in personally. Politics remains essentially a spectator sport; its ups and downs are followed and commented upon by the general populace, but it isn't of sufficient interest to warrant the direct involvement of the man or woman in the street.

The lack of grandiose displays of grassroots actions or attitudes in New Orleans may be a symptom of the city's diffuse character. There are many strongly identifiable racial and ethnic backgrounds: Cajun, Creole, African, French, English, Spanish, German, and Italian. But even within these groups there is little history of concerted community action.

Factions and frictions

The many different factions, and their frictions with other groups and with each other, are part of the reason that the author A. J. Liebling back in the 1950s called Louisiana "the westernmost of the Arab states," and compared the politics of New Orleans with those of Beirut. From politics to social clubs, it's not part of the local character to unite – or at least not to stay united for very long – in a common cause. Rather, it is part of the New Orleans tradition for members of a group to squabble among themselves, and then for some of the members to break away and form their own rival group.

In recent years, these breakaways have led New Orleans to have two groups of zoo supporters, two opera guilds, two ballet compa-

nies, two cancer societies, and more splintered political factions than anyone could care to count. Even the family connections for which New Orleans is known – people who work for Uncle Wardell or with Cousin Bubba – often

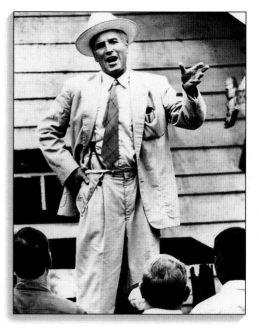

fracture to the point that brothers and cousins end up operating competing restaurants or working for competing political fiefdoms.

This diffusion is natural in a metropolitan area that is itself administratively and politically divided, with three principal parishes making up what is generally known as New Orleans. Orleans Parish is the city proper, with a black majority population. St Bernard and Jefferson parishes are predominantly white suburbs whose residents work in the city but pay few taxes for its support.

Because of the widespread skepticism toward politicians, people in New Orleans typically try to give them as little money to spend as possible.

LEFT: former governor, Huey P. Long.
RIGHT: Paul Newman as Earl Long in *Blaze*.

Some say New Orleanians simply hate to pay taxes, but it would be more accurate to say New Orleanians hate to give their money to politicians. While the United States grew out of the notion that there should be no taxation without representation, New Orleans seems to believe that the ideal political situation is representation without taxation. Candidates that propose even modest tax increases, no matter how badly the money is needed for the public coffers, do not get elected in New Orleans.

MAN OF MOTTOS

Huey Long, who as well as governor, also served as a US senator from Louisiana, had a favorite motto; "L'Etat, c'est Huey." (The State *is* Huey).

In recent memory, various exemptions have allowed up to three-fourths of the local homeowners to avoid paying any property taxes at all, even though the assessments are among the lowest of any major US city. In any given year, the local tax bills for people in New Orleans are likely to be one-third of those for the residents of Boston or Chicago.

Perhaps this is because taxation is historically connected with power, and New Orleanians are suspect of political power. The fact that there have been as many as six publicly funded police forces or five different government agencies that cut the grass provides comforting reassurance that no one is really in control. Some of this mistrust of power must date back to the days of Huey Long, the self-styled "Kingfish" who was elected governor of Louisiana in 1927 and erected what has been described as the closest thing to a dictatorship in American history. The Kingfish was a populist who spoke to and for the little people. Under his motto, "Every man a king," Long improved the roads, built hospitals, provided free school books for children, and expanded social welfare programs.

During his heyday, Long also put a brutal hold on the processes of democracy in Louisiana through his vast political patronage system. It wasn't enough for a fellow Democrat under Huey to be broadly loyal; to get a job, or keep one, Democrats had to prove their loyalty again and again, in terms of time and money and whatever else the Kingfish required. He brooked absolutely no opposition or dissension.

Here's a classic example of the way the Kingfish operated. In 1935, he approached Frank Costello, a New York gangster, and invited Costello to bring slot machines into New Orleans. The Kingfish promised no interference from local authorities. In exchange, Costello had to split the profits of the illegal gambling with Long, who planned to use the money to provide more welfare programs for the blind and disabled. The slot machines did come in, but only lasted a few months: Long was shot and killed later the same year by the son-in-law of a political opponent, a man who had been denied a job.

Keeping it in the family

Huey Long, who was just 42 when he died, continued to cast a long shadow over Louisiana politics, even as his younger and more colorful brother Earl took up the populist mantle and served three terms as governor. Earl Long, immortalized in Liebling's book *The Earl of Louisiana*, once got into a fight with a political opponent in an elevator and almost bit the other man's ear off.

Like his brother, Earl Long used unorthodox methods to achieve his often laudable goals, and both brothers were given to making offhand segregationist remarks to white crowds while promoting programs to help blacks. Earl Long once found the state legislature reluctant to approve his recommendations for better health-care facilities in black areas, so he made an issue out of the fact that some blacks and whites were being treated under the same clinic roofs. The legislature promptly approved the money for more black facilities and staff.

The Long legacy continued in Louisiana politics, most notably in the form of Huey's son Russell, a long-serving and influential US senator who was known for populist stands but also for serving special interests such as the oil, gas, sugar, and shipbuilding industries.

More recent examples of the Louisiana style in national politics can be seen in politicians such as John Breaux and Edwin Edwards. Breaux was

Edwin Edwards was convicted in 2000 of racketeering and extortion. "Life is full of ups and downs," he declared after the verdict. "Mine are just larger and more public than most."

Good guys

The more liberal strains of the Long legacy have not been totally lost in New Orleans, however. Hale Boggs, the popular US House Majority Leader killed in a 1972 plane crash, and his wife Lindy, who succeeded him and held his congressional seat for nearly two decades before stepping down, were both New Orleans politicians known for their honesty, integrity,

a Democratic congressman who voted with the Republicans when then-President Reagan made broad social services cuts in the federal budget. It was widely known that Breaux had been won over by the Reagan administration's promises of price supports for the sugar industry, which was a great contributor to the economy in Breaux' district and also to his own campaign funds. Asked if this meant his vote could be bought, the congressman said no, but "it can be rented."

Flamboyant former Democratic governor

LEFT: the flamboyant Earl K. Long served three terms as Louisiana's governor.
ABOVE: Long with President John F. Kennedy.

LONG TIME RUNNING

Earl Long was arguably the most colorful and brazen character Louisiana politics will ever see, a man famously reputed to have hollered, "That's a damn lie!" to deny his very public extramarital affair with the stripper Blaze Starr. Despite showing signs of insanity in his later years – apparently due to a series of small strokes – he remained a politician to the end. At one point, state officials acting with the blessing of his wife, Miz Blanche, committed Earl Long to a mental hospital. But a lawyer-crony went to court to seek his release, and Earl, still the governor, fired the state officials who might have testified that he was indeed crazy.

and humanity. Other noted city politicians included a pair of mayors in the 1970s and '80s, Moon Landrieu and Ernest "Dutch" Morial, the city's first black mayor. Their administrations did much to revitalize New Orleans.

But Landrieu and Morial, like subsequent mayors, were and still are handicapped by New Orleans' haphazard system of financing its public services. Some agencies have been deemed by the state government to be too important to leave to New Orleans politicians, so they were established outside City Hall.

> ### FORMAL TIMES
>
> More formal wear and fewer copies of the *New York Times* are sold per capita in New Orleans than in any other major city.

An example is the Sewerage and Water Board, whose duties include keeping the water out of a city that was built below sea level. Because the board raises its own money through a separate property tax not connected with the city's general operating funds, it has had plenty of money in recent years – none of which it wants to share for other city services. The Sewerage and Water Board had enough money to build itself a modern new headquarters while City Hall remained a dusty and run-down edifice.

The revenues for New Orleans' general city spending increased by barely 3 percent during a period when an increase 10 times that would not have been able to maintain services. As a result, services and payroll were trimmed. The few agencies with money are the ones that have been able, one way or another, to persuade city fathers to allow them to follow the Sewerage and Water Board example of having their "dedicated" tax revenues reserved for their use alone.

The city Recreation Department, on the other hand, has had its requests for budget increases rejected repeatedly by voters in recent years. When funds for the Society for the Prevention of Cruelty to Animals were slashed to the point that New Orleans no longer had dogcatchers to collect strays, the SPCA said it might have to ask volunteer patrols of young men with rifles to hunt down the growing packs of semi-wild dogs. New Orleans has a thriving charity scene, but it can take a lot for its residents to dig into their pockets. When Maxim Shostakovich, son of the late Russian composer Dmitri Shostakovich, resigned after five years as music director of the New Orleans Symphony, he said he hadn't been paid in a year. He received a standing ovation at his last concert, but no one organized a fund drive to raise money to keep him in his position.

Civic woes

Like other troubled US cities, many of New Orleans' money woes in the 1990s were precipitated by federal government budget cuts imposed in the 1980s. As a result, programs once funded by the federal government are suffering. Local health care has deteriorated to the point that syphilis is a near epidemic, and there is not enough staff to promote or carry out routine check-ups for children. Nearly half the kindergarten children entering New Orleans public schools have not had the standard immunization shots – free at local clinics, when staff is available – for common childhood diseases such as measles.

About 90 percent of the children in New Orleans public schools are black. Whites generally send their children to private schools, though a program of higher-caliber "magnet" public schools is aimed at drawing white families back to the state educational system, with some success. While historically a city where blacks and whites often mixed more closely than in some supposedly liberal cities of the north, New

Orleans changed when the federal government began building huge public-housing complexes. The "projects," as they are known, turned areas such as Desire, Lafitte, and Iberville into harsh urban ghettoes where local whites dread to tread. On the other hand, the city has entire neighborhoods dominated by a black professional and managerial class. Whites and blacks still mix fairly easily throughout New Orleans, and there is little sign of racism among the casual everyday throngs of upper middle-class whites and blacks from the nearby housing projects.

But race can still be a simmering political issue for some. The symbol of the white back-

Hedonism

For the most part, however, New Orleans remains a city of tolerance – tolerance for three Sazerac cocktails and a dozen oysters before lunch, tolerance for streets full of potholes, tolerance for jurors who delay a decision so they can have a big meal at the city's expense before going home. As S. Frederick Starr noted in *New Orleans Unmasqued*, this is a city where the people throw parties for politicians who are sent to jail, and then re-elect them when they get out on parole. It is a hedonistic town, where flood, fires, disease, hurricanes, and politicians have all taken a turn inflicting their own peculiar

lash for many of those is David Duke, the yuppie politician from the suburbs who tends to do embarrassingly well in state elections. Once a high-ranking Ku Klux Klan leader, Duke has tempered his rhetoric by using thinly coded statements about "welfare," "drug abuse," and "quotas" to build a following among whites who oppose affirmative action hiring and any government welfare program helping the black community.

LEFT: for a while, the city's infrastructure was so frail there was little money for dogcatchers.
ABOVE: high-profile politician David Duke was once a senior member of the Ku Klux Klan.

brand of damage. It is a town where economic equality is elusive, but many blacks eagerly put aside any injustices to join in the whites' tradition of dressing up and marching down Canal Street with their floats every Shrove Tuesday.

Most New Orleanians share the attitude of Louis Armstrong, born in the city in 1900, who said he had seen too many of those famous brass-band funerals – a dirge on the way to the cemetery, a joyous blast of upbeat jazz on the way back – to be afraid of anything that might happen tomorrow.

After all, no matter what tomorrow brings, everyone in New Orleans knows there's going to be another big party next year. ❏

MARDI GRAS

A season of parades and parties, revelry and romance, Mardi Gras is when the gaudy and the grandiose all come together for one gigantic blowout

There are rituals and there are ritual watchers. Just who and how many get to watch which ritual is part of the complexity of New Orleans' Carnival celebration, a festival so deep in social significance that ritual watching and observing the ritual watchers can become rituals in themselves.

"I like Carnival because it extends the good mood left over from Christmas," says the captain of a group known as the Phunny Phorty Phellows. That this person is identified here by a title rather than a name is yet another part of the ritual. In the New Orleans Carnival, tradition has it that Carnival organizations are headed by a captain whose identity remains secret. Most of the organizations have their kings and queens, but the captain is, like the president, the real hand of power.

In her wisdom, the captain hit upon a fundamental truth about the New Orleans Carnival, a truth that will be missed by most casual visitors: New Orleans, unlike most of the rest of the world, does not suffer from post-Christmas letdown because Twelfth Night (January 6), the date given by tradition as the last day of Christmas, is also the first day of the Carnival season.

Fat Tuesday

That first day, however, is not what the world has come to associate with Carnival. Instead, it is the Carnival season's last day – a movable date that was tailored by Christianity in order to put some religious significance to the pagan tendency to celebrate the arrival of spring. The Catholic church gave the celebration a spot on the calendar and a message. The spot was the day before Ash Wednesday, which is the first day of the solemn season of Lent. The message was essentially to celebrate today, for tomorrow you fast. Because this day was to be one of feasting, it came to be known as Fat Tuesday or, as the French would call it, Mardi Gras.

PRECEDING PAGES: Mardi Gras monarchy.
LEFT: the Rex parade.
RIGHT: Carnival is popular with gays.

New Orleans, founded by the French, adopted this celebration with vigor. Ironically, as the church became more lax about its rules for Lent, the city began to enjoy the best of both worlds. New Orleans still celebrated the coming of the season of penance, but without having to do the penance – the feasting with none of the fasting.

For most people the most visual manifestation of Carnival is the parade. During the two and a half weeks that precede Fat Tuesday, there are parades throughout the metropolitan area, with the best and biggest winding their way through the city's business district almost daily. The period from the Saturday before Mardi Gras through midnight of the big day is in effect a four-day weekend. During the late morning and early afternoon of Mardi Gras, the central event is the parade of Rex, King of Carnival. That night the season is drawn to a close as the Rex court meets that of the Mystick Krewe of Comus (a "krewe" is a Carnival organization) which began the parading tradition in 1857. By midnight it is all over and the police are clearing the streets. Lent begins with the sanitation workers and cleanup crews doing their penance.

Although the parades and revelry of the season's last days are what most visitors will watch, this is like staring at a mask without fully seeing what is behind it. For most locals the Carnival season affects them in many different ways through many different rituals. Behind the mask, there are stories to be told. And Southerners love stories.

For some, these begin as early in the season as Twelfth Night. On that evening, a group going

by the name of the Twelfth Night Revelers stages its Carnival ball – traditionally the first of the major society balls of the season. At one point in the ceremony, a wooden cake is presented and each of the year's debutantes is served a wooden slice. This gesture is supposed to represent the eating of New Orleans King Cake, a flat, oblong Carnival confection sometimes covered with icing and sprinklings of colored sugar, which is big business for local bakeries.

Baked into the cake is an object, perhaps a bean, maybe a small porcelain doll, but most often a tiny plastic baby. King cakes are served at parties and in offices throughout the season, the tradition being that whoever gets the slice containing the object is "King" or, as appropriate, "Queen," and has to buy the next king cake. At the ball of the Revelers, the cake takes on a more symbolic importance. Each of the slices has a silver bean in it, except for one, in which the bean is gold. The girl who receives that slice is the Queen of the ball and thus one of the first monarchs of the year.

Family values

"I grew up with it and I enjoy it," says the captain of one of the oldest (founded in 1884) high-society groups, the Krewe of Proteus. While the newer, less socially connected organizations tend to have fewer restrictions on their membership, the old groups remain connected to old family names. In this man's case, participation in Carnival is part of his family heritage, which he himself has enriched. Besides being captain of a group he has received two of the highest honors that Carnival society can give, having been chosen at different times to be Rex, King of Carnival, and Comus, the whimsical god whose parade is the oldest.

There are approximately 40 Carnival balls held throughout the season, of which only a few are those of high society. At some of the balls the purpose clearly is to have fun, but at those of the nobility the main business is the presentation of debutantes and the perpetuation of the debutante tradition. To society watchers the Carnival season is not merely watching parades, but also watching the society pages of the daily newspaper, *The Times-Picayune*, to see which families were best able to snare the crowns for their daughters. Huey Long, the former governor, once spoke of his vision of "Every man a king." It may be that for some

---

CARNIVAL LAW

Carnival is governed by a basic code of law – called tradition. Thus, according to tradition, all riders on the floats must remain masked; the identity of the kings of several groups remains secret, as does that of the captain; and there shall be no commercial advertising.

There many other rules, some unique to particular krewes; some just trying to preserve, for one night at least, old-world manners, such as the proper way for a debutante to be presented at the ball. No one takes the ceremonies so seriously that the ritual and pretense transcends into the real world. It is like wearing a mask, only to return to normality once it is taken off again.

the truer ambition is every daughter a queen.

Those rituals of the Twelfth Night Revelers are performed before a relatively small group of people, dressed in black tie and evening dress, who are there by invitation only. Elsewhere, on the same evening, another group will be staging its traditions in front of anyone who happens to be in its path. This is the Phunny Phorty Phellows, a reincarnation of a 19th-century Carnival group, who, these days, are not all fellows, not always 40 in number, although, sometimes, they are funny.

BIG BEADS

One recent Carnival, the largest of the Mardi Gras supply house sold 41 million pairs of beads.

Early in the ride, two king cakes are served: one to the male members and the other to the females. In the tradition of the Twelfth Night Revelers, those who get the slice with the foreign object become the Queen and the Boss (the Phellows' equivalent of King). Here the similarity ends, for these Phellows are not members of high society, but just folks out to glorify the trolley, the city, and its Carnival.

Purity, like virtue, faces many temptations. Carnival in its purest form shuns commercialism. To date, however, that bit of purity has been

Carnival time!

The krewe's tradition is to charter one of the city's streetcars and announce the arrival of Carnival season. The trolley waddles along its path through uptown New Orleans and into the business district. Banners hung from each side proclaim that "It's Carnival Time!" The Storyville Stompers, a traditional jazz band, is on board to provide music for the Phellows who have somehow mastered the ability to dance in the narrow aisle of a moving streetcar while in costume.

LEFT: at Mardi Gras, even the balconies dress up.
ABOVE: the Golden Age Carnival ball.

better preserved within the city than in the suburbs where financially troubled parading groups have sought corporate bailouts. Within the city, it is illegal for a parade to have visible commercial sponsorship. That applies to the participating vehicles and units within the parade as well. Those rules make the New Orleans celebration all the more attractive because it may be the only major festival in the world in which the costs are the burden of the participants and not that of the spectators, business, or government.

City Hall does assume the expense for police, fire, and sanitation overtime, but those costs are easily justified by the dollars in sales tax that the event generates each year. They call it

"The Greatest Free Show on Earth." That may be an overstatement, but there is something about Carnival that runs contrary to capitalist values. It is like a tranquil island in a sea of sharks.

"I like Mardi Gras because I can dress up and be anything I want to be," says Kathleen Joffrion, a local art director and artist. Joffrion, who in daily life has a penchant for fashionable dressing, creates her own makeshift costumes for Mardi Gras. One year her costume was based on an aqua-colored satin swimsuit worn over pink tights. Around her neck she wore a gold lamé clown collar, and to round off her outfit she had a pyramid-shaped hot pink cap, feath-

albums with pictures of the kids in their first Mardi Gras costumes or of relatives all dressed up for the one night they went to the ball.

Ancient and modern

Not all that is precious to Carnival is ancient. Carnival sometimes needs to bend with the breeze, and some innovations have managed to do this and still maintain the dignity of the past. In the early 1970s, two new krewes, Endymion and Bacchus, began to attract large crowds, creating larger and more spectacular parades. Few groups have parade floats as innovative as those of Bacchus; no parade, perhaps none in the

ered butterfly wings, and yellow rubber gloves. On her feet were tap shoes. What was she supposed to be? "I don't know," she answered, "that's just what I had lying around the house."

As the story goes, the date that the French first arrived in the vicinity of what would become New Orleans was March 3, 1699. It just so happened that this date was Mardi Gras of that year; so it can be said with some accuracy that from the moment the French arrived there has been Mardi Gras. With a history that is so ancient, at least by American standards, plenty of memorabilia relating to Carnival can be found around the houses of New Orleanians. As well as scraps of costumes, this can include yellowed family

world, is as large as Endymion's, which has over 1,000 members. In 1987, the Lundi Gras celebration was created, at which Rex, supported by music and fireworks, arrives by river to begin his reign on the day before Mardi Gras.

But what makes it all special, what makes the New Orleans Carnival different from being just another group of passing parades, is that loyalty to the past, preservation of tradition, appreciation for ritual. To those who really understand Carnival the season can be like a king cake – the fascination is not so much in the sugar coating, but in what is hidden inside. ❑

ABOVE: society in the swim.

Mardi Gras Indians

From late spring until Fat Tuesday of the next year, they scrimp and save, sew and weave to create – by hand – the ornate costumes of their rank and tribe. They are the Indians, the Mardi Gras Indians, and they form one of the most colorful subgroups within New Orleans' black community. The members of these "tribes" live in inner-city black neighborhoods and generally come from poor or working-class backgrounds. They spend enormous amounts of time, money, and effort to participate in neighborhood "gangs" that go by such names as Golden Blades, Yellow Pocahontas, and Creole Wild West.

Both the intricate and elaborate bead work associated with the "suits" of the uptown tribes, and the dazzling, more modern, sequined designs of the downtown gangs represent months of sewing. The culmination of the months of work is when the "beautiful" Big Chief emerges from his house with the members of his tribe on Mardi Gras morning, resplendent in a headdress and hand-sewn suit that represents the Chief's most complete statement of visual cachet. His raiment is a dazzling challenge to that of every other Big Chief in New Orleans.He'll be judged as the "prettiest," or not *as* pretty by the other chiefs he encounters, by the gang members who also "mask" in dazzling costumes, and by the neighborhood followers who celebrate the Indians as symbolically representing the dignity of all the residents of the black inner-city neighborhoods. Indeed, the Big Chief himself is most often from the workaday world of the longshoreman, warehouseman, bartender, hotel cook, taxi driver, or seaman.

The Big Chiefs and their Indian tribes have paraded through the byways of New Orleans' black culture since at least the 1890s (some say much earlier). The tradition reaches back to old and lost languages, back to a remembered or imagined tribal dignity, back to old values of courage and bravery, and back to non-Western concepts of male beauty, where the regal male plumage overshadows that of the female.

From 8am until nightfall, the streets fill with

RIGHT: Big Chief of the 9th Ward Hunters.

the music of the chief and his gang. Everyone keeps rhythm with bottles, combs, sticks, tambourines, and drums, and second lines (a New Orleans tradition, meaning to follow the parade) with traditional responses to the leaders' chanting of dozens of well-known song lines from a vast oral repertoire that is as much a part of the shared black culture as the most familiar gospel refrains.

Rhythms are based on West African drumming and dancing. Although to unfamiliar ears the chants are rough-edged and unshapely, Indian songs and rhythms have been a major influence on New Orleans' jazz, rhythm and

blues, and popular music at least since the 1930s, with a number of traditional songs entering the popular recorded music repertoire.

Come Mardi Gras, the invigorating chants and shouts are heard throughout the neighborhoods, in the streets, from balconies, and in and near the bar-rooms. The Indians sing and flaunt their finery until dark, when the spy boys, flag boys and, yes, even the Big Chiefs themselves, footsore, their shoulders aching from the weight of their head-dresses, their voices hoarse, their eyes bloodshot from too much drink and lack of sleep, make their way home to re-emerge on Ash Wednesday in the working-class livery of the everyday world. ❏

WHAT'S COOKIN'

Creole and Cajun food has won fans around the world,

but there's only one place to find the real thing

The conversations one most often overhears in New Orleans restaurants are not about politics or sport – they are about food. Joe Cahn, an expert on New Orleans food and former director of its School of Cooking, sums up the local attitude towards dining. He says, "In south Louisiana, food is not looked upon as nourishment, but as a wonderful way of life. We want to say 'Wow!' with every bite; to clap and cheer and make noises. With food, nobody is ever wrong, for it is the only thing in the world in which everybody is allowed to have a personal taste. To us, food is not only on the plate: it is also in the heart."

The key to enjoying New Orleans food is realizing that it is a separate cuisine, distinct from other American styles of cooking. It is very different even from traditional Southern cooking. New Orleans' Creole and Cajun food is America's most fully evolved regional cuisine; thick, worthy books were written on the subject over a century ago. Although the culinary revolution that has swept New York and San Francisco is evident in New Orleans, too, with many fine restaurants producing new – even new-style – food, Creole and Cajun have long dominated local cuisine and probably always will. The differences between the two types of cooking can be summed up in one phrase: Creole is city; Cajun is country.

Rouxful cooking

Creole dishes feature rich, creamy sauces made with a *roux* and can be found in most restaurants. The fare served up under the name "Cajun," however, is likely to be a substitute for the real thing. Cajun food is typically cooked in a pot, slung together with ingredients to hand, extremely tasty – and very ugly. Too unattractive for diners paying lots of money, restaurateurs feel, and so the tendency is to dress the dishes up with superior ingredi-

LEFT: Paul Prudhomme, owner of K-Paul's Louisiana Kitchen and a popularizer of the region's cuisine.
RIGHT: drinks on the half shell.

ents, possibly improving the taste but diminishing the authenticity in the process.

All of this is changing, anyway. Cajun cooking of a sort *has* moved to the city, and Creole food is far spicier than it used to be, a tip passed on from its country cousin. In fact, the two styles have merged so successfully that Paul

Prudhomme, owner and chef of K-Paul's Louisiana Kitchen, calls this blended local cooking "Louisiana food," and leaves it at that.

Two indispensable elements of Creole-Cajun cooking are local to the southeastern part of the state. First are the great raw materials, especially seafood. Crawfish exist in populations so large that they are often shoveled into sacks right off the shore by lovers of shellfish.

The second essential element is the collective local taste. All Orleanians eat Creole-Cajun every day, to the near-exclusion of other styles of food. This is the taste which began with the original French settlers and was later modified by their Spanish successors. The hands-on practitioners of the art of Creole cooking have almost always been black – so the food shows a heavy Caribbean influence as well.

Creole-Cajun food is potent. There's more pepper, especially red pepper, than in other American dishes. But beyond that there is an intensity of flavor from generous mixtures of salt, cream, butter, garlic, and herbs. An extremely common starting point in Creole-Cajun cooking is to sauté "the holy trinity" in a *roux*. The trinity consists of onions, bell peppers, and celery; the *roux* is a blend of flour and some kind of oil.

But New Orleans cooking is never static.

Some restaurants now dare to use no *roux* in any of their dishes – a policy that would have been considered heresy 10 years ago. An identifiable "nouvelle Creole" style has emerged, much lighter than the traditional cooking, but with flavors still intact.

Mumbo gumbo

The most emblematic dish of Creole-Cajun cuisine may well be gumbo. The name comes from an African word for okra – a frequently used ingredient in the gumbo pot. The okra is mixed with all kinds of shellfish, sausages, and poultry. It is somewhere between a thick soup and a

A LEXICON OF NEW ORLEANS FOOD

The Creole and Cajun cuisine of New Orleans is as delicious as it is diverse. But there are many terms indigenous to the food of the region which visitors might not be familiar with. Here are some of them:

Andouille: (ahn-doo-ee) A hot Cajun sausage made with ham and garlic.

Bananas Foster: A delicious dessert of bananas sauteed with sugar, butter and cinnamon, flambéed with brandy, and served over vanilla ice cream.

Boudin (boo-dan): Also a red-hot Cajun sausage, this one involving spicy pork, rice, herbs, and onions.

Cajun popcorn: Batter-fried shrimp or crawfish.

Dirty rice: Pan-fried leftover rice sautéed with green peppers, onion, celery, stock and giblets.

Etouffée (ay-too-fay): A rich, tomato-based sauce for crawfish or shrimp dishes.

File (fee-lay): Ground sassafras leaves used to season, among other things, gumbo.

Gumbo: A hearty soup made with rice, it comes in many varieties, including seafood and andouille.

Grillades (gree-yads): Squares of broiled beef or veal.

Red beans and rice: Traditionally served on Mondays, a wholesome dish of kidney beans mixed with rice, seasonings, spices, and sausage meat.

thin stew and lends itself to endless variation.

Most gumbo can be categorized as either seafood gumbo or chicken gumbo, although there are lots of hybrids. Many are thickened with a dark *roux*. Some of the best gumbo in New Orleans is "gumbo ya-ya," served at the restaurant called Mr. B's. Other places to look for excellent gumbo are the Gumbo Shop, Bozo's, and Bruning's.

Another popular, low-priced dish is jambalaya (pronounced *jum-bo-lie-ya*). Served on top of yellow rice, the best jambalaya consists of

A BUG'S LIFE

Crawfish are known locally as "mud-bugs," because they are found in abundance in the mud of Louisiana's freshwater streams.

the spring, when crawfish are around too.) Raw oysters on the half shell are still easy to find, despite decimation of the oyster beds and some question about the healthiness of eating raw shellfish. The great oyster bars are those found at Bozo's and the Acme Oyster House. Here you can stand and down the bivalves as they're opened, to the accompaniment of a glass of cold beer.

Oysters are also the subject of much creativity in the kitchen. Three oyster dishes in particular are worth trying. Oysters Rockefeller were

anything in the kitchen: sausage, vegetables, spices and, of course, seafood, dished up all together. Gumbo's only main rival in the soup department is turtle soup. Creole turtle soup is a far cry from the clear broth made with the chelonian elsewhere. Instead, it's a thick, chunky affair, powerfully flavored with lemon, cloves, *roux*, and the holy trinity.

The hardest decision one is faced with is whether to begin a New Orleans meal with oysters, shrimp, or crab. (This is compounded in

LEFT: a couple of New Orleans specials – crawfish and corn, plus crab and shrimp.
ABOVE: Arnaud's restaurant.

invented at Antoine's (*see page 88*), where they're still delicious. The sauce is a mélange of puréed greens tinged with anise. Oysters *en brochette* are broiled or fried with bacon on skewers, then moistened with browned butter; this is a favorite at Galatoire's. The third great oyster speciality is found mostly in Italian restaurants, always under different names but always locally described as being "something like oysters Mosca." Here the oysters are baked in a drift of bread crumbs, garlic, olive oil, and herbs. Try them at Mosca's.

On the entrée lists of New Orleans restaurants, seafood is king. A decimation of the city's two most popular fin-fish species – speckled trout and redfish – led to the popularization of a host of other superb Gulf fish: wahoo, *mahi-mahi*, red snapper, amberjack, grouper, flounder, puppy drum, mako shark, and yellowfin tuna, to name a few.

Arguably the best fish available from the waters near New Orleans is pompano. It has a smooth, textured, light gray flesh with just enough oil to make it rich without seeming overly "fishy." Pompano is best cooked with a minimum of fuss. Avoid *pompano en papillote* (except at Antoine's where it was invented), in which the fish's flavors are overwhelmed by a thick seafood sauce, all baked in a paper bag

You may run into soft-shell crawfish during the appropriate season, but these are almost always more interesting than good.

Crawfish in its more familiar guises is a far better treat. The two most familiar preparations with crawfish are as a thick, chunky bisque or *etouffée* (smothered with a light, spicy sauce) over rice. But during crawfish season (roughly Thanksgiving through the Fourth of July, with a peak in late April) the tail meat of these mini-lobsters is used in almost every imaginable way. The streets are literally strewn with the vivid orange/pink shells, cast away by outdoor diners and hunted down by stray cats.

that waiters love to open at the table. Also be wary of anything that even smacks of blackened fish. New Orleans' most famous culinary export can be delicious (as it is at K-Paul's, Brigtsen's, and a few other places) but it's usually terrible, a victim of crass commercialization.

Fish to fry

A number of restaurants deftly grill fish over open wood fires, but usually it is fried. Even New Orleans classics like *trout meunière* are more often than not fried. So are soft-shell crabs, a marvelous local delicacy. Big specimens abound in the spring and summer, but soft-shells are almost always available fresh.

WHERE'S THE BEEF?

The city's strengths in the seafood department do not mean the end of meat or poultry dishes. In fact, New Orleans is one of the best towns in America in which to eat a steak. Prime beef is the rule, served with a bubbling butter-and-parsley sauce.

Recipes featuring chicken, duck, quail, and other birds all have their Creole versions. The most traditional of them is chicken *bonne femme* – a roasted chicken covered with potatoes, onions, and garlic. This is a good choice at Tujague's or Antoine's. At Mosca's, they serve a platter of roasted chicken with all the garlic and olive oil you always wanted, but nobody would ever give you.

Most crawfish are served in their whole form, boiled to a peppery distinction. Boiled crawfish is the apex of shirtsleeves Cajun gourmandise. Gigantic mounds are polished off by men, women, boys and girls of every social stripe, leaving behind smaller mounds of shells and abandoned corn cobs. Even to the uninitiated, this activity quickly turns into a passion.

The Gulf of Mexico near New Orleans is the source of most of the shrimp eaten in America. Eating shrimp here is like eating lobster in

LOCAL LINGO

Watch your pronounciation when ordering crawfish, the locals' favorite seafood by far. Only marine biologists and Yankees call them "crayfish".

foods" is a muffuletta, a sandwich of Italian meats and cheeses, lavishly spread with olive salad stuffed between seeded buns the size of dinner plates. Near the French Market in the Quarter, Italian delis engage in competition for the "original" or "best" muffuletta. Another good lunchtime snack is the "po-boy," a submarine-shaped sandwich prepared on French bread and served "dressed" with a variety of meats or – including oysters, alligator, roast beef and gravy, or meat balls – and cheeses.

Maine: the best and freshest never get far from home. The premier Creole shrimp dish is barbecue shrimp – a complete misnomer, since there is no smoked aspect to the dish. It was the creation of the restaurant Pascal's Manale, with cuisine exemplifying the merger of Creole and Italian styles. Barbecue shrimps are gigantic, cooked with the head and shells on (do not order them where the shells are removed) in a sauce of butter, black pepper, and a little garlic. It's a real mess to eat, but an unforgettable taste. Not all New Orleans' cuisine comes from restaurants. One of the most delicious "street

LEFT AND ABOVE: from taters to gators; Cajun cookin'.

Sweet delights

The classic New Orleans dessert is bread pudding. This is not the poor man's dessert one finds in most of America, but a rich confection with custard and cinnamon. As with gumbo, bread pudding has as many different forms and tastes as there are chefs who make it, but a few stand out. The bread pudding soufflé at Commander's Palace is in a class by itself. The puddings at Arnaud's and Mr. B's, while more down-to-earth, are first-class.

New Orleans is also known for its hand-made candies. In season, fresh strawberries dipped in dark, or even white, chocolate are guaranteed to put on the calories. A perfect souvenir is a box of pralines (pronounced *praw-leens*), a sweet patty made with sugar, water, and nuts, with several variations available. One of the most common sights in the city is the white cart, driven by mules, of the Roman Candy Man. In 1915, Sam Cortese introduced New Orleanians to the taffy-like confection his family made in Italy, and it and they have been here ever since.

The essential adjunct to any New Orleans dessert is the dense coffee with chicory that Orleanians prefer. The chicory – originally a cheap herb extender of precious coffee, now added for its own distinctive taste – coats the sides of a mug with a visible, almost palpable,

brown layer. In the cafés in the French Market, the coffee is cut with an equal amount of hot milk, yet it still packs a potent punch. This is always accompanied by a *beignet* (pronounced *bin-yea*), a square-shaped pastry, similar to a doughnut without the hole, which is sprinkled with powdered sugar.

Wine lists in restaurants around town continue to improve. Consistently the best is that of Brennan's, which features lots of old vintages – especially Burgundys – sold at prices on the low side. Antoine's also has an extensive, reasonably priced cellar, strong on French wines. Commander's Palace led New Orleans into its appreciation of California wines and still main-

tains a fine list of them, along with a substantial array of French bottles. The Windsor Court Grill Room has bought several private collections over the years and has a list full of rarities. Andrea's had the first decent collection of Italian wines in the area, and they still maintain an interesting selection.

The first cocktail

As the town that once did a roaring trade in the production of absinthe (*see box on page 53*), drink is no stranger to these famed streets. Pat O'Brien's, which is home to the potent Hurricane cocktail, claims to have the largest volume of liquor sales in the entire world.

The first cocktail was supposedly invented in a pharmacy on Royal Street, by a Caribbean named Antoine Amedee Peychaud. Peychaud concocted "bitters" from a secret recipe that he later found went very nicely with brandy. He prepared this drink in an egg cup, which the French pronounced "huhk-tyay." This became "cocktay," and in time, "cocktail."

Although New Orleans is known for its high-octane spirits, don't forget about Dixie beer, the local favorite. The brewery is located on Tulane Avenue and is open to the public, while the beer can be ordered in any local bar.

New Orleans has a problem in common with other places with a predominant indigenous cuisine: other cooking styles are crowded out; even French, Italian and highly contemporary cooking here is almost always influenced by Creole tastes. But in this, as in many other cultural matters, the parochialism of the city leads to similar pleasures. Even though there has been a trendy sweep of pseudo-Cajun food emporiums which extend from coast to coast across America, you don't get that New Orleans taste anywhere but here in New Orleans.

Or, in the words of chef Paul Prudhomme: "Nowhere else have all the ethnic groups merged to combine all these different tastes. And the only way you'll know the difference, honey, is to live 'em." ❑

For a list of restaurants with addresses and phone numbers, see Travel Tips at the end of the book.

LEFT: Brennan's, on Royal Street, is famed the world over for its breakfasts.
RIGHT: Susan Spicer of Bayona, one of the best of the new-generation chefs.

BEHIND THE SCENES AT ANTOINE'S RESTAURANT

Although food fashions – many of them created in New Orleans – come and go, tradition prevails at the oldest family-owned restaurant in America

Antoine's Restaurant
Since 1840

Antoine's is the oldest family-owned restaurant in America. Its roots extend back over 150 years, when 27 year-old Antoine Alciatore, fresh from Marseilles by way of New York, opened Antoine's, originally a plain boarding house. Five generations later his great-grandson, Bernard Guste, presides over a virtual institution at 713 St Louis Street in the French Quarter, where loyal patrons tuck up to the same tables at which their grandparents dined, and are attended by waiters who train for seven years. The restaurant is a true family affair; the average length of employment is 40 years, and the night manager is Henri Alciatore, a descendant of Antoine's, and Guste's cousin. Over 35 years ago John DeVille was given a job peeling potatoes. By working hard and studying carefully he made his way up the food chain to become head chef, a position he shares with Michael Regua.

Although tradition is the keynote here, every so often the kitchen branches out and invents a new dish that instantly becomes a classic, like Oysters Rockefeller or *pompano en papillote*, named in honor of a visiting French balloonist. The restaurant consists of 16 small dining rooms that are dotted around the premises – up flights of stairs or down discreet corridors. Next to pictures of Hollywood celebrities hang the photographs of nine presidents, Princess Margaret and Princess Anne. The chefs also cooked for Pope John Paul on his visit, giving extra credence to that trio of ingredients – onions, bell peppers and celery – that locals use in their dishes and call the "holy trinity."

△ **SERVICE WITH A SMILE**
Employees line up outside the restaurant at 713 St Louis Street in the French Quarter. Waiters at Antoine's train for seven years.

▽ **JUBILEE TIME**
Keeping a watchful eye on the presentation of Cherries Jubilee is Bernard Guste, great-grandson of the restaurant's founder.

◁ **QUEEN OF THE BEANS**
Lucille Smith started at Antoine's in 1955, when she was only 23 years old. The average length of employment is 40 years.

▷ **ESCARGOT TO GO**
Velio Ortiz with perfectly prepared snails. Over the years the restaurant has catered to princesses, presidents and popes.

CALLING ALL FUTURE CHEFS

The emphasis of the three-hour culinary sessions held at the New Orleans School of Cooking is on fun, food and folklore. The food is traditional Cajun and Creole from Southwest Louisiana – dishes like gumbo, jambalaya, bread pudding, bananas Foster and pralines, while the techniques are delivered with a flourish and liberally seasoned with stories of the dishes' origins. Not to mention stories by their cooks: while chef/demonstrator Michael Devidts mixes a bowl of gooey bread pudding with gloved hands, he relates how he once shoehorned the strip bar and beery nightlife of Bourbon Street into a cultural program for foreign tourists. There is a lot of talk about seasoning, how dishes should be spicy flavorful, not spicy hot, and what that difference is. Condiments and cookbooks are for sale at the school, which is located at 524 St Louis Street. Classes are held Monday through Saturday from 10am to 1pm; the price includes lunch and recipes. Tel: 1-800-237-4841 or (504) 525-2665.

△ SWEET SQUEEZE
Pastry maestro John Maes with Baked Alaska. Tables at Antoine's can be scarce, so booking is recommended, tel: (504) 581-4422.

▷ OYSTERS ROCKEFELLER
Invented in Antoine's kitchens, the dish was named after the wealthy Rockefeller family because of the richness of its sauce.

A CONFEDERACY OF WRITERS

New Orleans is proud of its literary heritage. Some of America's greatest writers have lived and worked here – at times you can almost sense their spirits

The vibrance and diversity of life in New Orleans and its easy, laid-back attitude has long made the city a haven for writers. People with literary intentions want to walk the same streets their heroes walked and drink in the same bars; some hope to write the same great books. It is also a place where visitors can search out the haunts of writers like Sherwood Anderson, William Faulkner, and Tennessee Williams, whose *Streetcar Named Desire* immortalized Stanley and Stella and Blanche.

Writ large

New Orleans' literary register reads like a *Who*'s *Who* of American writers, with names like Walt Whitman, George Washington Cable, and Kate Chopin writ large across its pages. F. Scott Fitzgerald spent time here. The Beats made New Orleans a frequent destination, and William Burroughs, Jack Kerouac, and Allen Ginsberg all passed through town, chronicling their exploits for an entire generation. Charles Bukowski's early work was published by the French Quarter publisher, the LouJon Press, in the 1960s. Truman Capote, born in 1924, spent much of his life here.

Some visitors to the city decide to stay a while, taking a room in the French Quarter, settling in to write their own versions of the Great American novel, short story, play, or poem. Some of them make it, some of them don't. Some drift through, some stick around. It still happens.

Some writers grow up in New Orleans, leave for a while, and then come home to stay. Such was the case with best-selling novelist Anne Rice, who returned in 1988 after a 25-year exile in California. The First Street mansion Rice shared with her poet-painter husband and son is a frequent destination for sightseers, as well as

the setting for *The Witching Hour*, Rice's saga of a family of Garden District witches.

Rice devotees prowl the city in search of the places featured in her *Chronicle of the Vampires* (the series that has brought her international acclaim), looking for the cemetery where Lestat took his long sleep, or for the Royal

Street townhouse that was home to the vampire "family" of Louis, Lestat, and Claudia, the protagonists of *Interview with the Vampire*.

Perhaps better than any other writer, Rice's works evoke the sensuality and lushness of New Orleans. In an interview for *Lear's* magazine, she said: "Trying to come home, you run the risk of finding it pale in comparison to your memories, but New Orleans is such an intense place that I don't think memory can enhance it. For the first time, I'm actually able to write with the sound of the rain falling on the banana trees, the smell of the river breeze coming in the window; and every night, the twilight, the golden moment when the sky is shot with red

LEFT: storyteller Malia Brofle. New Orleans hosts the Tennessee Williams Literary Festival in March, and a writer's conference in July.
RIGHT: the Faulkner House Bookshop, 624 Pirate Alley, is where William Faulkner wrote his first novel.

and purple and gold, is just incredible. I don't think most people here appreciate the other-worldly quality of this city or understand the contrast that exists between Louisiana and the rest of the world. It's a place in the United States where you're not really in this country any more. It still is Third World, like being in the Caribbean."

New Orleans has been home to large numbers of women writers who have as their literary foremothers writers like Kate Chopin, whose *The Awakening* is now considered a feminist classic. Lillian Hellman (*Pentimento*, *An Unfinished Woman*), Sheila Bosworth (*Almost Inno-*

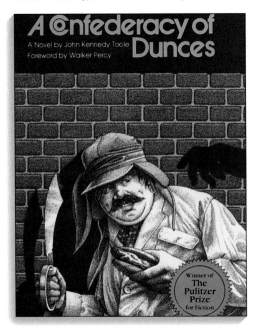

A Novel by John Kennedy Toole
Foreword by Walker Percy

A Confederacy of Dunces

Winner of The Pulitzer Prize for Fiction

A TRAGIC TALE

In 1969, a 30-year-old New Orleans native, John Kennedy Toole, committed suicide after despairing of ever seeing his work in print. After his death, his mother, Thelma Toole, haunted local bookstores and writers in quest of a publisher for her son's work, a rich and unique evocation of modern New Orleans. Finally, the amiable writer Walker Percy, the dean of Louisiana letters, took a look, liked what he saw, and recommended that Louisiana State University Press publish it. *A Confederacy of Dunces* won the first posthumous Pulitzer Prize for fiction, and has since been published in 16 countries, selling well over a million copies.

---

cent), Patty Friedman (*The Exact Image of Mother*), and Ellen Gilchrist (*In the Land of Dreamy Dreams*, *Victory Over Japan*) are only a few of the many writers with ties to the city.

The mysterious side of New Orleans has been a recurring inspiration. Chris Wiltz, for example, is the author of three mysteries set in New Orleans. Like Rice, Wiltz ventured to San Francisco, but she came home after only a year. Her romance with the city is ongoing, but she sees its less-benign side as well as its romance. "The past is written all over the face of the future in New Orleans," she said, "and darkness seethes beneath the atmosphere of bonhomie. Also, the living is easy here. Where else in the United States can you find an Old World city with built-in indolence? Writing requires a certain amount of indolence. Think-tank time, I call it."

Wiltz is part of a group of writers who chronicle the dark side of the city. Former policemen James Colbert, O'Neill DeNoux, and John Dillmann have all written mysteries or works of true crime with New Orleans as their focus.

City of exiles

Transplanted writers have also made themselves at home here. Cleveland, Ohio native George Alec Effinger chose the Big Easy over the Big Apple in 1971. Science-fiction writer Effinger is one of the most prolific writers in the city, with some 16 novels to his credit. He has also won the Hugo and Nebula awards, the two most prestigious awards in his field. Why does Effinger stay in New Orleans? His response is quite down to earth. "I like the slow pace. It's much cleaner here than in New York, and everyone is so nice. And you can get around without a car. The food, the music, everything else that goes on here... this city has everything I ever wanted."

Perhaps New Orleans' most famous literary exile-in-residence is the Romanian poet Andrei Codrescu, best known for his commentary on National Public Radio and for *A Hole in the Flag*, his memoir of the Romanian Revolution. Codrescu, who teaches at Louisiana State University in Baton Rouge, chooses instead to live in New Orleans, and occasionally he turns a sardonic eye on the city.

Describing a convention of booksellers in his essay, *The Mind Circus is in Town*, Codrescu wrote, "I'm not here for my good looks either. My publishers have me shaking hands with the world. At night, we do what we do so well. We party. The moon is full, the velvety air of romantic old New Orleans caresses the exposed arms and legs of the swaying couples under the banana trees. The siren song of Café Brasil throws erotic shivers through the throng. Reading is the farthest thing from our minds."

Despite its well-known literary heritage, not all writers have fared well in New Orleans. In 1969, John Kennedy Toole, a 30-year-old New Orleanian novelist, committed suicide. After years of trying to get publishers interested in his work, Toole could no longer cope with the agony of yet another rejection letter.

Literary spirit

An abiding inspiration for many young writers is the work of Louisiana's presiding literary spirit, the late novelist and philosopher Walker Percy, whose *The Moviegoer*, published in 1961, virtually defined the existential quest of an entire generation. Percy's search for meaning in the increasingly barren modern landscape won him an enthusiastic following. Many disciples journeyed across Lake Pontchartrain in the hope of an audience with this generous man.

In *The Moviegoer* Percy wrote, "The search is what anyone would undertake if he were not sunk in the everydayness of his own life. This

Ironically, the book was published to great acclaim after his death. *A Confederacy of Dunces* offered a new and unique vision of New Orleans. The adventures of hulking hero Ignatius Reilly, pushing his Lucky Dog cart around the French Quarter and chronicling his philosophy on Big Chief tablets, captivated an international audience. Toole portrayed New Orleans from the inside out, talking the talk and walking the walk the way the locals do, and the world embraced his vision.

LEFT AND ABOVE: The late John Kennedy Toole's epic tale of a New Orleans Lucky Dog vendor was a worldwide success.

morning, for example, I felt as if I had come to myself on a strange island. And what does such a castaway do? Why, he pokes around the neighborhood and he doesn't miss a trick."

Writer Seth Morgan, whose search brought him in to New Orleans at the end of a veritable orgy of drugs and drinking, liked to say that this was "the place where I ran out of highway." Inspired by a PEN award for a work about life in prison, he was determined to become a writer. After a period of great creativity, during which he wrote his critically acclaimed debut novel, *Homeboy*, a blackly funny and violent chronicle of prison life, Morgan died in a motorcycle accident. At the time of his death,

Morgan was at work on a New Orleans novel called *Mambo Mephisto*, in which he hoped to write "nothing less bold than the Mardi Gras novel as yet unwritten. A baroque and bustout tale of love foredoomed and sin unremitted spin between the bearded oaks, the streetcar lines, and lacework galleries of the Big Easy, a Gothic fable of helpless men and women who must 'in ignorance sedate roll darkly down the torrents of their fates,' gripped in the currents of those pasts which Faulkner taught are not even past but the stuff of the here and now, enigmatically shaping and informing the present."

While the city has inspired great fiction, New

Orleans has also nurtured a number of leading authors of nonfiction, among them Stephen Ambrose, author of multivolume biographies of presidents Nixon and Eisenhower, Carol Gelderman, biographer of Henry Ford and author Mary McCarthy, and Nicholas Lemann, whose bestselling *The Promised Land: The Great Black Migration and How it Changed America* was inspired by an awareness of race relations that began in his New Orleans childhood.

Of course writers need the support of their community to survive and prosper. Lured South by cheap rents and an inviting lifestyle, writers have to *live* in the place they have chosen.

Walk into the Quarter's Napoleon House or the Café Brasil in Faubourg Marigny and you will doubtless find a writer, leaning against the bar or hunched over a table, pen in hand. A week rarely goes by without an autographing or a reading in one of the city's many literary venues. The Maple Leaf Bar on Oak Street in Carrollton boasts the longest-running poetry reading series in the South. It began in 1979. Any Sunday afternoon at three o'clock, you can belly up to the bar, shove the beer bottles aside, and hear works-in-progress by local writers. Or, if you're lucky, you might arrive on a day when a well-known writer is reading.

Writers' gathering

The very private act of writing takes the public stage during the latter part of every March, when the Tennessee Williams/New Orleans Literary Festival celebrates the city's favorite playwright with a three-day extravaganza of plays, readings, panel discussions, and literary walking tours of the French Quarter. The Festival, international in scope, offers an appealing mix of new and established writers, and its book fair is a delight for every bibliophile.

Aspiring writers from around the country flock to the Big Easy in September for the New Orleans Writers' Conference. Sponsored by the University of New Orleans, the conference allows aspiring writers to meet editors, agents, and fellow authors for three days of workshops and manuscript evaluations. Some people come just to soak up the atmosphere that inspired so many others before them. Established and aspiring writers also come from near and far to visit the Maple Street Bookshops, the city's oldest local chain. Proprietor Rhoda Faust agrees that these are good times for writers. "Writers come here because a lot of great writing has been done here and a lot of great writing has been *set* here and that's very appealing and confidence-inspiring.

The same could be said of Boston, New York, and San Francisco, but New Orleans offers something more – a slower pace, less pressure, less competition within the community of writers. New Orleans is more tolerant than most cities, and it didn't become that way because it's politically correct. New Orleans has always been tolerant in a joyful way that seems more sincere. Writers seem to thrive in this atmosphere." ❏

LEFT: author Anne Rice (*see the* Further Reading *section in Travel Tips at the back of this book*).

Coping with the Myths

Some cities make people go weak at the knees just thinking about them. Paris is one such city; New York and London, for all their attractions, are not. New Orleans is probably America's best contender in the *femme fatale* sweepstakes, a description given an airing by the writer George Sessions Perry in 1947: "In some ways gaudy old New Orleans very much resembles an alluring, party-loving woman who is neither as virtuous as she might be nor as young as she looks… a *femme fatale* who has known great ecstasy and tragedy but still laughs and loves excitement, and who after each bout of sinning, does duly confess and perhaps partially repent."

New Orleans has other labels, too: The City that Care Forgot; The Big Easy. Writers have inspired so many myths about the town and its residents that sorting out fact from fiction can be an uphill task. Tennessee Williams, for instance, defined the archetypal Southern woman, perhaps for all time; invariably helpless, beautiful, neurotically dependent on men, and incapable of dressing in anything other than gorgeous peignoirs.

In fact, according to statistics published by the Department of Labor and the Census Bureau, far from being helpless, over half the women of working age have a job, and of all homes with households headed by women, around 40 percent hold the property in their own names.

But then, New Orleans isn't a traditional Southern town, another popular myth. Even though it is located in the South, culturally and geographically New Orleans is an island. Proof of this is in the accent, which is not the slow, lingering drawl found in nearby Alabama, but the brisk accent of farther north, probably due to the large number of Yankees and immigrants who made their homes here.

Socially, New Orleans is known for food, jazz and, of course, Mardi Gras. Many people think that Mardi Gras is the best or even the only time to visit, but when it comes to getting to know the city – its people and its way of life – it is probably one of the worst times to visit.

Some hotels slap on a hefty "festival charge" and popular restaurants are often fully booked. Many residents leave town entirely, preferring to celebrate at one of the smaller festivals held throughout the year.

These festivals are numerous – on average around three every two weeks – giving rise to New Orleans' reputation as a nonstop party town. But life can be hard in the Big Easy. Schools and roads and education are neglected to the point of ruin, paint is peeling off its

best-loved buildings, and the living are warned against visiting unaccompanied the cities of the dead. There are more policemen on the streets, and an encouraging reduction in serious crime. Unemployment is still high but it is no longer escalating, although according to some estimates, almost one in five households is living at or below the poverty level.

New Orleans' romantic character is tailor-made for myths. It always was and always will be. Some of these tales, however, are similar to the decorative filigree that graces the balconies of French Quarter apartments – they're attractive, well-loved and durable as iron.

But they can also be full of holes. ❑

RIGHT: Vivien Leigh as Blanche in the 1951 film of Tennessee Williams' *A Streetcar Named Desire*.

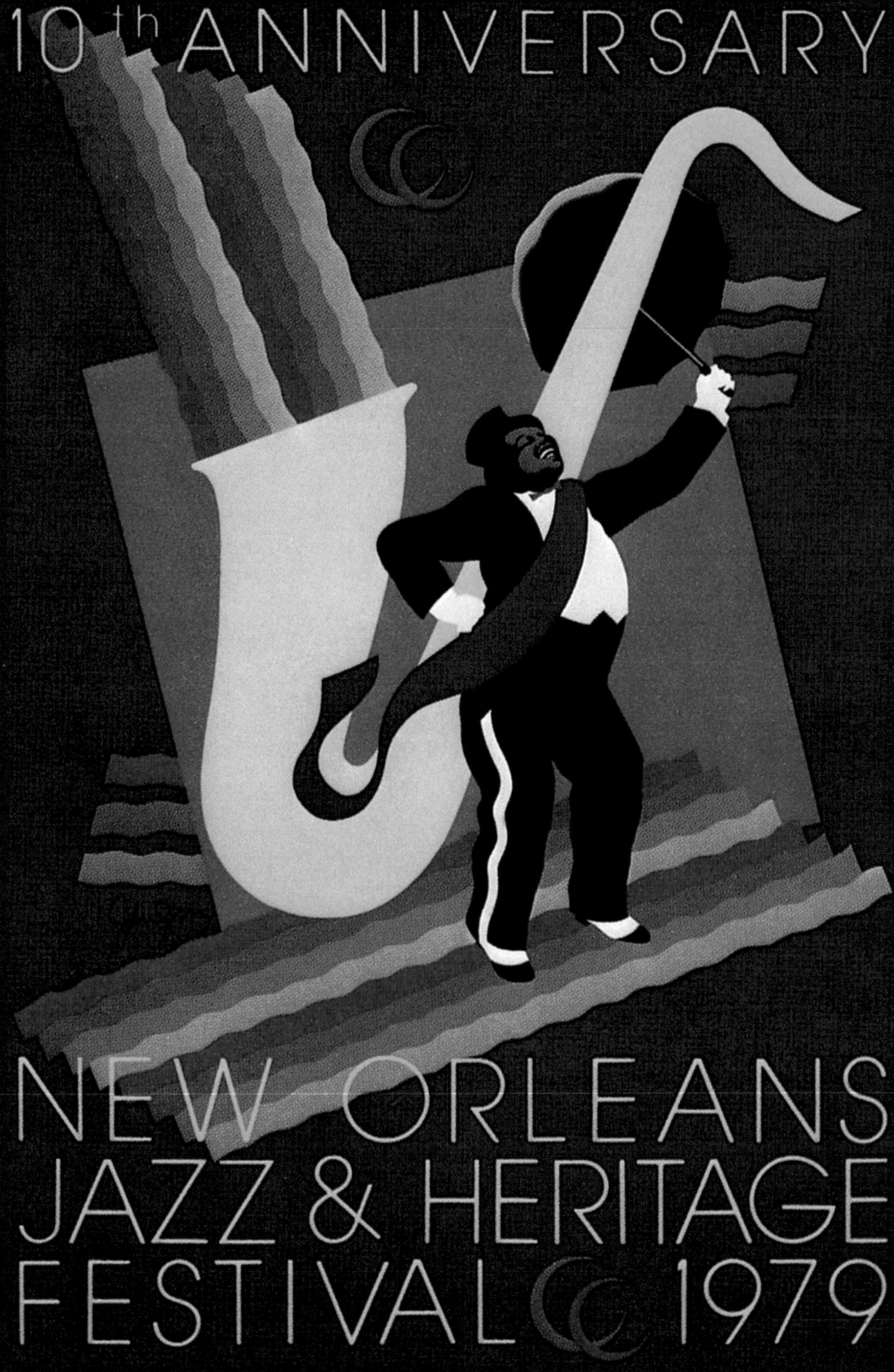
10th ANNIVERSARY
NEW ORLEANS
JAZZ & HERITAGE
FESTIVAL 1979

MUSIC: LET THE GOOD TIMES ROLL

New Orleans is celebrated as the birthplace of jazz, but music has been
the lifeblood of the city for much, much longer

In 1979, New Orleans R&B artist Ernie K-Doe mused, half in jest and half in earnest, "I'm not sure, but I'm almost positive, that all music came from New Orleans." If you qualify "all music" to mean "all authentic 20th-century American music" K-Doe's statement rings fairly true. The local music magazine *Wavelength* always carried this quote on its masthead.

One reason 20th-century American music might well have begun in New Orleans is because the city developed as a major cultural force long before it was officially annexed into the US in 1812 as part of the Louisiana Purchase. By the 1830s, full opera productions in a world-class opera house were presented here.

New Orleans-born composer and concert pianist Louis Moreau Gottschalk (1829–69) toured and performed in both America and Europe, where he was feted by the likes of Chopin and Berlioz. Well before the Civil War and the cultural unification of America, New Orleans had developed a distinct identity as a "musical city."

Walkin' to New Orleans

The town was also the only location in North America where African musical culture was celebrated. Jazz's first great saxophonist, Sidney Bechet, traces his love of music back to an ancestor who danced in Congo Square. Duke Ellington celebrated Congo Square in his "A Drum Is a Woman" suite. So what is Congo Square, and why is it important?

Located in Armstrong Park near the French Quarter – and also called Beauregard Square – the field that became Congo Square was used in the early 1880s by the Oumas Indians to celebrate their corn feasts. As New Orleans grew, the field was turned into a public square and on weekends, Congo Square was the site of music and dance performed by enslaved Africans who were permitted to congregate there.

PRECEDING PAGES: Ladies Zulu at Jazz Fest.
LEFT AND RIGHT: the New Orleans Jazz & Heritage festival is the highpoint of the musical year.

Old New Orleans was the only city which permitted slaves to sing in African languages, perform African dances, and use African instruments – notably the drum and the string instrument that became the banjo. This contributed significantly to the development of jazz and popular American music.

Pre-Civil War New Orleans boasted an unmatched quantity of both African and European musical activity. But it was only after the Civil War that a distinctive American musical form began to develop. Prior to the abolition of slavery, the descendants of enslaved Africans generally did not have the opportunity to develop their cultural expressions publicly. During the post-bellum period (the Reconstruction era of 1865 through 1877), newly emancipated African Americans began to move into the major cities. The official census notes that between 1860 and 1880 the black population of New Orleans more than doubled, growing from 25,000 to over 56,000.

This was the period of SA&PC (Social, Aid & Pleasure Clubs), benevolent societies established to provide both entertainment and social support during times of illness, death, or economic hardship. These organizations hired brass bands to play at social functions ranging from picnics and parties to weddings, births, and funerals. No other American city had such a strong network of benevolent societies among African Americans of both the laboring as well as the professional and artisan classes.

Turn-of-the-century New Orleans was a mixture of peoples and cultural influences. Both the German and Italian immigrant communi-

The birth of jazz

Jazz began as music to accompany outdoor social activity and not as brothel music, as is commonly thought. The Storyville legend of jazz's birth is probably based on the fact that the music's first major composer, Jelly Roll Morton, spent his formative years playing ragtime piano in Storyville. But jazz bands did not generally perform in brothels. Jazz autobiographies such as Louis Armstrong's *Satchmo* and Sidney Bechet's *Treat It Gentle* make clear the community and street origins of jazz as opposed to the mythical Storyville birthplace. It is ironic, however, that the closing of Storyville and the pop-

ties had extremely strong musical traditions, which found expression in numerous outdoor venues. The German Oom-pah brass bands were particularly popular. Additionally, America as a whole was high-stepping to the parade beat of John P. Sousa, and New Orleans was no different.

Also, at that time New Orleans was the major gateway port to the Caribbean and Central and South America. There were numerous public ceremonies, all involving music, to welcome officials, dignitaries, and other important people. On a more mundane level, the pawn shops were awash with instruments left behind from the Civil War.

HERE COMES THE BAND

It might seem obvious that New Orleans' cultural richness would promulgate the emergence of a new, hybrid musical form such as jazz. But the jazz band was not simply an extension of existing music, but a distinctly American combination of African cultural antecedents and European musical technique and tradition.

The African descendants who played music in New Orleans brought with them more than just a "jungle sound" which emphasized "undisciplined intonations and timbres." Buddy Bolden, Jelly Roll Morton, Freddie Keppard, King Oliver and, above all, Louis Armstrong, introduced the idea of outdoor processions for which the city is known.

ularization of records, as opposed to live music, marked the end of the first major jazz period. Although the 1920s became known as the "Jazz Age" in America, by then most of the major New Orleans jazz musicians were performing and recording in Chicago and New York. For example, it was there that Louis Armstrong cut the first classic recordings of jazz in the 1920s. New Orleans itself was experiencing a downturn that coincided with the introduction of rigid segregation known as "Jim Crow."

HITMAKIN' HEROES

New Orleanians Fats Domino and Dave Bartholomew have between them written over 200 songs. They helped create what became known as "rhythm and blues".

Fats Waller tradition, Antoine "Fats" Domino, the more flamboyant personality in a team known as Domino and Bartholomew. While Fats played the piano and sang, trumpeter Dave Bartholomew, who grew up playing traditional New Orleans jazz, was the songwriter and producer. By the early 1960s, when the Beatles dominated popular American music, Domino and Bartholomew were the first American artists to dethrone the mop-tops from the number-one spot on the US charts.

Following on the heels of the Domino/

Back to its roots

It was not until the jazz revival movement of the late 1940s and early 1950s that musical attention was again focused on New Orleans. By the late 1950s the same synthesis that produced jazz produced another major development known as "rhythm and blues," or R&B.

Although New Orleans was not the sole center for the development of this new musical form, the city did play a seminal role. The major focus of this resurgence was an ebullient pianist in the

LEFT: spiritual awakening.
ABOVE: Fats Domino was the first to dethrone the Beatles from the Number One spot in the US charts.

Bartholomew duo was songwriter, pianist, and producer Allen Toussaint, who was single-handedly the most important creative force in the resurgence of local music during the 1960s. Like composer and bandleader Duke Ellington, Toussaint had the ability to craft memorable songs to fit the individual talents of the people with whom he worked. From Ernie "Mother-In-Law" K-Doe and Irma "It's Raining" Thomas, to Aaron "Tell It Like It Is" Neville (one of the famous Neville Brothers) and Lee "Working In The Coalmine" Dorsey, to bands such as the Meters, in many ways Allen Toussaint was a credit to the spirit of Jelly Roll Morton.

After the 1960s, the national impact of New Orleans music waned. However, the New Orleans Jazz & Heritage Festival was born soon after. Since then "Jazz Fest," as it is commonly known, has grown to become the largest paid music event in the world, with an annual attendance of over 300,000 revelers, and an essential showcase for both new and established New Orleans artists.

The late 1980s saw a resurgence of interest in New Orleans jazz artists that has lasted through to the new millennium, brought about mainly

ON THE RECORD

Although jazz has roots in New Orleans, the first recording was, in fact, cut in The Big Apple by Nick La Rocca's ODJB band in 1917.

community. The city government does not give this important manifestation of black culture any economic support. Brass bands exist because the local community has made it a priority to fund them. After all, they play at parades, funerals, picnics, after baseball games, for private parties, wedding receptions, and similar social functions.

Visitors who come to New Orleans are often frustrated in their search to find "authentic New Orleans music." Invariably they are steered towards the French Quarter nightclubs and hotel

through the rise of jazz stars Wynton Marsalis, Branford Marsalis, Harry Connick Jr and Donald Harrison. Wynton Marsalis, in particular, has incorporated traditional New Orleans jazz into his composing and performing styles. Also garnering international acclaim are marching bands like the Dirty Dozen Brass Band, a band which mixes the traditional repertoire and instrumentation with contemporary rhythms and songs.

These modern brass bands receive both the opportunity to develop, and much-needed economic support from the SA&PCs. Often this aspect is overlooked by those who are unaware of how deeply the brass-band scene is rooted in the day-to-day life of the New Orleans black

lounges. Although there are fewer venues than in the past, the real music still exists in the various neighborhoods. More often than not, you can hear these bands in small taverns on the weekends and in the streets at funerals.

The ambience of venue and audience is often just as important as who is playing. For those who have a particular interest in the brass band tradition, October through early December is the best time to visit. During this period, on Sunday afternoons, many of the SA&PCs hold their annual parades. Dancing in the streets is the order of the day. ❏

ABOVE: fringe performers at Jazz Fest.

Jazz Fest

At the New Orleans Jazz & Heritage Festival, it's likely that a member of the Marsalis family will be playing. It could be Wynton on the Ray-ban stage, sharing a bill with the likes of Robert Cray or B. B. King. It could be father Ellis, a professor of music at the University of New Orleans, holding forth in the jazz tent. It could be brother Branford, whose "Makin' Whoopee" always raises cheers. If a Marsalis isn't playing, chances are a Neville Brother will be.

Despite the enormous crowds that pour into the Fair Grounds during two spring weekends (in April and May) – and crowds that are growing each year – Jazz Fest can still feel like a family affair. Neighbors greet neighbors at the stand selling crawfish po-boys or run into people they haven't seen for years at the children's tent. Jazz Fest attracts just as many locals as internationals, and the low-key ambiance of the world's largest paid music festival is one to be savored.

The hurly-burly in and around the main tents is like any big-city concert, but over near the gospel tent or the Musical Heritage stage, people are stretched out on the lawn having picnics or dancing the *fais do-do*.

It is these minor stages that are the real attraction of Jazz Fest. It is a cliché, but also the case, that most of the finest jazz, gospel, and blues musicians in the world will make an appearance; if not this year, then sometime soon. And many artists are likely to have local connections, like Eleanor Ellis, blues guitarist and vocalist, or C.J. Chenier, son of Cajun zydeco king, Clifton Chenier. The gospel singers often come from nearby high schools. With around 75 acts performing every day, it's impossible to make a poor choice.

The first local festival was a humble affair, funded by a $10,000 bank loan and held in Congo Square. That year, 1969, there were apparently more musicians playing than audience in attendance. Soon after, New Orleans' father-and-son team Arthur and Quint Davis joined with the festival's founder, New York-based impresario George Wein in an uphill

battle to fund the festival, but it was only years later, when the event transferred from Congo Square to the Fair Grounds, that the fest moved out of the red.

Initially, problems in finding sponsors held the festival back, but by 1983, Jazz Fest had become a major musical event and tourist attraction. Since then, its economic impact on the city has been considerable. The festival itself generates well over $60 million, and visitors bring in around $25 million during their stay in New Orleans. For music-lovers, the festival itself is a bargain. Tickets at the gate are so inexpensive that one social chronicler

worked out that each act costs under 25¢ to see. Combine this with great food, sunshine, plus parades and free workshops throughout the day, and a good time is ensured.

The only drawback to the Jazz & Heritage Festival is the weather. It may be unbearably hot, so bring sunscreen. It may rain, so bring plastic sheeting. Even if the sun is out, but the weather on previous days has been poor, be warned: straw spread over mud, which dries in the steaming swamp heat, means that indoor tents can be unbelievably smelly. But you won't find people complaining; only music of such quality could avoid the nose and go straight to the heart and feet. ❏

RIGHT: vintage posters like this one for the 1975 Jazz & Heritage Festival are now collector's items.

VOODOO

A lurid cocktail of witchcraft, tribal ritual and Catholic opposition,
voodoo exerted a sinister hold on the people of New Orleans

According to the *Encyclopedia of Witches and Witchcraft*, New Orleans is the traditional American headquarters of voodoo. Along with Miami, the Big Easy is one of the few cities in the US where almost everyone will have some knowledge about the subject, even if it is little more than after-dinner conversation.

There are thought to be around 50 million followers of voodoo around the world, although worshippers now prefer the term "verdoun" to voodoo, to distance their practices from the more lurid aspects of the faith. They believe that the work of various gods appear in all parts of everyday life and that pleasing (or appeasing) them will achieve spiritual prosperity.

Charming custom

New Orleans' heyday as a spiritual center was the mid-19th century, although even today token *gris-gris* (voodoo charms, often a small bag) can be bought with very little effort.The charms are the most obvious manifestation of the cult and have traditionally been used to attract members of the opposite sex, acquire money, achieve good health, or to ward off enemies. A genuine *gris-gris* (pronounced *gree-gree*) is one which is sacred by having been blessed with fire, water, earth, and air, and which contains several ingredients, the number of which must not exceed 13. It can be used for good or evil purposes.

Although the amulets bought in French Quarter tourist shops are innocent enough, there are still believers around. A local museum conducts "voodoo tours" for visitors and one (unconfirmed) report is that New Orleans policemen have been known to carry *gris-gris* for protection during their daily rounds.

In the mid-19th century, upper-crust Creoles pursued voodoo in much the same way that fashionable people of today latch on to the latest New Age development. It was a heated topic of conversation in the posh parlors of well-heeled New Orleanians, but much more than mere lip service was paid to the practice. Superstitious Creoles scrubbed their front stoops with brick dust to ward off curses and called regularly upon witch doctors and voodoo queens.

For 19th-century tourists, no trip to the Crescent City was complete without a visit to famed voodoo queen Marie Laveau. The strange and exotic voodoo ceremonies would draw enormous throngs of thrill-seekers. Reporters frequently turned up to view the rites, and local newspapers of the period were filled with detailed, sometimes shocking accounts of voodoo conclaves and voodoo-related activities. But the ceremonies witnessed by the hordes and the reporters were often just elaborate shows staged for the benefit of the curious outsiders. Voodoo was a mysterious, secretive cult whose more sinister aspects were carefully shielded from curious eyes.

LEFT: Marie Laveau, voodoo queen.
RIGHT: an 1880s French newspaper gave a gruesome account of Louisiana voodoo sacrifices.

Voodoo originated in the African kingdom of Dahomey (now the Republic of Benin). *Vodu* was the religion of the Dahomeans. The word vodu and its various forms – voodoo, voudou, vaudau, and even hoodoo – encompassed all aspects of the religion, including the gods, the cult, the cultists, and the rituals. One of the primary gods was Zombi (also called Damballah), which was a snake – usually a giant python. Among other things, the snake-worshippers believed that the first man and woman on earth were blind until the serpent gave them sight. The Bantu word *zumbi* means fetish, and the cult involved beliefs in sorcery and black magic.

When voodoo arrived in New Orleans, the cultists incorporated some of the characteristics of the Catholic Church. Statues of the Virgin Mary and pictures of saints sometimes adorned voodoo altars, but the tenets of this particular religion bore little resemblance to Christianity.

Voodoo rising

The first organized voodoo ceremony in New Orleans is said to have taken place in an abandoned brickyard on Dumaine Street. It was probably presided over by Sanite Dede, the first of the great voodoo queens. But repeated police raids on the brickyard drove the cultists out to

HOW VOODOO CAME TO TOWN

As well as being the center of the *vodu* religion, the kingdom of Dahomey was a major source of slaves. By 1700, some 20,000 were being sold annually, thousands of whom were transported to the islands of Martinique and Haiti (then called Saint-Dominique) in the French West Indies. The slaves took with them their voodoo, which flourished – it is still practiced in Haiti.

Although African slaves had brought voodoo to Louisiana as early as 1717, a series of bloody rebellions in Saint-Dominique in 1803 saw French planters and their slaves pouring into South Louisiana. Many settled in New Orleans, and voodoo became firmly established.

Bayou St John and Lake Pontchartrain. In 1817, the Municipal Council, fearful of voodoo-inspired slave uprisings, outlawed slave gatherings except on Sundays and in officially designated and supervised areas. Congo Square was one such legal meeting place. For many years the slaves gathered each Sunday afternoon in Congo Square (later renamed Beauregard Square, the plaza in Armstrong Park), chanting, beating their tam-tams, and dancing the Calinda and Bamboula. Congo Square drew large crowds of gawkers, but the activity there was mere window-dressing compared to the grotesque and orgiastic illegal rituals that took place around the bayou and the lake.

For practitioners of voodoo, St John's Eve (June 23) was the most important night of the year. Eyewitness accounts of St John's Eve ceremonies on the lakefront include lurid tales of half-naked cultists whirling in fantastic dances around a huge bonfire and a boiling caldron into which they tossed live frogs, black cats, and the ever-present snakes. Congo drums were beat with the leg bones of buzzards and the crowd chanted "Li grand Zombi" as the reigning voodoo queen danced with the python. It was

GIRL POWER

Voodoo was a matriarchy. Witch doctors paled in comparison to the strong queens – always free women of color, never slaves – who reigned over the rituals.

man of color who claimed to be a Senegalese prince, Doctor John was an enormous man whose ebony face was marked with hideous tattoos. In the 1840s, he bought a veritable harem of female slaves and a house on Bayou St John. He exerted great power over the Creoles, who flocked to his house to purchase charms and have their fortunes told. He seemed to see into their homes and knew their innermost secrets. In fact, he did – the servants in many prominent Creole homes spied and then sold him information.

LEFT AND ABOVE: Voodoo Museum exhibits.

said that the voodooists ripped live chickens apart, and ate them, and that sometimes in the throes of a frenzied dance they clawed, bit, and drew blood from each other. The presence of small coffins at the torchlit rituals led to the belief, widespread among Creoles, that white babies were kidnapped and sacrificed by the voodoos. The majority of voodooists were black, but there are many stories of whites – particularly young women – who participated in the rites.

The two most famous names in local voodoo lore are Doctor John and Marie Laveau. A free

When Doctor John died in 1884, writer Lafcadio Hearn wrote a flowery elegy that was published in *Harper's Weekly*.

Queen Marie

The name Marie Laveau is legendary in New Orleans. There were at least two voodoo queens named Marie Laveau – mother and daughter – and possibly others. The first was a tall, handsome, and mean-eyed woman who was said to have been the illegitimate daughter of a wealthy white planter and a mulatto. The reddish cast of her skin indicated some Indian blood. In 1819, at the time of her marriage in St Louis Cathedral to Jacques Paris, a native of Santo Domingo,

Marie was a devout Catholic. Paris mysteriously vanished shortly after the marriage, and she began calling herself the Widow Paris.

Working as a hairdresser, she listened to gossip and secrets while arranging the tresses of aristocratic white ladies. A few years after Paris vanished, Laveau became the mistress of a quadroon named Louis Christophe Duminy de Glapion, with whom she had 15 children. They lived in a cottage (long ago demolished) on St Ann Street between North Rampart and Burgundy streets.

LOVE POTION NO. 9

Stores in certain American cities stock a range of voodoo potions, most with highly descriptive names like Love Oil, Courting Powder, and Follow Me Drops.

The disappearance of her husband and her move into voodoo may or may not have been connected; in any case, by 1830 Marie was *the* voodoo queen and a force to be reckoned with. She is said to have eliminated other queens through the use of hideous *gris-gris*, literally "voodooing" them to death. One of her bad-luck charms was supposedly a small bag made from the shoulder of a dead body. The contents included bats' wings, cats' eyes, a rooster's heart, and an owl's liver. Keeping this company was a dried lizard, a dried toad and the smallest finger of someone who was black and had committed suicide. Any unfortunate receiving such a potent gift would certainly die.

Everyone in the city was terrified of Marie Laveau; she is said to have had police and politicians in her pocket. She reigned over the Congo Square rituals, and danced with the snake at the Lake Pontchartrain rites. Marie retired in 1869, and died in June, 1881. Long before her death, her daughter, born in 1827, had gained as much notoriety as Marie I, perhaps even more. Other queens reigned after these two women, but none ever had the power or the fame of the Laveaus.

The Laveau-Glapion tomb is in St Louis Cemetery No. 1, near the Basin Street entrance. The stark-white tomb is always adorned with burnt candles, flowers, and voodoo offerings. It probably holds the remains of the Widow Paris, and may also be the final resting place of the second Marie Laveau. Others maintain that Marie II, exiled by her family after the death of her mother, is buried elsewhere – in one of the "ovens" of St Louis Cemetery No. 2 and in at least three other cemeteries. Some say her spirit is restless and cannot be contained.

Modern mojos

Voodoo is scarcely the force it once was. It is not, however, dead. Believers still use the "mojo hand" – a small cloth filled with pieces of dead birds, animals, or people – to "fix" (hoodoo) someone or something. The most popular and potent *gris-gris* is a root called "Johnny the Conqueror," also known as High John and Big John. Big John has turned up in several blues recordings, such as Bo Diddley's "I'm a Man" and Muddy Waters' "Hootchie Cootchie Man."

Another voodoo-related blues tune is John Lee Hooker's "Crawling King Snake Blues." And in the 1960s, rock-and-roll piano player, Mac Rebennack, decked out in feathers and face paint, adopted the stage name Dr John.

Perhaps the most impressive proof that voodoo is still with us is in its use in modern medicine and psychiatry. According to the *Encyclopedia of Southern Culture*, doctors in respectable Southern medical schools have consulted voodoo doctors, especially with regard to the treatment of paranoid schizophrenics. ❏

LEFT: the graffiti-adorned tomb of Marie Laveau.
RIGHT: Ava Kay Jones, Voodoo Museum priestess.

THE FRENCH QUARTER

A detailed guide to the area, with principal sites clearly cross-referenced by number to the maps

Residents of New Orleans are far too self-confident to take offense at this description of themselves, written by Oliver Evans in 1959: "Hedonistic, complacent, extravagant where amusement is concerned, soft to the point sometimes of insincerity, tolerant to the point sometimes of decadence; but always vivacious, good-natured, well-dressed, and well-mannered – these are the characteristics of a typical New Orleanian. You might think, perhaps, that his vices outweigh his virtues; it depends on what you believe is important, but there is no denying that he is an easy fellow to get along with."

Although the city has many undeniably attractive neighborhoods, to most visitors New Orleans is the French Quarter. This area of 96 square blocks, laid out in a perfect grid by French engineers in 1721, encompasses what many people think about the city as a whole: that it is a town where an architect, a gourmet, or a roué is in hog heaven, according to that prolific scribe, Ibid.

Directions in this 1-sq. mile (2.5 sq. km) area are governed by the flow of the Mississippi river: the lower Quarter is the area from Jackson Square to Esplanade Avenue; the upper Quarter lies between Jackson Square and Canal Street. If in doubt, aim for the spires of St Louis Cathedral, the centerpiece of the square, and then head out once again.

The French Quarter is not a polished place. Its buildings can appear shabby; its streets are sometimes dirty. It is overrun with tourists. On sultry summer nights, shambling hordes of out-of-towners, intent on guzzling as many Hurricanes as possible, maraud through the narrow thoroughfares as if it were a playground for demented youths. Others, in daylight hours, shop until they drop in the tacky souvenir emporiums that have replaced many of the small specialist shops. Some people, in fact, wonder what all the fuss is about when it comes to the French Quarter.

The answer can be found on the quiet side streets, in tiny cafés where huge platters of red beans and rice can be bought for less than you thought possible. In the neighborhood clubs, where the melancholy sound of jazz mingles with the sweet scent of perfume. Or at dawn on a spring day, when the sun colors the old buildings with a glow so mellow that it cannot fail to lighten the step.

Some visitors mind the crumbling nature of the French Quarter, the faded buildings, and the sometimes eccentric behavior of its habitués. They prefer their attractions to have more gloss.

It all depends on what you believe is important. ❏

PRECEDING PAGES: the French Quarter at dusk; vaults of one of the "Cities of the Dead"; Oak Alley plantation, built in 1837, on the Great River Road, Louisiana. **LEFT:** fine-tuning the floats at Mardi Gras World.

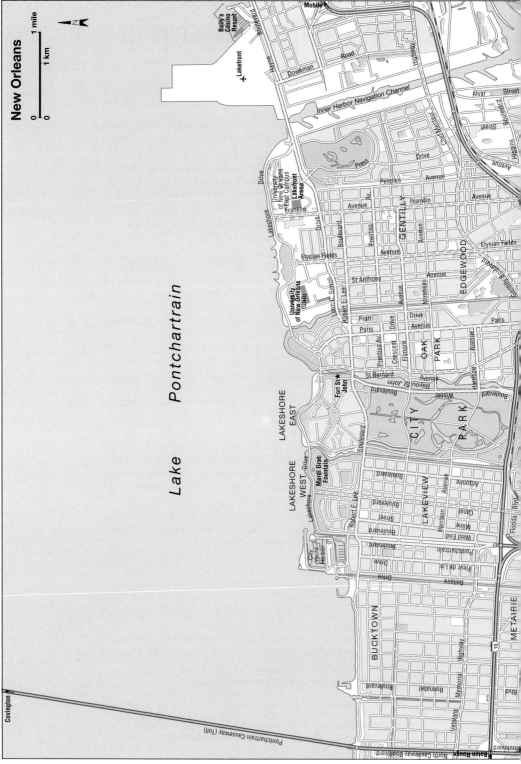

New Orleans

1 mile

1 km

Lake Pontchartrain

Bally's Casino Resort

Mobile

Lakefront

Inner Harbor Navigation Channel

Dowman

Road

Thrane

Boulevard

Highway

Alvar

Street

Chef Mentur

Higgins

Street

Boulevard

Avenue

Press

Drive

Peoples

Avenue

GENTLY

Lakeshore

Drive

University of New Orleans East Campus

Lakefront Arena

Franklin

Avenue

Franklin

Avenue

Prentiss

Avenue

Elysian Fields

Avenue

Elysian Fields

EDGEWOOD

St Anthony

Avenue

Avenue

University of New Orleans (UNO)

Leon C. Simon

Robert E Lee

Pratt

Drive

Mirabeau

Avenue

Gentilly Boulevard

Paris

Drive

Avenue

Paris

Prentiss Av

Drive

OAK

PARK

Crescent

Elmore

Avenue

St Bernard

Avenue

Fort St John

Bayou St John

Harrison

Wisner

Boulevard

LAKESHORE EAST

C I T Y

P A R K

Boulevard

LAKESHORE WEST

Mardi Gras Fountain

Boulevard

Boulevard

Antonne

Avenue

LAKEVIEW

Robert E Lee

Boulevard

Milne

Street

Canal

Harrison

Lakeshore Drive

West End

Boulevard

Florida Blvd

Pontchartrain

Boulevard

City Yacht Harbor

Fleur de Lis

Drive

Drive

Bellaire

BUCKTOWN

Bonnabel

Boulevard

Highway

Memorial

10

METAIRIE

Veterans

Florida

Blvd

Boulevard

Covington

Pontchartrain Causeway (Toll)

Baton Rouge

North Causeway Boulevard

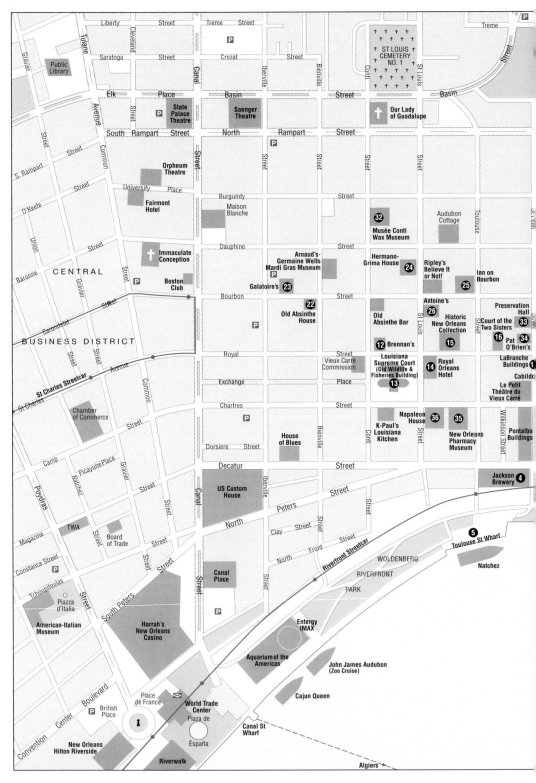

Liberty Street
Treme Street
Treme
Tulane
Cleveland
Gravier
Public
Library
Saratoga Street
Crozat Street
Canal
Iberville
Bienville
Conti
St Louis Street

ST LOUIS
CEMETERY
NO. 1

Elk Place
Basin Street
Rampart Street
Basin

Avenue
Street
State
Palace
Theatre
Saenger
Theatre
Our Lady
of Guadalupe

South Rampart Street
North Rampart Street

Common Street
S. Rampart Street
Orpheum
Theatre

O'Keefe Street
University Place
Fairmont
Hotel
Burgundy Street

Union Street
Maison
Blanche
Musée Conti
Wax Museum **32**
Audubon
Cottage
Toulouse

Baronne Street
Immaculate
Conception
Dauphine
Arnaud's-
Germaine Wells
Mardi Gras Museum
Hermann-
Grima House
Ripley's
Believe It
or Not!

CENTRAL
Boston
Club
Galatoire's **23**
24
25
Inn on
Bourbon

Gravier Street
Carondelet Street
Bourbon Street
Old Absinthe
House **22**
Old
Absinthe Bar
Antoine's **26**
Historic
New Orleans
Collection **15**
Preservation
Hall
Court of the
Two Sisters **33**
16 **34**

BUSINESS DISTRICT
St Charles Streetcar
St Charles
Royal Street
Vieux Carré
Commission
12 Brennan's
Louisiana
Supreme Court
(Old Wildlife &
Fisheries Building) **13**
St Louis
14 Royal
Orleans
Hotel
Pat
O'Brien's
LaBranche
Buildings **1**
Cabildo

Exchange Place
Le Petit
Théâtre du
Vieux Carré

Chamber
of Commerce
Chartres Street
Napoleon
House
K-Paul's
Louisiana
Kitchen
Conti
36 **35**
New Orleans
Pharmacy
Museum
Wilkinson Street
Pontalba
Buildings

Camp
Picayune Place
Gravier
Dorsiere Street
House
of Blues
Bienville

Poydras
Natchez
Decatur Street

TWA
Board
of Trade
US Custom
House
North Peters
Clay Street
Front Street
Jackson
Brewery **4**

Magazine
North Front
Riverfront Streetcar
WOLDENBERG
5
Toulouse St Wharf

Constance Street
Canal
Place
RIVERFRONT
PARK
Natchez

Tchoupitoulas
Piazza
d'Italia
South Peters
American-Italian
Museum
Harrah's
New Orleans
Casino
Entergy
IMAX

Boulevard
Place
de France
British
Place
World Trade
Center
Plaza de
España
Aquarium of the
Americas
John James Audubon
(Zoo Cruise)

Convention
Center
New Orleans
Hilton Riverside
1
Cajun Queen
Canal St
Wharf

Riverwalk
Algiers

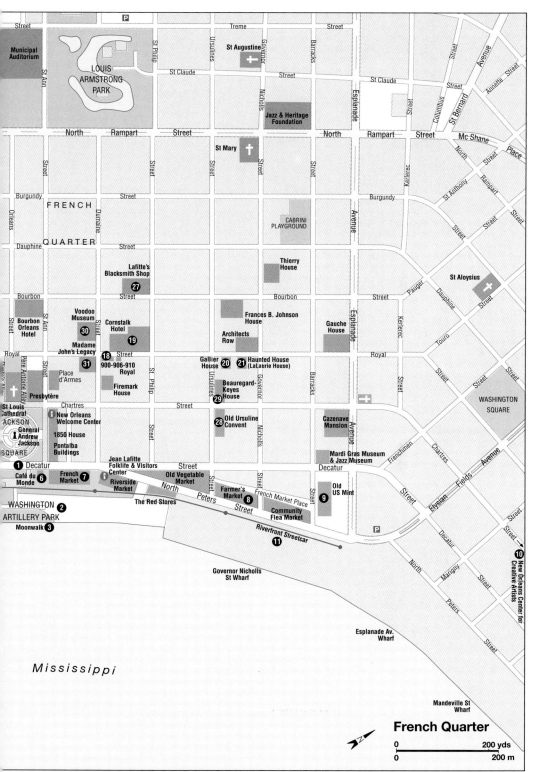

French Quarter

| 0 | 200 yds |
| 0 | 200 m |

AROUND JACKSON SQUARE

Map
on page
122

Jackson Square is the heart of the old city,
where the spirit of the past mingles with
the movie-makers of the future

Jackson Square is the centerpiece of the city's most famous attraction, the French Quarter. Also called the **Vieux Carré** (Old Square), the Quarter is the original colony of La Nouvelle Orleans. The buildings, most from the early to mid-1800s, are small and colorful, with steep gables, sloping roofs, dormer windows, and graceful fanlight windows. Many are painted in bright colors or pastels and festooned with ironwork galleries or gingerbread trim.

Surrounding the square is a flagstone pedestrian mall, the scene of circus-like activity. A black iron fence, which enwraps the park, is hung with paintings – the work of the many sidewalk artists whose easels are set up on the mall. Portrait painters, caricaturists, and landscape artists work, display their wares and await new business, seemingly oblivious of the jazz bands, tap dancers, clowns, and bongo players who provide day- and night-time entertainment.

Broad flagstone carriageways behind black cast-iron gates sweep from the street to secluded courtyards with tiered fountains and masses of lush tropical plants. Strolling through the Quarter, it is easy to imagine the place peopled with aristocratic Creoles, swashbuckling pirates, voodoo queens, and all manner of characters from the past.

LEFT: St Louis Cathedral was named for Louis IX of France.
BELOW: Dickens characters at Christmastime in Jackson Square.

Three languages

The past is very much cherished in New Orleans. Street signs in the Quarter come in three languages: French and Spanish, in fond remembrance of colonial days, and English. It seems almost a shame that Italian is missing. At the turn of this century the French Quarter was an Italian neighborhood.

The Vieux Carré Commission was established by the state legislature in 1936 to preserve the old colony, but, although the 19th-century buildings were here, the French Quarter as we know it did not exist until after World War II. The present Commission is composed of a group of dedicated preservationists who drive a hard bargain when it comes to exterior renovations. Still, the Quarter is hardly a polished and pristine place; it definitely has that "lived in look."

Bordered by **Chartres**, **St Ann**, **Decatur**, and **St Peter streets**, Jackson Square was known to the French Creoles as Place d'Armes and to the Spanish Colonials as Plaza de Armas. The park was originally a parade ground for the militia. The area around the drill field, with church and government buildings, was the center of social, religious, and political life. Grisly public executions sometimes took place in the square, as well as various ceremonies and celebrations.

Today, the former parade ground is landscaped with splendid magnolia, palm, and banana trees, flower beds and benches. Rearing up in the middle of the

Mime artist by a sign that reads "Plaza de Armas", the name given to the square by the Spanish.

BELOW:
Cathedral Garden was a 19th-century dueling ground.

park is sculptor Clark Mills' equestrian **statue** of **General Andrew Jackson** ❶, for whom the park was renamed in 1856. It was America's first equestrian statue and is a monument to the hero of the Battle of New Orleans, fought on the green fields of Chalmette in 1815. Each January 8, on the anniversary of the battle, solemn commemorative ceremonies are held in the square. During more frivolous occasions, such as the French Quarter Festival and La Fête, food booths and music stages are set up along the green.

St Louis Cathedral

Facing the park, stately **St Louis Cathedral** ❷ (tel: 525-9585; tours Mon–Sat, and Sun pm, except during services) rises above these earthy goings-on. Parishioners sometimes complain about the difficulty of keeping their minds on the spiritual with all the sensuous sounds emanating from the tap dancers and bongo players in the square. From time to time, to the delight of tourists, long white stretch limos with police escorts ease over the flagstones, bearing the wedding party of a wealthy socialite couple.

The first church on this site was a small wooden structure, designed in 1724 by Adrien de Pauger, the French engineer who surveyed the original colony. It was named for Louis IX, the 13th-century saint-king of France who fought in two Crusades. This first church was one of more than 850 buildings that went up in flames during the Good Friday fire of 1788. A wealthy Spaniard named Don Andre Almonester y Roxas bankrolled the construction of the new church, which was dedicated on Christmas Eve, 1794.

The present St Louis Cathedral dates from 1851. The stained-glass windows in the front of the church were gifts from the Spanish government. In 1964, the

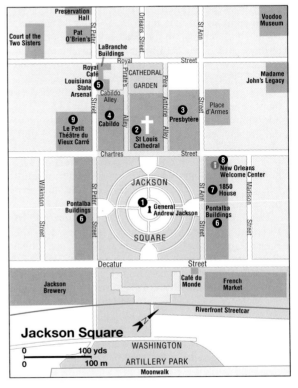

cathedral was elevated to the status of minor basilica by Pope Paul VI. Pope John Paul II visited New Orleans in 1987; in honor of the papal visit the mall in front of the cathedral was renamed Place Jean Paul Deux.

Map on page 122

Intriguing alleys

Pirate's Alley and **Père Antoine Alley** are flagstone passageways that cut alongside the cathedral and lead from the square to Royal Street. Romantics cannot stroll these cracked flagstones without imagining what life must have been like in 19th-century New Orleans. There are guides who tell of clandestine meetings in Pirate's Alley, when Jean Lafitte and Andrew Jackson were planning strategy for the Battle of New Orleans in 1812. Alas, not only were the alleyways constructed in the 1830s, long after Lafitte and his fabled band of pirates had disappeared, but Pirate's Alley was originally called Ruelle d'Orleans, Sud.

At 624 Pirate's Alley, the present site of the **Faulkner House Bookstore**, William Faulkner wrote his first novel, *A Soldier's Pay*. **Cabildo Alley** is a short passageway that leads from Pirate's Alley to St Peter Street. Père Antoine Alley (originally Ruelle d'Orleans, Nord) was renamed for a Capuchin priest, Father Antonio de Sedella, who arrived here in 1779. He was much loved by the French Creoles, who called him Père Antoine.

The Cabildo: papers for the Louisiana Purchase were signed here.

Cathedral Garden – the backyard, as it were, of the cathedral – lies between Pirate's Alley and Père Antoine Alley. The park is sometimes called St Anthony's Square and its centerpiece is a statue of the Sacred Heart of Jesus. The monument near the Royal Street gate was erected during the reign of Napoleon III to honor 30 French marines who gave their lives while serving others in a yellow fever epidemic.

BELOW:
Pirate's Alley.

Spanish treasures

The two historic buildings that flank St Louis Cathedral on Jackson Square are the Cabildo and the Presbytère. Both buildings date from the Spanish Colonial period and are now part of the Louisiana State Museum complex.

The **Presbytère** ❸ (tel: 568-6968; open Tues–Sun, except major holidays; fee), on the right as you face the cathedral, was begun in 1795. The two great fires destroyed both of the smaller structures that stood here. The Casa Curial, as it was called by the Spanish, or Presbytère to the French, was intended as a home for the priests who served the church, but was never used for that purpose. A part of the museum complex since the early 20th century, the Presbytère houses changing historical exhibits. The odd-looking object in the arcade is the Confederate submarine *Pioneer*, a relic of the War Between the States. In 1862, the Rebs sank it in Lake Pontchartrain, lest it fall into Yankee hands.

One of the most important structures in the city is the **Cabildo** ❹ (701 Chartres St.; tel: 568-6968; open Tues–Sun, except major holidays; fee). The building received its name from the Spanish governing council – that is, the *Cabildo* – which was housed here during the Spanish period. As he did with the Cathedral and the Presbytère, Don Almonester provided funds for the reconstruction of this building. Work began in 1795, but it wasn't fully completed until after the Americans took control of the city in 1803.

Much later, archaeologists discovered part of a wall from a 1750s police guardhouse that had been incorporated into the building. And it was in the room called the Sala Capitular on the second floor that transfer papers for the Louisiana Purchase were signed in 1803. When the Marquis de Lafayette made a ceremonial visit to the city in 1825, the Cabildo was his home away from home. In

BELOW: interior of St Louis Cathedral.

Map on page 122

the 19th century, when the city was divided into three separate municipalities, the Cabildo served as city hall for the First Municipality. It later housed the Louisiana Supreme Court. In 1988, 200 years after the monstrous conflagration that devastated the old town, a fire caused severe damage to the roof and upper floor. Miraculously, none of the museum's treasures was destroyed. It reopened in 1994 following a $6 million restoration.

Another part of the State Museum is the **Louisiana State Arsenal ❺** (not open to the public), behind the Cabildo at 615 St Peter. This was the site of the *calabozo*, or prison, in the Spanish Colonial period. After the Louisiana Purchase, when the Americans gained jurisdiction, a state arsenal was built here.

Legacy of a colorful woman

The buildings lining St Peter and St Ann streets are the **Pontalba Buildings ❻**, identical structures which were constructed in 1849 and 1850 and named for the colorful woman who financed and saw to their completion. She was Micaela Almonester, daughter of the Don who financed, among other things, the reconstruction of St Louis Cathedral, the Cabildo, and the Presbytère. While still in her early teens, Micaela married her first cousin, Joseph Xavier Celestin de Pontalba, and moved with him to Paris. That the couple later divorced is undisputed, but events surrounding the separation are murky. According to one version, Micaela's father-in-law objected to the divorce and, in a heated argument, shot and wounded her. She then wrenched the gun from him and shot him dead. Another version has it that the old baron shot her and, thinking her dead, turned the gun on himself. In any case, he died and she didn't. She obtained her divorce, returned to New Orleans, and threw herself into civic activities.

BELOW: the square's Presbytère houses historical exhibits.

Map on page 122

By the mid-1800s, as the American Sector was growing more and more affluent, Micaela de Pontalba made up her mind to promote the French Quarter and create jobs for the Creoles. She financed the building of the two apartment houses, which, in the European style, have commercial establishments on the ground floor and living space on the upper floors. Her architects were the estimable James Gallier and Henry Howard, and the lady herself was often seen up on a ladder, overseeing the work. The initials "A" and "P", for Almonester and Pontalba, are worked into the ornate ironwork of the balconies.

Each building consists of 16 rowhouses: 12 units facing Jackson Square, two facing Decatur Street, and two facing Chartres Street. The "lower" Pontalbas, on St Ann Street, are the property of the State of Louisiana, and the "upper" Pontalbas on St Peter Street belong to the City of New Orleans. ("Lower" and "upper" refer to the downriver and upriver sides of Jackson Square.)

Though Jackson Square is one of the noisiest places in the city, the apartments in the Pontalbas are among the Quarter's most coveted. In the lower Pontalbas, the Louisiana State Museum maintains the **1850 House** ❼ (523 St Ann St.; tel: 568-6968; open Tues–Sun, except major holidays; fee), which gives visitors a chance to see how upper-class Creoles lived in the 19th century. In addition to the canopied beds and other antiques, the apartment exhibits a kitchen filled with old-timey things and a display of antique dolls.

BELOW: Le Petit Théâtre is the oldest continually operating community theater in America.
RIGHT: a view of the Vieux Carré.

A warm welcome

Adjacent to the 1850 House, the **New Orleans Welcome Center** ❽ (529 St Ann St.; tel: 566-5031; open daily) has a wealth of free information, including maps, brochures, and advice. The **Louisiana Office of Tourism** (tel: 568-5661) shares space with the New Orleans Welcome Center and provides helpful information to visitors who plan to explore other parts of the state.

Across St Peter Street from the Cabildo is a balconied pink stucco building that houses **Le Petit Théâtre du Vieux Carré** ❾, the oldest continually operating community theater in America. It began in 1916 with a group called The Drawing Room Players that first mounted its productions in a private home and later moved to space in the lower Pontalbas. In 1919, the company moved to the present location.

The building that houses the theater is a faithful reconstruction of one that was completed on this site in 1797. The interior of the theater has a charming old-world ambience, and the inner courtyard is lovely.

Up the street from Le Petit, at 632 St Peter, a plaque notes that Tennessee Williams wrote *A Streetcar Named Desire* in an apartment in this building. Williams scholars say the playwright was inspired by the streetcar that used to rattle down Royal Street.

Just around the corner from the theater, on Chartres Street, is yet another New Orleans institution. La Marquise pastry shop is a French pâtisserie with wonderful croissants, Napoleons, éclairs, coffees, and other delectations. There are a few tables in the two tiny rooms and a pleasant courtyard with umbrellas to shield against the sun's rays. La Marquise is a delightful interlude in anyone's day. ❑

THE RIVERFRONT TO THE FRENCH MARKET

Map on pages 118–19

Fringed surreys, "Red Lady" streetcars, sugar-coated donuts and spice-scented markets are just a few of the attractions in this part of the French Quarter

F ringed surreys drawn by mules wearing silly hats and faded flowers are a common sight in the French Quarter. These half-hour carriage tours are a pleasant, old-worldly way to see the local sights, and the guides' spiels are entertaining if not necessarily accurate. An oft-repeated example of misinformation is that given by the carriage driver who solemnly informed his fares that the Presbytère in Jackson Square was the Presbyterian Church.

The pitch where the drivers ply their trade most avidly is **Decatur Street ❶**, the busy thoroughfare between Jackson Square and the Riverfront. Restaurants, delis, and coffeehouses line its perimeters, which is fitting, for the street ends up near the open-air food emporium, the French Market.

Just across Decatur from Jackson Square is **Washington Artillery Park ❷**, a broad split-level expanse of concrete and cast iron. Steps and ramps lead from the sidewalk to a **promenade** with box trees and park benches. This is a superb place to get a picture-postcard overview of Jackson Square and the Mississippi river. Street performers are often out in full force entertaining the sightseers, and the mournful sound of a jazz trumpet is never far away.

PRECEDING PAGES: the French Quarter al fresco. **LEFT:** carriage tours are available. **BELOW:** riverfront transportation.

Walking on the moon

From here you can walk down and across the Riverfront streetcar tracks to **Moonwalk ❸**, a wooden walkway smack on the river. (It was named for former New Orleans mayor Moon Landrieu.) This is one of the finest places in town to watch the ever-changing parade of tugs, fanciful river boats, and serious cargo ships and tankers on the river. The best time of all is at sunset, when both the sky and the water are streaked with brilliant scarlet color.

Directly across the river is the residential section of Algiers (*see page 205*). The great bend of the river at Algiers Point is the *bête noire* of river boat captains who must negotiate the sharp turn. Just upriver is the Crescent City Connection, which is the bridge from the east to the west bank of the river. At night the bridge, ablaze with yellow lights, looks like a long golden chain stretched across the river and reflected in the water. (As an example of how the Mighty Mississippi wreaks havoc with directions here, the West Bank is due east of the East Bank.) Quarterites love to relax on a Moonwalk park bench and dreamily contemplate their river. Oftentimes street musicians play here for tips, which can either enhance or destroy the mood, depending on the talent of the performer. Unfortunately, this is a pretty good place to be harassed by panhandlers. Shoeshines are also easy to come by in this area.

Sax appeal on the Moonwalk.

The large building on the riverside of Decatur at St Peter Street is the **Jackson** (or **Jax**) **Brewery** . The restored structure dates from 1891, and for many years Jax Beer was brewed here. In 1984, it was converted into a festival marketplace. Jackson Brewery is connected to a sister property, the Jackson Brewery Millhouse, another restored building containing shops and eateries. A block along toward Canal Street is the third of the Jackson Brewery Corporation's festival marketplaces, called, interestingly, The Marketplace. Many of these restaurants offer views of the Mississippi, with both indoor and outdoor seating.

Paddle steaming

The ever-colorful steamboat *Natchez* (tel: 586-8777; twice daily harbor/jazz cruises, nightly dinner/jazz cruises; fee) docks behind the Jax Brewery at the **Toulouse Street Wharf** ❺. An authentic paddle wheeler, this great white floating wedding cake offers delightful calliope concerts as passengers board for sightseeing cruises. The wonderful off-key calliope wheezes out old-time tunes that can surely be heard throughout the southeastern United States, if not the entire Western Hemisphere. **Woldenberg Riverfront Park**, an extensive landscaped area, with trees, statuary and park benches, stretches along the river all the way to the Aquarium of the Americas in the Central Business District.

Food, not surprisingly, is nearby. **Café du Monde** ❻ (813 Decatur St.; tel: 581-2918; open 24 hours daily) is an open-air pavilion at the corner of Decatur and St Ann streets, on the downriver side of Washington Artillery Park. Open all day and all night, the café is a New Orleans legend, as popular with locals as with tourists; the café has been on this spot for more than a hundred years. This is the place for *café au lait* and *beignets*, either to start the day, finish it, or help get through it. New Orleanians who've painted the town red usually stop here before heading home in the dawn's early light.

BELOW: the open-air Café du Monde has been on its French Quarter site for over a hundred years.

The *beignets* are heavily cloaked in powdered sugar, and more often than not so are the people trying to eat them. As is the case with many New Orleans foods, it is impossible to eat them neatly.

Café du Monde is the notable upriver anchor of the **French Market** ❼ (tel: 522-2621), a shopping complex with colonnades, arcades, specialty shops, and outdoor cafés. This is a great place to shop for gifts and souvenirs of the city. Shoppers of one kind or another have been doing business here since the early 1700s, when there was a trading post on this site. Today's street vendors are hardly a new phenomenon; only the styles and goods have changed.

In the old days, Sunday mornings in the French Market gave true meaning to the term "festival marketplace." Creole shoppers haggled loudly over everything from ice cream to live chickens to jewelry, while vendors sang out clever rhymes to hawk their wares. An itinerant dentist would arrive with a brass band to drown out the howls of unanesthetized patients.

There are still bands playing in the French Market, but they're more for toe tapping and hand clapping than tooth pulling. Open-air cafés such as the Gazebo are great places to take in the sounds of Dixieland, and free concerts are regularly held in **Dutch Alley**.

Map on pages 118–19

Concert schedules are available at the **Dutch Alley information kiosk** at the foot of St Philip Street. Park Rangers at the **Jean Lafitte** National Historical Park Service's **Folklife & Visitors Center** (916–918 N. Peter St.; tel: 589-2636; open 9–5 daily) in Dutch Alley offer free tours of the French Quarter and the Garden District, and supply information about the city and the region.

Mysterious pirate

One thing which isn't lacking in New Orleans is information about Jean Lafitte himself. Or perhaps we should say disinformation – so many legends abound concerning this pirate/patriot that even the spelling of his name is in dispute, being variously Lafitte (with one "f") or Laffite, with two "f" and one "t". The most romantic amalgam of these various tales is that Jean Lafitte was a 19th-century French buccaneer and smuggler who attacked Spanish ships sailing near New Orleans. Lafitte's brother, Pierre, sold black slaves to "quality households" around town, including the nuns at the Ursuline Convent. Jean received a presidential pardon for his smuggling activities for aiding Andrew Jackson in his war against the British, but, born to be a sinner, he soon returned to piracy. This time Lafitte attacked American, rather than Spanish, ships. Hotly pursued by the US Navy, he sailed away in his favorite ship, *The Pride*, and was never seen again. How much of the tale is true is anyone's guess.

The **Farmer's Market ❽** (open 24 hours daily) is the downriver link in the French Market's chain of supplies. Farmers from the surrounding areas have been bringing their fresh produce to this site for more than 160 years. Sightseers and locals cram the aisles of the open-air shed, picking through bins of fresh fruits, vegetables, garlic, and pecans. There are also booths piled with wallets,

BELOW: Farmer's Market is open 24 hours a day, every day of the week.

Memorabilia from Mardi Gras can be admired at the Old US Mint.

jewelry, and other nonedible market goods. On weekends, a well-attended open-air **Flea Market** takes place at the rear of the Farmer's Market.

The market is now a peaceful place compared to what occurred on this site between 1840 and 1870. In those days, Gallatin Street was a two-block stretch along the riverfront docks between Barracks and Ursulines streets. Lined with brothels and gin mills, it was among the toughest, meanest places in the world. Murders, mutilations, and mayhem went with the territory, and those who valued their lives steered clear of it. One of the bars is said to have been decorated in a mortuary motif. Bartenders were dressed up like undertakers, liquor bottles were stored in little coffins, and drinks were spiked with creosote. Not so much as a trace of Gallatin Street remains today, not even the name.

At the point where the Farmer's Market trickles into Barracks Street, the actual streetcar named *Desire* used to be on display at the Old US Mint. A tribute to Tennessee Williams' world-famous play of the same name, the restored car came from the old Desire streetcar line that inspired the playwright. The Desire line is no longer running; only a bus carries that name. Think how theatrical history might have been changed if there had never been such a streetcar line: "A Bus Named Desire" just doesn't have the same flair.

In Mint condition

BELOW: Cajun fish seller displaying the day's catch in the French Market.

The **Old US Mint** ❾ (400 Esplanade Ave.; tel: 568-6968; open Tues–Sun, except major holidays; fee) itself, which fronts on Esplanade Avenue, houses exhibits of two phenomena identified with the Big Easy city – Mardi Gras and jazz. The **Mardi Gras exhibit** is ablaze with sparkling gowns, crowns, scepters, and other carnival paraphernalia. Across the hall, the **jazz exhibit** contains a

well-documented history of this famous tradition, as well as sheet music and instruments used by famed musicians, including one of Louis Armstrong's first trumpets and also one of his white handkerchiefs. The building houses an excellent jazz archive, which is available free to *bona fide* researchers.

The Mint, a massive three-story Greek Revival structure, was constructed in 1835 on the site of an old Spanish fort. One of the first regional branches of the United States Mint, it produced about $5 million a month in coins. However, it was in operation for less than 30 years; the mint was closed in 1862 when Union forces occupied New Orleans during the War Between the States.

Ladies in red

As part of a development called Riverfront 2000, Audubon Institute has extended Woldenberg Riverfront Park downriver as far as the Governor Nicholls Street Wharf, providing more open space and a plant conservatory. Also in this vicinity, near **Mandeville Street Wharf**, the **New Orleans Center for Creative Artists** ❿ opened its $21.8 million facility at 2800 Chartres in 1999. The new facility incorporated some old abandoned warehouses which were restored and merged with new structures. NOCCA has been training musicians since 1973; among its graduates are Harry Connick, Jr, and Wynton Marsalis.

At Esplanade Avenue, the **Riverfront streetcar** ⓫ begins its breezy ride alongside the river. These "Ladies in Red" consist of seven vintage streetcars painted red with gold trim as a historical reference to the old French Market line which followed the same route. They carry around 5,500 people every day, and are a great way to get home. By the year 2001, the St Charles Avenue and Riverfront streetcars will be connected via a Canal Street streetcar system. ❏

Map on pages 118–19

TIP

Unless otherwise listed, all telephone numbers are preceded by the area code **504**.

BELOW: selling food in the French Market dates back to the early 1700s.

NEW ORLEANS' NICKNAMES

New Orleans inspires immense affection, and with affection usually comes nicknames. Few American cities have as many, fewer still have names that suggest such a strong sense of identity. Although most people will be familiar with the sobriquets "The Big Easy," "The Crescent City," and "The City That Care Forgot," here are some nicknames that may be less familiar:

- City of Saints and Sinners
- City of the Southern Pride
- Super Bowl City
- Jumbo Gumbo Pot of the South
- Gator Town
- Queen City of the South
- Parade City USA
- Home of Dixieland Jazz
- Nola (for New Orleans, Louisiana)
- Saint City (for the town's football team)
- City of Festivals
- City of Dreams
- City of Mystery
- City of the Chefs
- The Sleeping Beauty

ROYAL STREET

*Royal Street is the picture postcard image of the city,
a combination of well-preserved residences, historic hotels and
expensive shops offering a flavor of 19th-century affluence*

Map on pages 118–19

I n the 19th century, the intersection of Conti and Royal streets was the banking center of the French Quarter. The police station now occupies the porticoed Greek Revival mansion at 334 Royal Street, but it was built in 1826 as the Bank of Louisiana. Its handsome gate and fence were modeled after those at Lansdowne House in London.

Across the street is a balconied building that once housed the Old Bank of the United States. Nearby, at 403 Royal, are the premises of the old Louisiana State Bank, the last work of architect Benjamin Henry Latrobe. He designed the Bank of Pennsylvania in Philadelphia and later contributed to the United States Capitol in Washington, DC.

Money, as you may have gathered, is the keynote to Royal Street. Enjoyment of its pleasures is enhanced if you happen to have a lot of it, for this is the place to find upscale boutiques and fine restaurants, or that perfect "gentleman's gift," a hand-tooled snuffbox from one of its antique emporiums. For those without bank notes to spare, window shopping on Royal Street is pretty pleasant, too. Just as a visit to New Orleans isn't complete without a visit to Bourbon Street 'round midnight, a trip to the French Quarter isn't complete without a stroll along Royal.

PRECEDING PAGES:
Cornstalk Fence,
Cornstalk Hotel at
915 Royal Street.
LEFT: sunshade
and flagstone.
BELOW: former bank
at 403 Royal.

Fine and famous edifices

World-famous **Brennan's** ⑫ restaurant (tel: 525-2302) is located at 417 Royal. This building was constructed around the turn of the 19th century as a residence for the maternal grandfather of French Impressionist painter Edgar Degas. Shortly thereafter it was bought by the Banque de la Louisiane, and the initials "BL" were worked into the wrought-iron balcony that fronts it.

Across the street from Brennan's, occupying the entire 400 block, is a white marble building. This handsome structure, built between 1907 and 1909 to house the Civil District Court, has undergone a $19 million renovation and now houses the **Louisiana Supreme Court** ⑬ and the 4th Circuit Court of Appeal. When the city purchased this whole square in the early 20th century, buildings razed to make way for the new structure included the former site of Antoine's restaurant. This fine baroque edifice – which some older locals still refer to as the "**old Wildlife and Fisheries building**," in reference to a longtime tenant – featured strongly in Oliver Stone's film *JFK*. The steps provide a stage for performers.

At the corner of Royal and St Louis streets, the posh **Omni Royal Orleans Hotel** ⑭, called locally the "Royal O" (tel: 529-5333), sits on a historic site. St Louis Exchange Hotel, designed by noted architect

J.N.B. dePouilly, opened here in 1838. Much has been written to describe the splendor of this opulent property, with its great cupola, columns, and graceful archways. One of these archways was incorporated into the Royal O, which was built in 1960. In the lobby of the present hotel is a large painting of the St Louis Hotel, which boasted – besides an exchange and, of course, guest rooms – public baths, a bank, and shops. (Incidentally, the Esplanade Lounge in the lobby of the Royal O is an elegant place to enjoy pastries, flaming coffees, and piano music in the evening.) Running through the lobby of the old hotel was the St Louis-Toulouse stretch of the Exchange Passage, also designed by dePouilly.

Exchange Passage

Exchange Passage led from the Merchants Exchange Building at Royal and Canal (the site now occupied by the French Quarter Holiday Inn) through the center of three blocks, including those in the 400 block of Royal where the old Wildlife and Fisheries building now is, and eventually to the Cabildo, which was in those days the city hall. The route was well-trod by Creole businessmen who had city business to transact and who attended the slave auctions that were held at the St Louis Hotel. (The auctions took place between noon and 3pm, and the accommodating bar manager of the St Louis Hotel bar, Philippe Alvarez, served free lunches to anyone stopping in for a drink during that time.)

The only remaining sections of Exchange Passage (now referred to as **Exchange Place**) are from Canal to Conti streets and from St Peter to Pirate's Alley. That latter segment is now **Cabildo Alley**; as part of Exchange Passage it led to the city hall. The "Fencing Masters' Houses" at 618 and 620 Conti reflect how fencing lessons were *de rigueur* during that era of many duels.

BELOW: guests live in style at French Quarter hotels.

Map on pages 118–19

During the day, when Royal Street is blocked off to vehicular traffic, itinerant musicians and other performers take to the middle of the street to entertain passers-by. The most popular "stages" are the corners of **St Louis**, **Toulouse**, and **St Peter streets**. The quality varies, of course, but the majority are quite good. There is an outstanding pony-tailed piano player, who rolls his upright around, parks it, and sits down to play ragtime. Banjoists and guitarists are much in evidence. A black female contralto, whose voice is rich and mellow as she belts out acappella spirituals, can be heard from up to three blocks away.

In the middle of the block, between St Louis and Toulouse streets, is the courtyard of the television studio WDSU. In the early 19th century, two famous cabinetmakers worked in New Orleans: François Signouret and Prudent Mallard. Their ornately hand-carved canopy and tester beds, armoires, and tables can be seen in historic homes all over the state. This house at **520 Royal**, with its courtyard, was built for Signouret in about 1816. The courtyard is lovely and open to the public during business hours.

A blonde, a castle and a fortune

Across the street and down the block from WDSU, the well-established and interesting **Historic New Orleans Collection** ⓑ (533 Royal St.; tel: 523-4662; open Tues–Sat; Williams Gallery free; fee for tour of house) is pretty much what the name says it is: a collection of maps, documents, and memorabilia to do with the history of New Orleans. The **Williams Gallery** on the ground floor has changing exhibits of regional art, and there is an excellent research library here.

The building itself, which surrounds a lovely courtyard, was erected in the late 18th century as a residence for the Merieult family. According to Stanley Clisby

BELOW: the Historic New Orleans Collection is housed in a lovely mansion with connections to Napolean; tours are recommended.

Shopping for old lace in one of Royal Street's fancy stores.

Arthur in *Old New Orleans*, Napoleon Bonaparte, anxious to secure a political alliance with Turkey, made repeated attempts to purchase Catherine Merieult's mane of blonde hair, for the sultan of Turkey required a blonde wig for one of his sultanas. A fortune, and even a castle were offered, but each time Catherine rejected the emperor's request. This home was one of the handful of structures that survived the fire of 1794 and tours are well worth the nominal fee. In 1998, the Historic New Orleans Collection opened an impressive new research facility at 410 Chartres Street.

Another property with a fine courtyard is the **Court of the Two Sisters** ⓰, a restaurant in the 600 block (tel: 522-7261). Named for two sisters who had a variety store here in the late 1800s, the restaurant does a jazz buffet every day. Next door, the building that houses the Old Towne Praline Shop (which makes some of the best pralines in the new town) also has a lovely courtyard. In the 1800s, the famous coloratura soprano Adelina Patti stayed in this house, which was then a private home, during the time she was appearing in the opera.

First Skyscraper

A souvenir shop presently occupies the ground floor of 640 Royal Street, otherwise known as **New Orleans' First Skyscraper**, which was built between 1795 and 1811. An atmospheric old party, with peeling pinkish-gray facade and wrought-iron balconies, this house is known variously as the Pedesclaux-LeMonnier House, 'Sieur George, as well as the First Skyscraper. The initials "YLM" worked into the balcony railing stand for Dr Yves LeMonnier, for whom the house was originally built. George Washington Cable, a 19th-century New Orleans novelist, used this house as the setting for his short story *'Sieur George*.

BELOW:
Royal interlude.

QUADROON BALLS

In the 19th century, balls were held for the purpose of introducing young and beautiful quadroon girls (a quadroon had one-quarter black blood) to affluent Creole gentlemen. The young women were escorted to the balls by their mothers, each of whom hoped that her daughter would become the mistress of a wealthy Creole. When a satisfactory arrangement was worked out, the mistress's mother could be assured that her daughter would be supported and taken care of, for many Creole men maintained two separate households – one for his wife and their children, the other for his quadroon mistress and their children. Reams have been written about the quadroon balls, and there are varying accounts of the nature of these soirées. According to some historians they were glittering and glamorous occasions; other reports testify they were nothing more than brawls. Suspicious Creole wives would adopt different personas, and – disguised as men – would attend the balls themselves to find out what their men were up to. In addition, a great deal of voodooing went on in New Orleans at this time, and *gris-gris* and other voodoo charms were fairly common. Countless duels were fought over beautiful young quadroon women during the era of the balls.

Some say that the fourth floor was added sometime after the house was built, in order for it to retain its "tallest" title.

The **corner of St Peter and Royal** is said to be the most photographed place in New Orleans. The **Royal Café** is housed in one of the LaBranche Buildings, which were built around 1840 and are notable for their exquisite cast-iron galleries. There are actually 11 **LaBranche Buildings** ⓱ – separate three-story row-houses – lacing down the 600 block of St Peter Street to Cabildo Alley. Cast iron was introduced in New Orleans in 1850; these buildings originally were undoubtedly festooned with simpler wrought (handworked) iron.

Balls and nuns

At 717 Orleans Avenue, a few steps from Cathedral Garden, massive white paneled doors open onto the lobby of the **Bourbon Orleans Hotel** (tel: 523-2222). From the lobby, a spiral staircase leads to the mezzanine and the restored **Quadroon Ballroom**, which is today a handsome meeting room.

The Orleans Theatre once occupied this site and, adjacent to it, stood the Orleans Ballroom. These and many surrounding buildings were destroyed by fire in 1816, but the ballroom was rebuilt the following year.

The ballroom was the setting of some of the famous – or infamous – quadroon balls (*see box opposite*.) In fact, this was not the only site for the balls; they were held at various locations all around the French Quarter. This particular ballroom was purchased in 1873 by the Catholic Sisters of the Holy Family, an order of black nuns, and went on to became a convent and school. In 1964, the Sisters moved out to the suburbs and a part of this structure was incorporated into the Bourbon Orleans Hotel.

Map
on pages
118–19

BELOW:
taking a brake
on the way to work.

Map on pages 118–19

Among the well-nurtured legends of New Orleans is one concerning the ghost of a naked quadroon slave girl said to float around the rooftops in this area on cold winter nights. She is supposed to have been a quadroon whose lover was an elite Creole. When she demanded that he marry her, he said he would – but only if she would demonstrate her love by spending the night on the roof naked. It was the middle of winter and, of course, she froze to death.

Royals on Royal

Trivia question: Who was America's first Princess of Monaco? No, not the actress Grace Kelly. The first was a woman named Alice Heine, whose great-grandmother – the Widow Miltenberger – built the handsome houses at **900–906–910 Royal** ⓲ in 1838 for her three sons. Ms Heine, born in 1910, became a duchess when she married the Duc de Richelieu, and a princess when she became the wife of Prince Louis of Monaco. The Princess Monaco café, which is now closed, was named in honor of this lady.

Across the street, at 915 Royal, is a well-known landmark, the **Cornstalk Fence**, behind which sits the **Cornstalk Hotel** ⓳. Of ornate design, involving cornstalks, ears of corn and morning glories, the cast-iron fence was shipped from Philadelphia sometime after 1834. The fence has a twin in the Garden District, surrounding the stunning house known as Colonel Short's Villa.

Another of the Quarter's house museums is the **Gallier House** ⓴ (1118–1132 Royal St.; tel: 525-5661; tours Mon–Sat; fee – combination tickets for Gallier House and the Hermann-Grima House are available). It was built in 1857 by the well-known architect James Gallier, Jr, as a home for him and his family. Gallier's father, James Gallier, Sr, was also a famous architect whose work can be seen all over town. The senior Gallier was an Irishman whose real name was Gallagher; he Gallicized it after he arrived in New Orleans. Open for tours, the house is beautifully furnished and well-researched. It is a fine example of how the well-heeled Creoles of the 19th century lived.

Sometimes it seems as if every nook and cranny of New Orleans is inhabited by a ghost. A host of them is said to hang out at 1140 Royal, in what is known as the **Haunted House** ㉑. According to local lore, in 1831 this was the residence of Madame Delphine LaLaurie, a socialite who entertained lavishly. But her guests gossiped about the condition of the lady's slaves; they were emaciated, and appeared to be terrified. A neighbor reported seeing Madame LaLaurie beating a small slave girl, who later fell from the roof. Madame LaLaurie was hauled into court, but was merely fined. In 1834, when a fire broke out in the house, neighbors broke down doors and discovered in a smoke-filled room seven chained and starving slaves gasping for breath. A newspaper account implied that Madame LaLaurie set the fire, and a mob gathered in front of her home. The LaLauries escaped and the mob destroyed the house.

In 1837, the building was bought and restored, and is now a private residence. It is not open to the public, but some people insist they can hear hideous shrieks emanating from the house on dark, stormy nights. ❏

BELOW: it's a dog's life. **RIGHT:** the corner of Royal and St Peter street is one of the most photographed (and filmed) sites in the city.

BOURBON STREET

A carnival of high-octane bars, belting music and bawdy fleshpots,
Bourbon Street attacks the senses as fiercely as the liquor
that shares its name

Map
on pages
118–19

An initial stroll along Bourbon Street might lead one to believe it was named for the intoxicant. New Orleans' best-known thoroughfare – locals just call it "the Street" – has more bars than you can shake a swizzle stick at. All kinds of bars – jazz, piano, gay, straight, sleek, sleazy, historic, topless, bottomless, and oyster. Many who come here, especially during particularly festive occasions such as Mardi Gras and the Sugar Bowl, feel obligated to try to drink Bourbon Street dry. When people let their hair down on Bourbon, they let it way down. (Beware: There are unsavory folk here who have creative ways of relieving the inebriated of their valuables.) Actually, the name of the thoroughfare was carefully chosen by the unscrupulous John Law when the colony was founded. The Duke of Bourbon was a major investor in Law's Mississippi Company, and it was thought polite to give the street his name. Law was nothing if not wise to political expediencies. Bourbon Street is famed even more for its music than for its proliferation of watering holes. You can hear the street before you set foot on it. Bourbon has far and away a greater concentration of music clubs than anywhere else in town and possibly in the world.

Bourbon Street blues

Within a six-block stretch you can hear hard rock, rhythm and blues, Dixieland, honky-tonk piano, Irish music, gutbucket (lowdown mean blues), Cajun and zydeco, can-cans, karaoke, and occasionally a bagpiper in full regalia pumping out *Scotland, the Brave.*

It isn't even necessary to go inside to be entertained. Doors of the clubs are flung wide all year round, and the music pours out and floods the streets. Almost any place that serves mixed drinks has "go-cups," so you can take your libation along as you stroll.

Mingling with the music are the sounds of the sidewalk tap dancers, young black kids who dance for dimes and, they hope, dollars. Break dancers are also out to entertain sightseers, spinning and gyrating on blankets they've spread out in the middle of the street.

Barkers, like those at carnival sideshows, stand outside the various clubs and keep up a running spiel, advising passers-by of the wonders to be seen inside. When doors are left open to let in a breath of "fresh" air, the topless/bottomless wonders can sometimes be glimpsed. Outside is the continuous din of merrymakers roaming up and down the street and in and out of bars.

During Mardi Gras, things, shall we say, intensify. There are so many people jamming the streets on Fat Tuesday that it's almost impossible to move. Every balcony on Bourbon is crowded with people, most of them not entirely sober, who toss beads and other

PRECEDING PAGES: street music. **LEFT:** Dixieland denizen. **BELOW:** Lafitte's Blacksmith Shop.

trinkets to the shrieking throngs. Incidentally, regardless of what you've been told, there is no ordinance or even tradition that *requires* women to bare their breasts on a Bourbon Street balcony during Mardi Gras. The law does prohibit the throwing of souvenirs from balconies, but it is not enforced. Midnight of Mardi Gras night presents one of the most incredible sights imaginable. Every square inch of street and balcony is covered with revelers who wish to continue reveling. But at midnight Mardi Gras is officially over and Ash Wednesday begins. No one wants to go home, and it takes a long time to clear the street. The devout go to church, but there are parties that last till dawn.

Many Bourbon Street establishments change owners and names on a regular basis. One new attraction, however, is set to become an "instant classic." This is the **Storyville District** (125 Bourbon Street, tel: 410-1000), a complex showcasing New Orleans' finest – jazz and food – set up by Jazz Fest supremos George Wein and Quint Davis, along with restaurateur Ralph Brennan. Three rooms with state-of-the art sound systems feature music (most of it live) from noon until 1pm, with special performances in the evening.

New Orleans is the only city in America (other than Las Vegas) without a closing law. Bars and clubs are open 24 hours a day, 'round the clock.

Absinthe minded

A tour of Bourbon Street proper (as if that word could be applied to this thoroughfare) begins at the **Old Absinthe House ㉒**, 238 Bourbon, an old, well-established institute of higher imbibing. It was built in 1806 as a commercial-cum-residential structure, and is typical of an *entresol* house. *Entresol* is a French word meaning mezzanine, and in this context it meant a half-story between the upper and lower floors. Used for storage, it was lit by the arched fanlights on the lower floor windows. As for absinthe – that's a whole new story (*see page 53*).

(*see page 53*)

BELOW:
Bourbon Street is full of bars: topless, bottomless, and oyster.

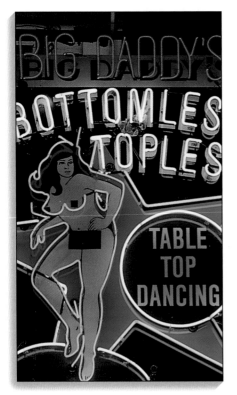

It's true that the main fame of Bourbon is due to its music and bars, but the street is a mixed bag. Sophisticated **Galatoire's ㉓**, one of the city's old-line French Creole restaurants, has been on Bourbon since its founding in the early 20th century (tel: 525-2021). Around noon on any given day (except Monday when the restaurant is closed), a quiet, well-dressed crowd queues up in front for lunch, for reservations are not accepted; their garb in sharp contrast to the short-shorts and T-shirts worn by casual Quarterites and sightseers. In the next block are the smart green awnings of the **Royal Sonesta**, one of the city's fine hotels (tel: 586-0300). Its balconied rooms are much coveted during Mardi Gras, for those who don't want to sleep. In the 500 block, tucked in among the girlie shows and gay revues, Chris Owens does classy Vegas-style shows in her own club.

Just off Bourbon, at 820 St Louis Street, is the **Hermann-Grima House ㉔** (tel: 525-5661; tours Mon–Sat; fee). One of several house museums in the Quarter, this one is an American-style townhouse that dates from 1831. It was built for a man named Hermann, who later sold it to a Grima; hence the name. The mansion itself is handsome, but of particular note are the restored outbuildings that surround pretty ornamental gardens. There is a 19th-century kitchen, where, during the winter months, Creole cooking demonstrations take place. The **Inn on Bourbon** sits on a historic site at Bourbon and Toulouse streets. A plaque on the building notes that the French Opera House stood here for more than half a century, until it burned down in 1919. New Orleans was the first city in America in which opera was performed (though not on this site). Creoles were much enamored of opera, and performances in the 1,800-seat theater were standing room only. Lavish parties were sometimes held in the theater following a performance, and were attended by anyone of importance in the "ruling class." Notice that the curb curves inward here, to accommodate the horse-drawn carriages that pulled up to let off ladies and gentlemen in their fancy dress.

Gentlemen and smugglers

Antoine's , one of the city's most famous restaurants, is located on St Louis Street, between Bourbon and Royal streets (*see page 88*). In 1840, Antoine Alciatore founded this restaurant, and it's still operated by his descendants. Antoine's is housed in a lovely old building dating from 1868 that's lavishly garnished with pale-green ironwork. Below Jackson Square, in the lower Quarter, Bourbon Street is mainly residential – and much quieter. At Bourbon and St Philip streets, the musty old **Lafitte's Blacksmith Shop** is a little cottage that looks like it's about to collapse. Ownership records of this neighborhood bar date back to 1772, but it may be even older. The legend persists that this building housed a blacksmith shop that was a front for local heroes Jean and Pierre Lafitte's smuggling and slave trading activities. What is certain is that the construction of this cottage, known locally as brick-between-posts, is of the kind used in the earliest buildings in the city (*see page 158*). ❑

Map on pages 118–19

In 1990, Dixie Beer launched Blackened Voodoo Lager. The state of Texas banned it, siting occult overtones. The story made national newspaper headlines, and Voodoo sales soared.

BELOW: much of what you may desire can be found here.

THE UPPER AND LOWER QUARTER

Map on pages 118–19

There is a lot to savor away from the main streets of the French Quarter – world-class jazz, other-worldly voodoo, and another world entirely of historic houses and convents

O ne way to distinguish between an out-of-towner and a resident is whether they say "outer" or "lower," "inner" or "upper" when speaking about the French Quarter. Locals refer to the lower Quarter and the upper Quarter, because directions, as usual, follow the flow of the river. The lower Quarter is the area from Jackson Square to Esplanade Avenue, which is vaguely "east" on a map; the upper Quarter lies between Canal Street and Jackson Square. The description is used here because this chapter skips across the remaining French Quarter streets faster than a tap-dancer's toes.

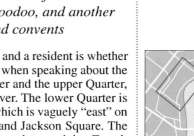

LEFT: the best traditional jazz in the world can be heard in this former stable.
BELOW: the Napolean House was built in 1814.

First in this country

Holding title to the "oldest" or "first in this country" is dear to the hearts of New Orleanians. Local historians still argue over which is the oldest structure in the Vieux Carré. It is undoubtedly true that the sole building to survive the 1788 fire intact is the **Old Ursuline Convent** ㉘ (1100 Chartres St.; tel: 529-3040; tours daily 10am–3pm, Sat and Sun 11.15am–2pm; fee). It is the only remaining example in the city of pure French Creole architecture and one of the oldest buildings in the Mississippi Valley. As such, it is of national importance (*see photo on page 29*).

The large structure, with its portico, pediment, and dormer windows, was designed in 1745 by Ignance François Broutin, who was at the time Louisiana's Engineer-in-Chief, for the Ursuline nuns who arrived here from France in 1727. It was completed in 1753, and replaced the previous convent on this site, built in 1743, which had to be demolished soon after its construction. Here the sisters conducted the first Catholic school, the first Indian school, the first Negro school, and the first orphanage. The nuns prayed in the convent chapel during the 1815 Battle of New Orleans. Andrew Jackson, the hero of the battle, came to the convent afterwards to thank them for their prayers. The Louisiana State Legislature convened in this building from 1831 till 1834, the convent having been moved to a downtown location. It now contains the archives of the Archdiocese of New Orleans. Guided tours take in the formal gardens, the first floor, with its ornate furnishings and artifacts, and the splendid St Mary's Church.

Across the street from the convent, at 1113 Chartres, the **Beauregard-Keyes House** ㉙ (1113 Chartres St.; tel: 523-7527; open Mon–Sat 10am–3pm; tours on the hour; fee) is a house museum which is open to the public. Many New Orleans houses have aliases; this one is also known as the Le Carpentier House. Of

The French Quarter isn't just for tourists; over 3,500 residents live here, too.

course, therein lies a tale. The porticoed Greek Revival raised cottage was built in 1826 for Joseph Le Carpentier, a New Orleans auctioneer who was the grandfather of New Orleans-born world chess champion Paul Charles Morphy. After the War Between the States, when it was a boarding house, General P.G.T. Beauregard – the man who ordered the first shot at Fort Sumter, which began the war – rented rooms here for a brief period. In the 1940s, the house was bought by novelist Frances Parkinson Keyes, who lived and wrote here till her death in 1970, using the slave quarters as her studio. The many books she wrote about the region include *Dinner at Antoine's* and *Steamboat Gothic*. The lovely walled garden adjacent to the house is included in the tour.

Voodoo doings

An only-in-New Orleans phenomenon is the Historic New Orleans spooky **Voodoo Museum** ③⓪ (tel: 523-7685; open daily; fee), at 724 Dumaine Street between Royal and Bourbon. Though rather small and dimly lit, it is filled with all manner of voodoo doings, including dolls, potions, and *gris-gris*. There's a large portrait of Marie Laveau, the famous 19th-century Voodoo Queen, and, in a back room, a voodoo altar. The museum folk conduct guided voodoo tours of the city, as well as a night-time visit to observe a voodoo ritual.

Some historians insist that the house known as **Madame John's Legacy** ③① (632 Dumaine St., tel: 568-6968, open Tues–Sun, except major holidays; fee) predates the Old Ursuline Convent and should be crowned "oldest in New Orleans." A beautifully restored West Indies-style structure, typical of the homes built by the early planters, it has a sloping roof, dormer windows, and a broad gallery with slender wooden colonettes. The present house was built in 1788–89,

BELOW: spoiled for choice with things to do.

Map on pages 118–19

immediately after the great fire, for Don Manuel Lanzos. However, the furor is due to the fact that an earlier house stood on this site.

In 1725, it was built for Jean Pascal, a sailor who was killed during the Natchez Massacre of 1729. Pascal's widow lived here until 1777. Defenders of its "oldest" title say that the house was only partially destroyed by the fire, and when it was rebuilt much of the earlier structure was utilized. (Such things are important to Southern historians.) Madame John's Legacy was given its unusual name after a character in 'Tite Poulette, a short story written in the 19th century by George Washington Cable. The house was restored and is furnished with Louisiana antiques by the Louisiana State Museum, its present owner. There are two exhibits in the house: "Goin' Cross My Mind: Contemporary Self-Taught Artists of Louisiana," and "History and Legends of a National Landmark."

History in wax

The **Musée Conti Wax Museum** ❷ (917 Conti St.; tel: 525-260; open daily; fee) is New Orleans' answer to London's Madame Tussaud's. It traces the history of the city through a series of tableaux, beginning with the story of pioneer explorer La Salle. The wax figures, dressed in period costumes, are amazingly lifelike and presented with great pizzazz. The eyes of the voodoo dancers in the Marie Laveau scene are alarmingly realistic. All the city's heroes and villains are here, including General Andrew Jackson, pirate/hero Jean Lafitte, slave-beater Delphine LaLaurie – even Napoleon Bonaparte, depicted sitting for some reason in a bathtub while discussing the details of the Louisiana Purchase.There is also a **Chamber of Horrors**, appropriately lit and properly ghoulish, and, a bit inexplicably, a figure of the singer Michael Jackson.

BELOW:
a Hurricane at Pat O'Brien's bar is as potent as its name.

Map
on pages
118–19

The 700 block of St Peter Street has two establishments worth mentioning. Grungy, world-famous **Preservation Hall** ❸, at No. 726, situated in a former stable, presents some of the best traditional jazz in the world (tel: 522-2238 in the daytime; 523-8939 at night). There's no bar, but you can get a "go-cup" next door from **Pat O'Brien's** ❸, another well-known bar. Pat's is in an historic structure constructed around a stunning courtyard. It was built in 1791 and occupied by the first Spanish Theatre in the US. Louis Tabary's troupe of actors and musicians, refugees from the West Indies, also performed in this theater.

J.N.B. dePouilly, who designed many 19th-century New Orleans homes and tombs, was the architect of the house at 514 Chartres, now occupied by the **New Orleans Pharmacy Museum** ❸ (tel: 565-8027; open Tues–Sun; fee). It was built for druggist Louis J. Dufilho, who was America's first licensed pharmacist. DePouilly worked on this house at the same time as another of his projects, the fabulous St Louis Hotel, was under construction across the street. A pharmacy museum since the 1930s, it contains many strange and wondrous things: ancient prescriptions and sinister-looking medical implements, *gris-gris* potions, exotic herbs, and a handsome rose-colored Italian marble soda fountain from 1850. There are lots of colorful apothecary jars and containers for such essentials as leeches. This is a fabulous, musty old place in which to poke around, and you can step into the pretty courtyard to catch a breath of fresh air.

BELOW: exhibits in the Museé Conti Wax Museum trace the city's history.
RIGHT: polishing the image.

A Boney part

Today, the **Napoleon House** ❸, a few doors over at 500 Chartres, is one of the most popular bars in town. An atmospheric place, with memorabilia of the Little Corporal everywhere, it was built in 1814 as the private home of New Orleans Mayor Nicholas Girod. Although constructed more than 10 years after America gained control of the city, the house is an excellent example of how the French architectural influence continued here. As for its name, the story goes that Girod was a great admirer of Bonaparte and organized a syndicate to rescue the former emperor from exile on St Helena and bring him to New Orleans. The third floor of the mayor's house is said to have been added as apartments for the expected exile. According to some sources, a schooner was dispatched under the command of the swashbuckling Dominique You, one of Lafitte's men. Napoleon died before the rescue attempt could be accomplished.

Much of the lower Quarter contains residential property, for, far from being just a tourist attraction, the French Quarter is home to about 3,600 inhabitants. Appearances can be deceptive: behind shuttered, inconspicuous facades are houses of grand proportions, many attached to spacious courtyards that vie for elegance with gardens in the Garden District. Other properties are delightful, if shabby, hovels.

Quarterites are a mixed bunch: architects, poets, aristocrats, and waitresses are neighbors in the Vieux Carré. The living is easy. Cars are not only unnecessary but a liability. Virtually everything can be found in the area, at almost any hour. Quarterites tend to stay up late and, if they have the money, retire from working early. Once bitten, they will rarely live anywhere else. ❑

NEW ORLEANS' NOTABLE ARCHITECTURE

The city is an architectural museum; the local domestic buildings are a mosaic of all the cultures that have lived here for the past 300 years

The predominant construction methods in the early French Quarter were *colombage*, mortise and tenoned timbers, and *brique-entre-poteaux* (brick between posts). But after the fires of 1788 and 1794, which destroyed most of the wooden structures, the Spanish legislated to put a cement coat over the bricks and posts, and also introduced flat, tiled roofs. Suddenly, this former French colony looked like a town in Spain. But architectural hybrids from a variety of cultures were commonplace: the raised plantation-style Pitot House (*south bedroom, above*) at 1440 Moss Street, is a combination of French Colonial and West Indian influences. A typical Creole cottage was four equal-sized rooms with an outbuilding containing the slave quarters and the kitchen, isolated because it generated heat. New Orleans architectural "specials" include the *entresol*, a residential and commercial building; the shotgun, often built to house immigrants and which maximized a tiny plot of land; and the camelback, with one story at the front and two stories at the rear. The Preservation Resource Center conducts architectural tours, for details *see Travel Tips*.

△ **CAPTAIN'S FOLLY**
One of two similar houses on Egania near the Bywater district, built by a captain for himself and his son in the style of a steamboat.

▽ **CREOLE COTTAGE**
This West Indian-style cottage at 1440 Pauger is allegedly where pirate Jean Lafitte and drunken cohorts invented the game of craps.

▷ **CREOLE TOWNHOUSES**
Creole townhouses like this one at 641 Barracks are three floors high, with exterior walls made of stucco over brick. The second floor has a balcony.

▷ **BRICK BETWEEN POSTS**
This detail from the St Pierre Hotel (1780) on Burgundy is an example of the French Quarter architecture *brique-entre-poteaux*, also called "brick between posts."

JAMES GALLIER, ARCHITECT

James Gallier, Sr arrived in New Orleans from New York in 1835. An Irishman by birth and an architect by accident, he worked in London before moving to the US in 1832. He was inspired by the New York architect Minard Lafever, generally considered the father of Greek Revival in America. Gallier's first commission was the St Charles Hotel, the grandest structure in New Orleans until it burned down in 1851. His next major project was to complete St Patrick's Church. Critics wrote "it surpasses every attempt at a similar order on this side of the Atlantic, and, when completed, may proudly challenge comparison with any modern parochial edifice in Europe." His signature structure is Gallier Hall, overlooking Lafayette Square. It was the New Orleans City Hall from 1852 to 1957, and also the seat of the Reconstruction government after the Civil War. Gallier passed the business to his son, James Gallier, Jr, after poor health and failing eyesight forced him to retire in 1849.

◁ **SHOTGUN HOUSE**
The name comes from the story that a blast fired from the front door would travel through every room and exit through the back door.

△ **FIRST FLUSH**
Designed by James Gallier, Jr, the Gallier House on Royal Street was one of the first to have a flush toilet (*above*) and running water.

▷ **1445 PAUGER STREET**
The house at this address is a Creole cottage remade into French Colonial.

GREATER NEW ORLEANS

A detailed guide to the area, with principal sites
clearly cross-referenced by number to the maps

Greater New Orleans is a well-kept secret. The French Quarter so dominates most people's perception that the rest of the city recedes into the background. A pity for visitors; a bonus, perhaps, for New Orleanians, who recognize a *lagniappe* when they see one. A *lagniappe* (pronounced lan-yap) is common parlance for a treat, a little reward, a pleasant "something extra." From the attractions and universities Uptown to the 19th-century charm of Algiers, to the art galleries of the Warehouse District: these are bonuses to a visit to New Orleans. None is far away. Most can be reached without a car. All are less crowded than the French Quarter and less commercial, too.

New Orleans' above-ground cemeteries are spread throughout the city. So are live oak trees, the most famous being the Dueling Oaks in City Park, the site of many a swashbuckling dare. Audubon Park, designed by Frederick Law Olmsted, the man who created New York's Central Park, has antebellum embellishments, plus several white alligators. Plantations, strung along the Mississippi like pale pearls on a necklace, can be visited in a day or a stay stretched to a week.

But New Orleans is not just 19th-century elegance. The Central Business District is home to the soaring Superdome, where 76,000 thoroughly modern football fans cheer college teams in the Sugar Bowl to victory every year, caring not a fig for cast-iron filigree, Andrew Jackson, or the "Wah." The Ernest N. Morial Convention Center ranks third in the US in terms of convenient exhibit space. Cajun Country and the swamps surrounding it are increasing in popularity annually as people begin to realize there is life beyond the borders of the French Quarter.

The gateway to Greater New Orleans is Canal Street, one of the widest thoroughfares in the country. Canal Street is the dividing line between uptown and downtown, or, locally, upriver and downriver. (New Orleanians also refer to "riverside" or "lakeside" when explaining directions.) Uptown is also a geographical location, an elegant neighborhood which contains the campuses of Tulane and Loyola universities.

Most Mardi Gras parades take place along Canal Street, and with them there is massive attendant paraphernalia. The largest parades, Endymion and Bacchus, feature a combined total of 75 floats and 60 marching bands. Their 2,300 members throw around 2½ million doubloons to avid spectators. In fact, the "Greatest Free Show on Earth" generates more than half a billion dollars for the city of New Orleans. Which isn't a bad *lagniappe*, when you think about it. ❑

PRECEDING PAGES: the Mississippi River at Algiers Point.
LEFT: the streetcar is always a desirable way to travel.

CITIES OF THE DEAD

*New Orleans' cemeteries are little towns of above-ground tombs,
some resembling simple cottages, others elaborate mansions – and
all built around a network of trees or paths*

Map
on pages
116–17

Visitors to New Orleans may not be dying to tour the local cemeteries, but the city's unique burial grounds are among the top sightseeing attractions. However, for personal safety, visitors should always view the graveyards in the company of an organized group *(see Travel Tips section for details)*.

In contrast to the lush green lawns, landscaping, and headstones of grave-yards in most other US cities, the old cemeteries in New Orleans are notable for their above-ground tombs and mausoleums. Called **Cities of the Dead**, they look like small towns with tiny windowless houses and buildings whose front doors are stark white marble slabs. The tombs are lined up, row after row, with brick or stone walkways laid out in front. The oldest are stepped-top tombs of handmade brick, with inscriptions that have long since faded. Some of the tombs are small and very simple, others are toy-like versions of court houses, banks, and grand Garden District mansions, and still others are elaborate monuments featuring gleaming white marble statuary. Many are surrounded by ornate cast-iron fences and frilly grilles. The largest and most spectacular tombs are those of the city's many benevolent societies.

LEFT: someone to watch over me.
BELOW: details of the tombs are elaborate and poignant.

Burial above ground

There were essentially two reasons for the custom of above-ground burials in New Orleans. The first had to do with Mother Nature, and the second had to do with the mother countries, France and Spain. With regard to the former, much of the city is four to five feet (1–1.5 meters) below sea level, and graves that were dug in the ground rapidly filled with water. (The 20th-century drainage system now makes underground burials possible.) In addition to that practical consideration, New Orleans French and Spanish Creoles were always fond of emulating fashions in Europe, where above-ground burials were customary.

In the 19th century, many grand tombs were graced with *immortelles*, ornamental wreaths made of wire, beads, and glass. They were usually imported from France, where they were quite the rage. In 1883, Mark Twain wrote sarcastically of this artificial ornamentation: "The *immortelle* requires no attention; you just hang it up, and there you are; just leave it alone, it will take care of your grief for you and keep it in mind better than you can; stands weather first rate, and lasts like boiler iron." It is not recorded whether Twain influenced the demise of the *immortelle*, but the ornament is no longer used as a decoration on tombs.

All Saints Day (November 1) is a day of remembrance and a religious, as well as a bank, holiday in New Orleans. For weeks before, New Orleanians are busy cleaning, repairing, and freshening up family tombs. Early in the morning of All Saints Day, people begin arriving at the cemeteries, and thousands of chrysanthemums are placed on the tombs. The flowers are often fashioned in the shape of crosses. By evening there are throngs of people around the graves, and a surprisingly festive atmosphere.

First and No.1

The city's first officially designated cemetery no longer exists. It was laid out in around 1725 on St Peter Street, between Burgundy and Rampart streets, and was in use for about 70 years. The great fire of 1788 destroyed virtually all of the city, and an ensuing epidemic of yellow fever took hundreds of lives. City officials closed the cemetery, and in 1789, **St Louis Cemetery No. 1**, the oldest extant graveyard, was established.

This new cemetery was laid out back of town in a swampy area bordered by the present Basin, Treme, St Louis, and Conti streets. It was established during the Spanish colonial period, and the Spaniards followed a centuries-old custom of building a wall around the graveyard. The wall vaults, which are about 12 feet (3.5 meters) high and 9 feet (2.5 meters) wide, are called "ovens" because of their resemblance to bakers' ovens. They were used for multiple burials, often by families who were unable to afford individual, private tombs.

Visitors are often curious to know how so many people could be buried in a single vault. The answer is, a year and a day after a body is interred, the tomb is opened, the remains are swept to the back of the vault, and the remainder of the casket is taken out, thus creating room for another permanent resident. Most private tombs have two vaults, one above the other, and a lower receptacle in which bodies are placed after removal from the vault.

Brunswig mausoleum, Metairie Cemetery.

BELOW: ashes to ashes; dust to dust.

RIGHT: Tiffany window, Tilton tomb.

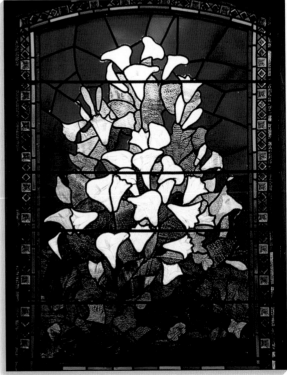

As a rule, the tombs in St Louis No. 1 are not quite as ornate as those in the later cemeteries, but this site is the final resting place for many prominent early Orleanians. Among them are **Etienne de Bore**, who was the city's first mayor and the first person to granulate sugar successfully. Others include Paul Morphy, a 19th-century world chess champion; Myra Clark Gaines, whose 65-year lawsuit over land ownership was one of the longest and most complicated of the 19th century; **Blaise Cenas**, the first US Postmaster in New Orleans; the two wives of William C.C. Claiborne, the first American Governor of Louisiana, whose tombs bear remarkably similar inscriptions; **Bernard de Marigny**, a fabulously wealthy Creole for whom the suburb Faubourg Marigny is named; and **Marie Laveau**, the city's most infamous voodoo queen, whose tomb is usually adorned with voodoo charms and brick-dust crosses. (Another Marie Laveau may be buried in St Louis Cemetery No. 2.)

No. 2 and No. 3

Some of the more elaborate tombs are those of the Italian Mutual Benevolent Society and the French Society, and the five-tiered structure of the Portuguese Benevolent Association. At the rear of the cemetery there used to be a Protestant section, but, in the 1830s, due to an extension of Treme Street, most of the graves were emptied and the remains moved. Only a small, rather desolate part of the Protestant burial ground can still be seen today.

St Louis Cemetery No. 2, which stretches between Iberville and St Louis streets along North Claiborne, was consecrated in 1823. As well as containing the tombs of 19th-century New Orleans mayors **Pitot** and **Girod**, and pirate captain **Dominique You**, who fought with Andrew Jackson in the Battle

Map on pages 116–17

TIP

November 1 is a public holiday, and is when locals spend time at their family tombs. Individuals might want to visit the cemeteries on that day, otherwise it's wiser to join an organized tour.

BELOW: large tombs are often used for multiple burials.

Map on pages 116–17

of New Orleans, the cemetery boasts tombs designed by J.N.B. dePouilly.

When the French architect arrived here in the 1830s, having graduated from the Ecole des Beaux Arts, he brought with him sketches of Père Lachaise cemetery in Paris. The sketchbook still exists, and the influence of the famous French cemetery can clearly be seen in the dePouilly-designed tombs in New Orleans.

The worldwide popularity of the Greek Revival style was, quite literally, carried right to the grave. It was during this period that such flourishes as Ionic, Corinthian, and Doric columns, pediments, and other such ornamentation began to turn up in the New Orleans cemeteries. The best dePouilly designs in St Louis No. 2 are the society tomb of the **Orleans Cazadores** and those of the **Peniston-Duplantier**, **Miltenberger** and **Grailhe** families. DePouilly's final resting place is in a wall vault located between St Louis and Conti streets.

St Louis Cemetery No. 3, the newest and largest of the St Louis cemeteries, is on Esplanade Avenue near the entrance to City Park. It opened in 1854. The entrance is through a broad, ornate iron gate, and the paved roads are wide enough for cars. The mortal remains of many priests and nuns are enshrined here, and there are several "society" tombs: the Young Men's Benevolent Association's; the United Slavonian Benevolent Society's, and the unmistakably Greek, very ornate mausoleum of the Hellenic Orthodox Community.

Metairie Cemetery

The largest and most photographed of the city's many cemeteries is **Metairie Cemetery**, at Metairie Road and Pontchartrain Boulevard. The cemetery covers 150 acres (60 hectares) and contains more than 7,000 graves. It was established in 1872 on the site of the old Metairie Race Course, and the plan for the cemetery follows the oval shape of the racetrack. Unlike other New Orleans cemeteries, Metairie is notable not only for the number of spectacular tombs and mausoleums but also for the lovely landscaping and pretty trees.

The oldest tomb in the cemetery is that of the **Duverje** family of Algiers. Erected in the Algiers cemetery in about 1848, it was dismantled and moved to Metairie in 1916. There are a number of extremely flashy mausoleums in Metairie, notably the pyramidal **Brunswig mausoleum**, which features a large marble sphinx, and the gaudy Romanesque Revival tomb of Salvatore Pizzati, an immigrant who amassed a fortune by importing tropical fruit. The marble-winged angels clasping each other atop the **Aldige tomb** commemorate a wife and daughter who drowned at sea. Architect **James Gallier, Sr,** also perished at sea, and he lies beneath a handsome monument that bears a touching inscription written by his son.

Four statues, representing Faith, Hope, Charity, and Memory, surround the base of a 60-ft (18.5-meter) shaft on the **Moriarity tomb**. An equestrian statue of Confederate General Albert Sidney Johnston tops the tomb of the **Army of Tennessee**. The body of Jefferson Davis, who died in New Orleans in 1889, was interred for four years in the tomb of the **Army of Northern Virginia**. The remains of the Confederate president were later moved to Richmond, Virginia. ❏

BELOW: knockin' on heaven's door.
RIGHT: Metairie was established in 1872 on the site of a racetrack; the landscape still follows the shape of the track.

CANAL STREET TO THE WAREHOUSE DISTRICT

Map on page 174

A World Trade Center, a major arts center,
four museums and four international plazas are
grouped around the streets where Mardi Gras reaches its peak

C anal Street, one of the widest shopping streets in America, leads all the way from the Mississippi River to City Park Avenue, near City Park. A broad, tree-lined street with tall, graceful lampposts, it serves as a gateway to the river, a signpost towards the Central Business District, and the dividing line between Uptown and downtown.

Bronze plaques in the base of each lamppost commemorate the four governments whose flags have flown over the city: France, Spain, the Confederate States of America, and the United States. As a holdover from the early days, street names change when crossing Canal from the French Quarter.

At the foot of Canal Street – that is, the riverside end of the street – the striking **World Trade Center** ❶ rises 33 stories above the city. Plans have been announced for a $68 million conversion of the first 18 floors of the WTC to a hotel, possibly to operate under the Crowne Plaza umbrella. The higher 15 floors will also be renovated and leased to foreign consulates, business and professional firms, and other trade-related organizations.

PRECEDING PAGES: jazz procession to the Pearly Gates. **LEFT:** view from the World Trade Center. **BELOW:** Riverwalk.

Casino culture

Just across the street from the World Trade Center, the Rivergate Exhibition Center, built in the 1960s, was demolished to make way for a casino, but the "land-based" casino on Canal Street has had an extraordinary history, with a script resembling a Marx Brothers laugh fest. In 1995, Harrah's began construction of a Greek Revival building, then almost immediately went bankrupt. A flurry of lawsuits ensued, so to speak. However, in late 1998, **Harrah's** announced that all problems had been resolved, and that a 100,000-sq. ft. (9,290-sq. meter), $213 million casino would open here shortly. With 2,840 slots and 114 gaming tables, the casino would have five themes – Jazz Court, Mardi Gras Court, Court of the Mansion, Smuggler's Court, and a Court of Good Fortune.

Directly behind the World Trade Center, lying alongside the river, is **Plaza de España** ❷, a broad open expanse of colorful tiles whose centerpiece is a splendid fountain that bubbles up to 50 feet (15 meters). One of four "foreign plazas" in the area, **Spanish Plaza**, as it is better known, was a Bicentennial gift to the city from Spain in 1976. A large bronze equestrian statue of Bernard Galvez, an early Spanish governor of Louisiana, stands at its entrance. The **Canal Street Wharf** ❸ and the **Poydras Street Wharf** ❹ along Spanish Plaza are the departure points for the sightseeing riverboats. The ferry that

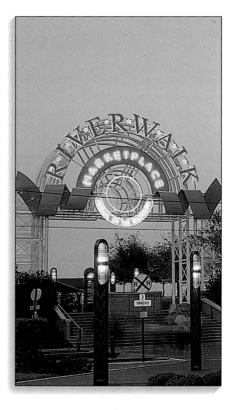

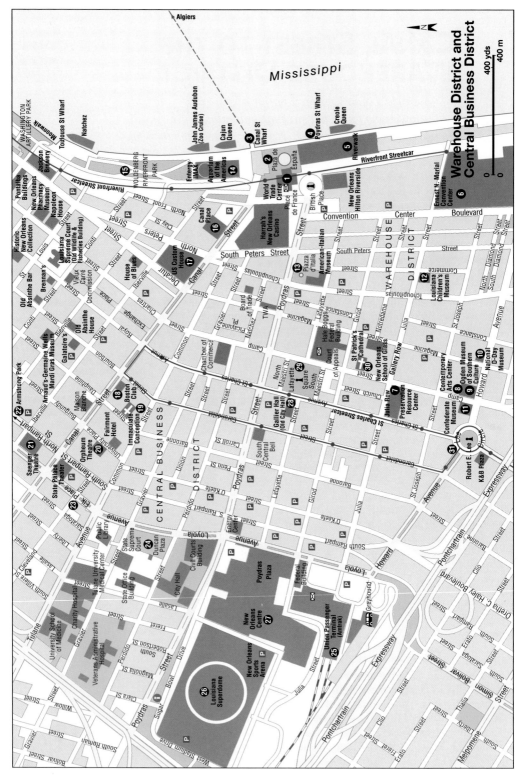

Warehouse District and Central Business District

crosses the Mississippi to Algiers Point (taking both pedestrians and vehicles) also puts in at the Canal Street Wharf.

On Lundi Gras (literally, Fat Monday – the night before Fat Tuesday, or Mardi Gras), the city hosts a huge, free-to-the-public masked ball in Spanish Plaza, with music and fireworks. The mayor is on hand to kick off this final 24 hours of Mardi Gras and to welcome Rex, who arrives by barge to make his first Carnival appearance. This is the signal for a free-for-all of drinking, dancing and general merry-making.

Map on page 174

Canal Place Mall. The area has lavish hotels and is good for shopping.

Riverwalk

The front doors of **Riverwalk** ❺, a festival marketplace, open onto Spanish Plaza. This multimillion-dollar complex occupies one of the sites of the 1984 World's Fair. The long, split-level collection of shops, restaurants, and fast-food outlets extends upriver from Spanish Plaza all the way to the Ernest N. Morial Convention Center. Smack adjacent to Riverwalk is the Hilton Hotel, on Poydras Street. One of the largest hotels in the Gulf South, the Hilton is aslosh with restaurants, bars, and lounges (and, of course, guest rooms), including the sleek club of clarinet-playing native son, Pete Fountain. The Hilton also has one of the city's best health clubs.

Paralleling Riverwalk, Convention Center Boulevard runs along to meet up with the **Ernest N. Morial Convention Center** ❻, which also sits on one of the 1984 World's Fair sites. With the third expansion of the facility, the center has well over 1 million sq. feet (93,000 sq. meters) of space. This building is easily big enough to swallow up all 27 floats of the Krewe of Bacchus, which mounts one of the most spectacular parades of Mardi Gras. The 700-member

BELOW:
Spanish Plaza.

Many galleries in the Warehouse District are housed in high-ceilinged, restored old premises.

Krewe parades through the streets the Sunday night before Mardi Gras and winds up in the Convention Center for its annual bash.

The greatest free show on earth

The madness called Mardi Gras begins to reach fever pitch the Friday night before Fat Tuesday. During the weekend and on through Fat Tuesday there are parades every day and every night. The downtown parades all march along Canal Street. Thousands of people line the routes, and by the big day as many as a million people throng the area. Offices are closed, and Canal Street becomes one of the main venues for the "greatest free show on earth." (*See below for some Mardi Gras facts.*) At the upper end of Convention Center Boulevard and Riverwalk, in the area surrounding Julia Street, is the revitalized and trendy **Warehouse District**.

From the 1830s until around the Civil War, Julia Row – the block of Julia Street between St Charles Avenue and Camp Street – was one of the most fashionable addresses in town. The 13 brick townhouses on the Uptown side of Julia Street were known as the "13 Sisters." However, around the turn of this century, this area began to deteriorate. For many long years it was distinguished only by old abandoned warehouses and factories. Fortunately, Julia Row has been restored and is once again a chic address. Now known as **Gallery Row**, the street is lined with upscale contemporary arts galleries, all housed in high-ceilinged restored warehouses. The **Preservation Resource Center ❼**, whose offices are in Gallery Row, was one of the driving forces behind the restoration project. In addition to its displays of the city's historic structures, the Center does occasionally conduct guided architectural tours.

NOLA BY NUMBERS

Although Nola (**New Orleans, Louisiana**) is not known for having clear geographical directions, the city is a whiz with numbers. Here are a few to consider:

● 8	Parishes (counties)
● 14	Miles from the airport to the CBD
● 23.87	The length of the Lake Pontchartrain Causeway (in miles)
● 60	Average low temperature in fall (°F)
● 65	Public libraries
● 90	Miles from the mouth of the Mississippi
● 200	Limousines and buses
● 940	Churches, including 3 synagogues
● 1,600	Taxis serving the downtown area
● 15,000	Costumed maskers aboard the 350 flatbeds on Fat Tuesday
● 25,650	Hotel rooms filled during Mardi Gras weekend (so book early)
● 240,000	Cruise passengers sailing from the port
● 455,000	Music fans at a recent Jazz Fest
● 476,625	Population of Orleans parish
● 500,000	King cakes sold each year between January 6 and Fat Tuesday

SoHo of the South

This area is the leading center for visual arts in New Orleans. Since 1984 more than 20 art galleries have opened here, leading to the formation of the prestigious Warehouse District Arts Association. The revitalization of this district actually began in 1976, with the opening of the **Contemporary Arts Center ❽** (900 Camp St.; tel: 523-1216; open daily; fee). The sturdy and handsome, four-story 19th-century warehouse that houses the CAC was given a major facelift in 1990, when ten local artists assisted the architect, Stephen Bingler, with the renovation plans. As well as showcasing local artists, the center hosts drama, dance, and performance art shows.

Map on page 174

There's a flourishing style scene around the CAC, the nearby galleries and local watering holes, which escalates in the fall with the beginning of "the season." Gallery owners from other parts of the US have gravitated to the area, with an eagerness that has led to one magazine describing the Warehouse District as "the SoHo of the South" (after the district in New York).

All this activity is not simply window dressing. An art columnist for the *Times-Picayune*, Roger Green, identified a local artistic movement, which he called "Visionary Imagists," in which artists and sculptors "give expression to fantastic visions, rendered meticulously and tending towards moralization, often cloaked in absurd humor."

At press time, a flurry of cultural construction was underway in the area, with two major museums due to open near to two existing museums. The impressive **Ogden Museum of Southern Culture ❾**, which is one-of-a-kind, will trace the story of the visual arts in the American South, and showcase the best of the past, present, and future of southern culture. Not far away, the

BELOW: the building that begat a neighborhood and an artistic movement.

National D-Day Museum ⑩ will commemorate the day the US, Britain and Canada invaded the beaches of Normandy. Renowned historian/biographer Stephen Ambrose, whose home is in New Orleans, was among the advisers.

Cultre vultures can also visit two other museums. On Camp Street, housed in a brooding Romanesque building, the **Confederate Museum** ⑪ (929 Camp St.; tel: 523-4522; open Mon–Sat; fee) contains Civil War memorabilia, including personal effects of Jefferson Davis, president of the Confederate States of America, and General Robert E. Lee's campaign chest. A statue of Lee can be seen in nearby Lee Circle (*see page 189*). The **Louisiana Children's Museum** ⑫ (420 Julia St.; tel: 523-1357; open Tues–Sat and Sun pm; fee) is a first-class facility, offering hands-on exhibits that are both educational and fun.

International plazas

New Orleans has other foreign plazas as well as Spanish Plaza, and they're all grouped near to each other back up towards the World Trade Center. An unflattering statue of Sir Winston Churchill stands in **British Place**, a circle of green grass near the front entrance to the Hilton Hotel. On Poydras Street near Tchoupitoulas Street, **Piazza d'Italia** ⑬, featuring a fountain shaped like Italy, pays tribute to the more than 200,000 Italians who live in the city. This is, not surprisingly, the scene of much festivity during the annual Columbus Day celebration, and there is a small museum. Piazza d'Italia "starred" in the opening scene of the film *The Big Easy*. **Place de France** has a small, but quite bright, gold-plated statue of Joan of Arc, which is located on the "neutral ground" (*see page 183*) across from the World Trade Center.

The modern structure anchored on Canal Street across from the wharf is the $40 million **Aquarium of the Americas** ⑭ (tel: 581-4629; open daily; fee). The 1 million-gallon (3.75 million-liter) aquarium houses over 10,000 fish, reptiles, birds, and foliage indigenous to North, Central, and South America. Major exhibits are the Caribbean Reef Environment; the Amazon Rainforest Habitat; the Mississippi River and Delta Habitat; and the Gulf of Mexico Exhibit. In its own wing of the aquarium complex, the **Entergy IMAX Theatre**, which soars five-and-a-half stories high and has an 11,500-watt digital sound system, shows stunning nature-related films.

The aquarium complex sits in pretty, landscaped **Woldenberg Riverfront Park** ⑮, in which locals like to loll and read a book or build castles in the sky while gazing out over the river traffic. The much-appreciated park stretches along the Mississippi from Canal Street downriver all the way to the Governor Nicolls Street Wharf below Faubourg Marigny.

Across Canal from the casino, **Canal Place** ⑯ is a classy indoor mall whose tenants include Saks Fifth Avenue, Gucci, and Brooks Brothers. Built around a stunning atrium, the mall connects Canal Street with Iberville Street in the French Quarter. On the third level there is a food court, four first-run cinemas, and the **Southern Repertory Theatre** (333 Canal St.; tel: 861-8163). The upscale Westin Canal Place Hotel sits on top of the mall; glass elevators purr up to its posh marbled lobby on the 11th floor.

BELOW:
the Confederate Museum contains the personal effects of President Jefferson Davis.

Custom House

Occupying the entire next block, heading away from the river, is the gray, granite **US Custom House** ⑰ (423 Canal St). This behemoth is on the site of the former Fort St Louis, which guarded the 18th-century French city. Work began on the Custom House in 1848 but was halted by the unpleasantness known in these parts as the War of Northern Aggression. New Orleans fell to the Union forces in 1862, and this building was General Benjamin "Spoons" Butler's headquarters (his nickname resulted from his alleged penchant for pilfering the finest Southern silver).

The building was then called Federal Prison No. 6, and at one time held 2,000 Confederate soldiers. Construction was not completed until 1881, long after the war ended. It still has a rather unfinished look due to the empty niches on the exterior walls. The niches were meant to hold statues but, for reasons unknown, they were never put in place.

Despite its austere exterior, the Custom House is worth a visit to see the **Great Marble Hall**. Hailed by the American Institute of Architects as one of the finest examples of Greek Revival architecture in this country, the marbled hall measures 95 feet by 125 feet (29 meters by 38 meters) and is 54 feet (16.5 meters) high. Fourteen Corinthian columns, each 41 feet (12.5 meters) high and 4 feet (1 meter) in diameter, support a dramatic skylight.

On the riverside wall there is a huge marble bas-relief depicting the Great Seal of the State of Louisiana, which is flanked by General Andrew Jackson and Jean Baptiste le Moyne, Sieur de Bienville, and the founder of the city of New Orleans. The Custom House is a strong contender to be the future home of the Audubon Institute's **Living Science Museum**. ❑

Map on page 174

TIP

Unless otherwise listed, all telephone numbers are preceded by the area code **504**.

BELOW: the Aquarium of the Americas.

THE CENTRAL BUSINESS DISTRICT

Map on page 174

This is New Orleans' "skyscraper city" where the heart of commerce beats right next to historic churches, pretty theaters and the soaring Superdome

I n the earliest days, a vast plantation owned by the Jesuits extended upriver from what is now the French Quarter. In 1763, the Jesuits were expelled from Louisiana (the order was subsequently re-established here); their land was confiscated and sold at public auction. This area comprises much of today's Central Business District (which locals call the CBD), which is roughly bordered by the Mississippi River, Canal Street, Loyola Avenue, and Howard Avenue. It also includes the Riverwalk complex and the Warehouse District, which were discussed in the preceding chapter (*see page 173*).

The Jesuits' land passed on to Bernard Gravier and his wife, Marie. Following a fire in 1788 that virtually destroyed the original French Creole city, the Graviers began to parcel the former plantation into lots, developing it into the city's first *faubourg* (suburb). The *magazins*, or warehouses, along the river led to the name Magazine Street; Camp Street was named for the camp of huts in which the slaves lived; and Poydras and Girod streets were named for investors in this real estate venture. The suburb was first called Ville Gravier, but, after the death of his wife, Gravier changed the name to Faubourg Ste Marie in tribute.

PRECEDING PAGES: the CBD at night. **LEFT:** the space-age Superdome. **BELOW:** the Orpheum Theatre.

The American Section

After the Louisiana Purchase, Anglo-Americans began to pour into New Orleans. Snubbed by the Creoles, they settled in Faubourg Ste Marie and in time the suburb became known as the American Section. By the 1830s, New Orleans was an officially divided city with separate city governments for the Creoles and the Americans.

Dividing the American Section from the French Quarter was a wide stretch of land along which a canal was to have been built. The plan for the canal was never actually implemented, and the land designated for it became a neutral ground on which the Americans and the Creoles sometimes skirmished. The median down the center of Canal Street – and in fact, all medians – is still known to most people in New Orleans as the "neutral ground."

Within the boundaries of the CBD are "progressive" glass-and-concrete skyscrapers and quaint cast-iron buildings. This area is home to the sprawling Superdome, the high-tech, high-rise convention hotels and several important monuments. At Canal and Carondelet streets the St Charles streetcar takes on passengers for its Uptown ramble through the Garden District and beyond (*see pages 193 and 201*) .

The white, three-story Greek Revival building at 824 Canal Street was designed by James Gallier, Sr, as

a home for the Mercer family. It now houses the exclusive **Boston Club** , an elite private club founded in 1841. Around the corner from the Boston Club, at 132 Baronne Street, is the Jesuit **Church of the Immaculate Conception** ⓲. The exotic Spanish-Moorish building, with twin onion domes and horseshoe arches, is a standout, and well-worth seeing. Built in 1930, it is a replica of a church that stood on this site in 1857. The early church fell into disrepair and had to be demolished.

The interior of the more recent church is no less dramatic than the exterior. Much of it – notably the cast-iron pews and bronze gilt altar – was retained from the 19th-century church. The statue of the Virgin Mary was to have stood in the royal chapel at Tuileries, but that plan was swept away along with the royal family during the Revolution of 1848. Much later, the New Orleans congregation bought the statue in France for the sum of $5,000.

Academia and vaudeville

A pleasant shortcut from Baronne Street to University Place is through the plush blue-and-gold lobby of the Fairmont Hotel: **University Place** is so named because this was the original home of Tulane University. Founded in 1834, the university moved Uptown in 1894. The **Orpheum Theatre** ⓴ (129 University Place; tel: 524-3285) is almost directly across the street from the Fairmont. Built in 1918 and boasting an elaborate Beaux Arts facade, the theater has been home to the Louisiana Philharmonic Orchestra. In its early days it was one of the major stops on the Orpheum vaudeville circuit; many top performers, from Harry Houdini to Bob Hope, played the theater.

Touring companies and other top-name entertainers are booked into the

BELOW: the blue ceiling inside the Saenger Theatre has "stars" that twinkle when the lights are lowered.

Saenger Theatre ㉑ (143 N. Rampart St.; tel: 524-2490) at the corner of Canal Street. Its surroundings are tacky, but this theater has a lovely Italian Renaissance auditorium, replete with statuary and "stars" that twinkle in the ceiling.

Map on page 174

Armstrong Park

Rampart Street, the lakeside border of the French Quarter, has for many years been in a disgraceful state of repair. The stretch between St Peter and Canal streets is fairly safe during daylight hours, but visitors should avoid walking alone on any section of Rampart Street after dark. **Armstrong Park** ㉒, whose entrance is at St Ann Street, is dangerous.

This is a particular shame, since an entertainment complex sits within the park. The New Orleans Ballet and New Orleans Opera perform in the **Mahalia Jackson Theatre for the Performing Arts** (tel: 565-7470), and the nearby **Municipal Auditorium** (tel: 565-7470), the site of many a Carnival ball. Many Mardi Gras parades end in Armstrong Park, and sometimes floatriders will rid themselves of a last stash of "throws" in this section of Rampart Street. A handy thing for bead-collectors to bear in mind.

Old Congo Square, which many historians believe was the birthplace of jazz, is situated in front of Municipal Auditorium. Also called **Beauregard Square**, this is where 18th- and 19th-century slaves gathered each Sunday afternoon to chant and dance to the accompaniment of tam-tams. The etiology of jazz aside, *Armstrong Park is not the place for unsuspecting tourists*, and despite looking extremely inviting from the street, it is, sadly, really only safe to venture into with the large crowds that attend the arts performances staged here.

During the day it *is* safe to stop in **Our Lady of Guadalupe Church** (411 N.

ABOVE AND BELOW:
Armstrong Park is thought to be the birthplace of jazz. Today it is the site for both local and international performing arts groups.

TIP

Although New Orleans' crime rate has dropped dramatically, visitors should still be wary of walking around Basin Street, Rampart Street and Armstrong Park, even in the daytime.

Rampart Street). This small, unpretentious church dates from 1826, when this area was on the fringes of the city. Originally called the Mortuary Chapel, it was built near the cemeteries as a "burying chapel" for victims of yellow fever and cholera. To the right of the entrance is a statue of St Expedite. According to local legend, a crate arrived at the church marked "expedite," and the statue inside was duly mounted. That may be true, but St Expedite also figures prominently in voodoo culture.

Basin Street, of song and legend, parallels Rampart Street. This, too, is an extremely unsavory, unsafe thoroughfare. St Louis Cemetery No. 1, the city's oldest extant cemetery, is located on Basin Street behind Our Lady of Guadalupe Church (*see page 166*).

Lewd and lascivious

A notorious housing project occupies the site of Storyville, the city's old red-light district, which was itself notorious. In the mid-19th century New Orleans, never exactly a tame town, seems to have been awash with "lewd and lascivious women." An outraged city alderman introduced a bill that set down boundaries within which prostitution could be practiced. The bill passed, and in 1897 Storyville was established. Storyville was bounded by Iberville, St Louis, North Robertson, and Basin streets, and within that area some classy establishments flourished, along with tough bordellos. Jazz musicians entertained in the parlors, and on the street corners ragtag groups called "spasm bands" held forth.

Storyville thrived for 20 years, before being closed in 1917 by order of the United States Navy. Absolutely nothing remains of the red-light district, and visitors are strongly advised not to go exploring here.

BELOW: the Sugar Bowl is one of the hightlights of the sports events held at the Superdome.

For one block, between Canal Street and Tulane Avenue (an extension of Common Street), Basin Street is called **Elk Place ㉓** – so-named for the Elks Club that used to be located here. The **statue** at Canal and Basin streets is of **Simon Bolivar**. In the tree-shaded neutral ground of Elk Place, the sidewalk is carved with all the historic events and dates that make up the city's past. Upriver of Elk Place, Basin Street becomes **Loyola Avenue**. At the corner of Tulane and Loyola avenues is the main branch of the New Orleans Public Library. Charity Hospital and the medical schools of Louisiana State University and Tulane University are nearby on Tulane Avenue. Heavily trafficked Loyola Avenue zips smartly along, whizzing past **Duncan Plaza ㉔** and the **Civic Center**; the landscaped lawn of the plaza rolls out before **City Hall**, the **State Office Building**, and the **State Supreme Court Building**. A few blocks along Loyola Avenue is **Union Passenger Terminal ㉕**, for interstate buses and Amtrak trains. Although busy during the day, neither the terminal nor the plaza is a place to be after dark.

Map on page 174

Super statistics about the Superdome:
- *it is 27 stories high*
- *it covers 52 acres*
- *dome covers 9 acres*
- *parking for 5000 cars and 250 buses*

Stupendous Superdome

Poydras Street is another of the CBD's main drags. Like Canal Street, it is a wide boulevard whose foot stands near the Mississippi. If the streets of the CBD didn't fan out to follow the river's curves, Poydras would parallel Canal Street. The street is notable for its plethora of towering, streamlined office buildings.

Not far from the Civic Center, the stupendous **Superdome ㉖** (Sugar Bowl Drive; tel: 587-3810; tours daily; fee), hunkers like a giant spaceship on Poydras Street. The Dome is home to the New Orleans Saints football team and host of the famous annual Sugar Bowl college football game. More Super Bowl games have been played here than in any other city.

BELOW: although famous for its sports events, the Superdome also plays host to trade fairs and other conventions.

Gallier Hall is the most beautiful Greek Revivial building in New Orleans. Ionic columns support figures representing Justice, Liberty and Commerce.

In addition to sports events, the Dome has been the arena of everything from Rolling Stones concerts to a Republican National Convention. It opened in 1975, cost upwards of $180 million, and is touted as the largest facility of its kind in the world. The statistics are mind-boggling. It encompasses a total land area of 52 acres (21 hectares) – the dome alone covers more than 9 acres (3.6 hectares) – and has on-premises parking for 5,000 cars and 250 buses. It rises to a height of 27 stories; the diameter of the dome is 680 feet (209 meters). More about the Superdome can be learned on one of the daily guided tours.

Behind the Superdome is the newly-built **New Orleans Sports Arena**. The 20,000-seat arena is to be home to the New Orleans Brass professional hockey team, affiliated with the minor league East Coast Hockey League. It is hoped a professional basketball team may also take up residence here.

Super Centre

The Superdome, New Orleans Centre, the Hyatt Regency Hotel, and Poydras Plaza form a veritable community along Poydras Street. The most stylish kid on the block is the pretty, pink **New Orleans Centre ㉗**, which is a high-rise complex of offices and shops. Macy's and Lord & Taylor are the best-known of its many stores. **Poydras Plaza**, of which the Hyatt Regency is a part, also contains offices and shops, and has been a fixture for many years.

At St Charles Avenue, Poydras Street forms the lower border of Lafayette Square, the city's second oldest square. Gallier Hall faces the square, adding a distinguished air. In the 19th century, when the city was split into separate municipalities, this area served the Americans in the same way that Place d'Armes (now Jackson Square) served the Creoles. Gallier Hall was their city hall, Lafayette Square was a social center, and St Patrick's Cathedral (across the square) was the Irish American answer to the French St Louis Cathedral.

BELOW: St Patrick's Cathedral.

Gallier Hall ㉘ is the most splendid surviving Greek Revival building in the city. It was designed by noted architect James Gallier, Sr (*see page 159*), and constructed between 1845 and 1850. Ionic columns support an elaborate pediment on which there are figures representing Justice, Liberty, and Commerce. Gallier Hall remained the seat of city government until the present City Hall was completed in 1957. Here, on April 29, 1862, not long after Admiral Farragut shouted the famous words, "Damn the torpedoes, full speed ahead!", Union forces took possession of the city.

In the parlor of the hall, the bodies of Jefferson Davis, P.G.T. Beauregard, and city mayors have lain in state. Since 1958, the hall has been administered by the New Orleans Cultural Center Commission. The building contains offices and is not open to the public. A highlight of Mardi Gras takes place here, when the Rex parade pauses and the King of Carnival, on his float, exchanges toasts with the mayor.

Lafayette Square ㉙ dates back to 1788, when it was laid out as part of Faubourg Ste Marie. Centerpiece of the landscaped square is a tall bronze statue of Henry Clay, who served in the US Senate in the 19th century and frequently visited New Orleans. A statue of John McDonogh, a benefactor for whom several of the city's public schools are named, stands on a garlanded pedestal facing St Charles Avenue. The square is a beehive of activity during business hours, but it is not at all a safe place to be after the sun goes down.

Map on page 174

St Patrick's Cathedral

To the Irish Catholics who came to New Orleans it seemed that in St Louis Cathedral, God spoke only in French. They first built a small wooden church on this site, and then laid plans for a grand cathedral. Charles and James Dakin were the original architects for **St Patrick's Cathedral ㉚** (724 Camp St.; tel: 525-4413; open Mon–Thur 9.15am–3pm, Fri 10.30am–3pm), and they patterned the church after York Minster in England. There were structural problems in the marshy area, and James Gallier, Sr, was called in to assist. The cornerstone was laid in 1838, and the church was completed in 1840. The interior is stunning, with a vaulted, ribbed ceiling and handsome stained-glass windows. Three huge murals behind the main altar were painted in 1841 by Leon Pomarede.

A few blocks up at Howard Avenue, traffic whips all around the towering **Robert E. Lee statue** at **Lee Circle ㉛** (*also see page 178*). The Confederate general died in 1870, and his admirers immediately began a fund-raising drive to establish a monument in his memory. At that time, New Orleans was still under Reconstruction rule, and that fact, plus difficulties in raising money, delayed completion of the statue until 1884. Dignitaries at the unveiling included Jefferson Davis and P.G.T. Beauregard, the Fort Sumter Confederate general. The bronze statue stands on a 60-foot (18.5-meter) pedestal, with the general resolutely facing North. In a city where Eastern Avenue steadfastly runs north and south, this is about the only place in town where direction actually means anything. ❏

BELOW: Robert E. Lee at Lee Circle. The Confederate general is facing North, in order to safeguard the city from Yankees. Ex-president Jefferson Davis attended the unveiling of the statue.

NEW ORLEANS FOR KIDS

Despite its steamy reputation, New Orleans is still a place where parents with kids won't feel completely chained to a hotel room. Here's a sampling of what's around for small-time tots: rollicking streetcars and the Roman Candy Man. High-kicking parades with giant floats and marching bands. Fireworks, museums, and spooky haunted houses. Nature centers, petting zoos, the Aquarium and riverboat rides. Two national magazines, *Your Family* and *Parenting*, have rated the Louisiana Children's Museum as one of the best in the country. And City Park's "theme park for children," Storyland, has been touted as one of the most imaginative. There's the Musée Conti Wax Museum, the IMAX Theatre, plus the white alligators in Audubon Zoo. Further afield are swamp tours and all of Louisiana, which, in true Southern style, thinks "family" is sacred. Even that rowdiest of celebrations, Mardi Gras, replete with drag queens and party kings, can be manageable. The Children's Museum offers special programs like mask-making, and an ex-schoolteacher has set up personalized Mardi Gras tours specially for kids. To be taken, of course, while the grown-ups slip off and get — low-down and steamy. Details from the New Orleans Convention and Visitors Bureau, tel: 1-800-672 6124. Ask for their kids' brochure.

THE GARDEN DISTRICT

When New Orleans was one of the wealthiest cities in America, prosperous merchants built lovely homes upriver from the French Quarter

Map on page 194

A ccording to some sources, by the 1800s New Orleans was the wealthiest city in the United States. Cotton, sugar, and timber had made local Americans (as opposed to Creoles) millionaires, and they built elegant, sometimes fanciful homes in an area upriver from the Vieux Carré. The 1830s ushered in what is known as the city's Golden Age, a period of boom-town prosperity that lasted until the Civil War. Even after the war, splendid homes continued to be built in this suddenly desirable part of New Orleans.

Growth was spurred by the opening, in 1835, of the New Orleans and Carrollton Railroad along what is now **St Charles Avenue**. The St Charles streetcar, itself a National Historic Landmark, is the oldest continuously operating street railway system in the world. By the time the city of Lafayette was annexed by New Orleans in 1852, the Garden District, as the area became known, was already a very posh residential section of town.

The district is bordered by Magazine Street, and Jackson, Louisiana, and St Charles avenues. It's possible to get a tempting taste of the area by driving along the main thoroughfare, **Prytania Street**, which is lined with handsome homes. Or, take the St Charles streetcar, get off at Jackson Avenue, and simply wander around. Organized tours are also available.

PRECEDING PAGES: Garden District home and owner. **LEFT:** the Carroll-Crawford house. **BELOW:** vegetation runs riot in the Garden District.

Greek Revival

The most obvious – but not necessarily the purest – architectural style in the Garden District is Greek Revival. By the early 19th century, the enthusiasm for classic antiquity that began with the excavations in Pompeii, Herculaneum and Greece had reached a crescendo. The Garden District is aslosh with Ionic, Doric, and Corinthian columns; Greek key motifs; ornamental molding; and fanciful details.

But other styles are also in evidence. With the Victorian Age came pointed Gothic arched windows with diamond-patterned lights; ornate Italianate mansions inspired by the Italian Renaissance; the mansard roofs and bull's-eye dormer windows of the Second Empire; and the fussy busyness of Eastlake and Queen Anne-style houses, with all kinds of spindlework, wooden beads, turrets, and trim. The lavish wrought- and cast-iron garnishes on the houses rival the most fanciful grillework in the French Quarter, and beveled and leaded glass embellish many of the houses' doors.

Among the famed architects who worked in New Orleans during the Golden Age were Jacques Nicholas Bussiere dePouilly, a graduate of the Ecole des Beaux Arts in Paris; James and Charles Dakin, whose work includes St Patrick's Cathedral on Camp Street; James Gallier, Sr; James Gallier, Jr; and Henry Howard, who designed Italianate mansions in the Garden District, as

The Caribbean Room Restaurant of the Pontchartrain Hotel is famous for its calorie laden, but scrumptious and awesome, dessert called Mile High Pie.

well as Nottoway and Madewood, two restored plantations that can be seen to the west of New Orleans.

The area's status as a "center for gardens" was assured from the very beginning, when the levee guarding the Mississippi broke, flooding several plantations, leaving them virtually bankrupt and depositing a fertile layer of silt. The district's advantageous position above the river provided a higher elevation and better drainage. Vegetation flourished. In contrast to the Creoles, whose homes were built around lush, hidden courtyards, the Americans surrounded their estates with landscaped lawns and gardens. The aptly named district of gardens is thick with magnolia, palm and banana trees, camellias, azaleas, and thousands of species of subtropical plants and flowers.

Mile-high pie

At the junction of Josephine Street and St Charles Avenue, the snappy canopy of the **Pontchartrain Hotel** ❶ (2031 St Charles Avenue, tel: 524-0581) has long been one of the city's landmarks. The traditional, old-world hotel is one of the finest in the city. Don't, under any circumstances, miss dessert.

The structure directly across the street once housed the Restaurant de la Tour Eiffel. The building was designed and built for the restaurant that was for many years on the second level of the Eiffel Tower in Paris. Because of structural damage to the tower, it was necessary to remove the restaurant. It was meticulously disassembled, then shipped across the Atlantic, and ultimately reconstructed on this site. It opened with much hoopla in 1986, and enjoyed a couple of years of popularity before going bankrupt. This is now the **Red Room** ❷ (tel: 528-9759), a posh supper club, all gussied up in seven shades of red.

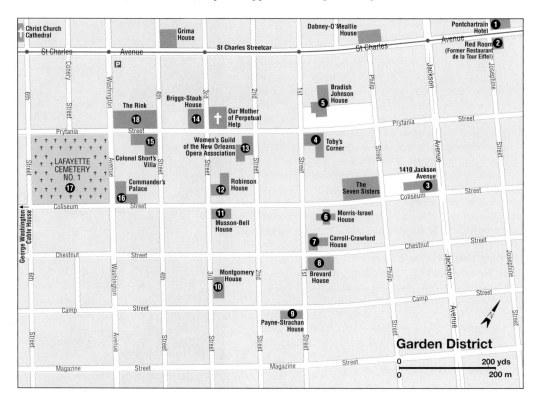

Garden District

Walk along Jackson Avenue toward the river. At **1410 Jackson Avenue ❸**, (corner of Coliseum Street), the impressive plantation-style house with Greek Revival flourishes and belvedere was built in 1856 for a cotton factory owner named Henry Sullivan Buckner.

Map on page 194

Raised cottage

At the corner of Jackson and Coliseum, turn right and go along the side of the Bruckner House on Coliseum Street. At Philip Street turn right again, and then left on Prytania Street, to reach **Toby's Corner ❹** (also called the Toby-West-feldt House) at 2340 Prytania Street. The rather simple (though hardly small) Greek Revival-raised cottage was built around 1838 for Thomas Toby, a Pennsylvania businessman. "Raised cottage," of which there are many examples in New Orleans, refers to a style of house in which the living quarters are on the upper level as protection from flooding. The lower floor, which is the marshland equivalent of a cellar, is usually used for storing non-valuable items.

Across the street from Toby's Corner, at 2343 Prytania Street, is the lavish **Bradish Johnson House ❺**. Designed by New Orleans architect James Freret, who studied at the Ecole des Beaux Arts, this Second-Empire house dates from 1872. Since 1929 it has been the Louise S. McGehee School, for girls.

Turn left at the corner of Prytania and First and walk down First Street toward the river. Wrapped in elaborate, identical ironwork, the **Morris-Israel House ❻**, at 1331 First Street, and the **Carroll-Crawford House ❼**, at 1315 First Street, are Italianate mansions designed by William Jamison and built in 1869. At 1239 First Street, the rose motif in the cast-iron fence is carried over into the galleries of the stately **Brevard House ❽**. Novelist Anne Rice bought and restored the

BELOW: headquarters of the Women's Guild of the New Orleans Opera Association.

BELOW: the
Bultman House

house, and used it as the setting for her best-selling novel, *The Witching Hour*. Rice's other Garden District properties include the former St Elizabeth's orphanage at 1314 Napoleon Avenue, now a repository for the novelist's vast doll collection and the site of her annual Halloween party.

The imposing **Payne-Strachan House 9**, at 1134 First Street, was built in the mid-1800s. In 1889, Jefferson Davis, former president of the Confederate States of America, fell ill while traveling through New Orleans en route to Beauvoir, his home in Mississippi. Unable to continue the trip, he was brought here to the home of his friend Jacob Payne, where he died.

Less rigid, more romance

By the time most of these existing houses were built, the layout for gardens in the Garden District had become more romantic and less rigid. Grounds surrounding the earliest houses had tended to be formal, their symmetrical lines following the European tradition for precise, highly stylized lawns. It was only later that planting began to be adapted for local purposes. Trees began to be placed well away from windows, to allow access to cooling breezes, and emphasis began to be placed on southern exposures, to ensure a warm spot to sit during the chilly winter months.

The interesting bracket-style **Montgomery House 10**, at 1213 Third Street, is the only one of its kind in the Garden District. It was built in 1868, after the Civil War, when most of the South was suffering under Reconstruction.

Going along Third Street toward St Charles Avenue, you'll pass the handsome Italianate **Musson-Bell House 11**, at 1331 Third Street. It was built in 1853 for Michel Musson, a New Orleans Postmaster, uncle of French Impressionist painter Edgar Degas. The Mussons later moved to 2306 Esplanade Avenue, and it was there that Degas stayed for several months and completed 17 paintings. That house, called the **Degas House**, is now a bed-and-breakfast. In the next block, surrounded by a white fence, is the splendid two-story Italianate **Robinson House 12**, at 1415 Third Street. Believed to have been the first house in New Orleans with indoor plumbing, it was built in 1864–65, during the Civil War, for a Virginian named Walter Robinson.

Continue along Third Street and turn right on Prytania Street to see the lovely house at No. 2504. The grand Greek Revival mansion with the octagonal turret houses headquarters for the **Women's Guild of New Orleans Opera Association 13** (tel: 899-1945 for tours – groups of 20 or more only).

Backtrack one block along Prytania to find the **Briggs-Staub House 14**, at 2605 Prytania. Dating from 1849, and attributed to James Gallier, Jr, it is a fanciful and very distinctive Gothic Revival House. An identical little guest house sits in the side lawn.

In the next block **Colonel Short's Villa 15**, 1448 Fourth Street, is a knockout in the Italianate style. Henry Howard designed it in 1859, the year he concocted Nottoway Plantation upriver. It was built for a merchant, Col. Robert Henry Short. The cast-iron cornstalk-and-morning-glories fence is almost identical to one at 915 Royal Street in the French Quarter.

The delightful, turreted Victorian mansion at 1403 Washington Avenue is home to the Brennan family's famed **Commander's Palace** restaurant (tel: 899-8221). The ubiquitous New Orleans jazz brunches originated at Commander's, and are still considered to be the best in town. Held on both Saturdays and Sundays, booking is essential during peak seasons.

Map on page 194

Historic skating rink

Directly across the street is **Lafayette Cemetery** ⓱, bordered by Washington Avenue, and Coliseum, Prytania, and Sixth streets. It was established in 1833 as the burial ground for the City of Lafayette. Through the iron gates you can see the white above-ground tombs that are typical of New Orleans graveyards, but unfortunately, it is not safe to wander around alone.

At 2727 Prytania, the small, multilevel shopping mall called **The Rink** ⓲ was built in the late 1800s as the Crescent City Skating Rink. For two houses that are actually in the Uptown area (*see page 201*), but belong to the Garden District in style, go along Prytania to Eighth Street, turn left and walk down to **1313 Eighth Street**. The well-known 19th-century writer George Washington Cable lived in this raised cottage, and Mark Twain was among the literary luminaries who visited. Nearby, at 1525 Louisiana Avenue, is the **Bultman House**.

Magazine Street borders both the Garden District and the Irish Channel. This street is lined with Creole cottages and once-grand Victorian mansions that now house antique shops offering pleasant browsing. But do bear in mind that, unless otherwise noted, homes in the Garden District are private residences, and are not generally open to the public. An exception is made during Spring Fiesta, when some home owners allow tours. ❑

BELOW:
Commander's Palace restaurant with the *pièce de résistance*, bread pudding soufflé.

NOTABLE NEIGHBORHOODS

New Orleans is a series of neighborhoods – some old and established, some up and coming. These are the ones that will be of most interest to visitors

Map on pages 202–03

The neighborhoods in this chapter – Uptown, the Irish Channel and Algiers – could not be more different. Uptown is old and established, with a wonderful park, some of the finest homes in the city and two handsome and respected universities. The Irish Channel has a rough-and-ready charm that is especially evident on St Patrick's Day, when the entire area, it seems, dons shamrocks and green. Algiers, across the Mississippi River from the French Quarter, dates from 1719. Its shabby streets are filled with Victorian and Greek Revival houses standing side-by-side with tumble-down shacks, making a visit to the area's Mardi Gras World an architectural tour with surprises around each corner.

Uptown

The best way to get an overview of the sights in the Uptown district is on the city's movable museum, the **St Charles Streetcar**. The carriages clang and rumble from Canal Street all the way up historic St Charles Avenue, turn with the bend of the river at Carrollton Avenue, and wheeze to a stop at Palmer Park. There you can pay another fare and return to the Central Business District. The section of St Charles Avenue between Lee Circle and Jackson Avenue is not at the moment visually promising, lined as it is with fast-food chains and run-down houses. Known as the **Lower Garden District**, this area, like the Warehouse District, is, however, undergoing a renaissance as young, upwardly mobile folk buy and renovate these once-grand houses.

Above Jackson Avenue, things pick up considerably, and anyone interested in in-depth details should probably opt for a guided tour of Uptown. Both sides of St Charles Avenue are adorned with handsome homes, many of them magnificent Greek Revival mansions. One such place is the **Dabney-O'Meallie House ❶** at 2265 St Charles Avenue. As the avenue stretches upriver, homes are newer and styles more eclectic. Some of the St Charles Avenue landmarks to look for are the two Gothic-style churches: the Episcopal **Christ Church Cathedral ❷** (No. 2919), which dates from 1887; and **Rayne Memorial Methodist Church** (No. 3900), built in 1875. The **George Washington Cable House ❸**, just off the avenue at 1313 Eighth Street, was discussed in the previous chapter (*see page 197*).

The imposing **Bultman Funeral Home** (3338 St Charles Avenue) is the place to be laid to rest, and behind it, on Louisiana Ave, is the **Bultman House ❹**, built by architect William Freret in 1857 as his private residence. Nearly a century later the Bultman house was the inspiration for the set of dramatist Tennessee Williams' *Suddenly, Last Summer (see photo page 196).* The verandahed **Columns Hotel ❺**, 3811 St Charles Avenue, tel: 899-9308), was built as a private home in

PRECEDING PAGES: St Charles Streetcar. **LEFT:** Irish dancing, Irish Channel. **BELOW:** the Columns Hotel.

The St Charles Streetcar is the best-value tour in the city. A round-trip takes about 1½ hours, traveling from Canal Street to Palmer Park; it also takes in the Garden District, the University area, Audubon Park and Audubon Zoo.

1884, and as well as a wonderful place to stay, has been the set for films, including Louis Malle's 1978 *Pretty Baby*, starring Susan Sarandon and Brooke Shields.

The **Sully House** ❻ (No. 4010) is an elaborate Queen Anne structure, replete with gables, gingerbread trim and towers, designed by Thomas Sully as his personal residence. The stunning **Sacred Heart Academy** ❼ (No. 4521) is a prestigious girls' school that was built around the turn of the 20th century and is run by the Sisters of the Sacred Heart. One of the most exotic houses in the city is the **W.P. Brown House** ❽ (No. 4717), a Richardsonian Romanesque mansion with dramatic Syrian arches. Surrounded by manicured lawns, this house was built about 1902 at a cost of a quarter of a million dollars. The **Milton H. Latter Memorial Library** ❾ (No. 5120) is a Beaux Arts mansion that dates from 1907. In the 1940s, it was the home of silent screen star Marguerite Clark and, in 1948, was donated to the city. It's a fine place to sit and read Gothic Southern novels.

Gone with the truth

There are people in New Orleans who will tell you that scenes from *Gone With The Wind* were filmed at **Tara** ❿, the house located at 5705 St Charles Avenue. This isn't true. Scarlett O'Hara's famed fictional home was a movie set in Hollywood, but the plans for Tara *were* used in constructing this exact replica, which was completed about 1941. The **Wedding Cake House** ⓫ (No. 5809) is an elaborate Colonial Revival concoction that looks very much like… a wedding cake. Similar in flavor is the whimsical **Castle House** ⓬ (No. 6000).

Campuses belonging to Loyola University and Tulane University almost overlap on St Charles Avenue, but that frontage is only a tiny portion of each campus. Both are highly landscaped, with lawns and a variety of palm trees and magnolias.

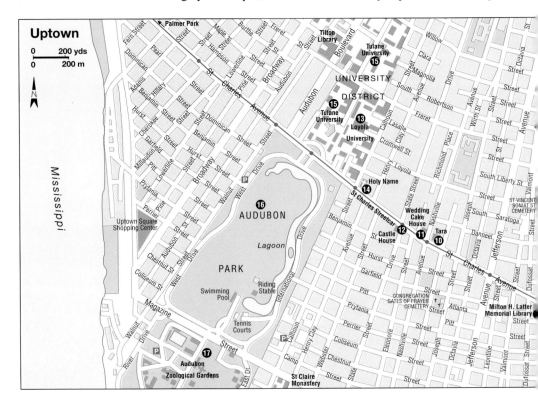

Uptown

Loyola University ⓭, the largest Roman Catholic university in the South, dates from 1840 when the Jesuits established the College of the Immaculate Conception downtown. The school moved to its present location in 1911. The university covers five city blocks and has an enrollment in excess of 5,000 students. Owned and operated by the Jesuits, Loyola is especially famed for its Law School. Facing St Charles Avenue, adjacent to the main building, the large Gothic-Tudor **Holy Name Church** ⓮, built in 1918, serves as the parish church for this section of the city.

Map on pages 202–03

An urban oasis

Neighboring **Tulane University** ⓯ also began as a downtown school. It opened in 1834 as the Medical College of Louisiana (in 1847, the name was changed to the University of Louisiana), and was located at Common and University Place. The school was rechristened in memory of Paul Tulane, a wealthy New Orleans merchant who, on his death in 1883, left a bequest to the school. In 1894, the university moved to its present location. With an enrollment of more than 13,000 students, the school sprawls over 110 acres (45 hectares).

Tulane, like Loyola, has a well-respected Law School. It also has an internationally acclaimed medical school, and its **Tilton Library**'s excellent research facilities include the New Orleans Jazz Archives and the Middle American Research Institute, which has extensive collections of pre-Columbian art. The prestigious Sophie H. Newcomb College for Women, once a separate institution, is now a part of the university.

Directly across St Charles Avenue from the campuses, the 340-acre (138-hectare) **Audubon Park** ⓰ is an urban oasis for which the word elegant is not inappropriate. The beauty of its oak trees rivals that of those in City Park. Not surprisingly,

Loyola University, well known for its law school, was established in 1840 and, later, moved Uptown in 1911.

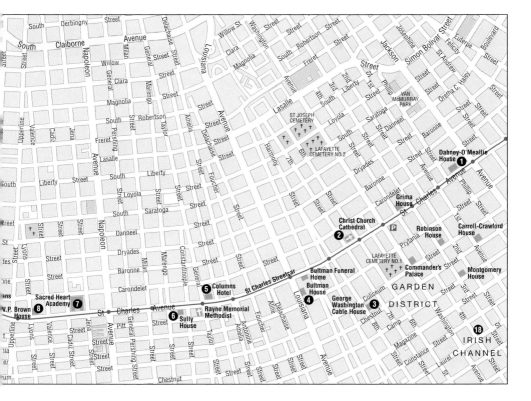

The white alligators in Audubon Zoo are a major attraction for visitors. White 'gators in the wild are rare, as their pale color makes them easy prey.

BELOW: a captured moment in beautiful Audubon Park.

this being New Orleans, the park is on the site of a former plantation. In the 18th century, the park was part of an estate owned by Etienne de Bore and his son-in-law, Pierre Foucher. In 1795, de Bore discovered how to granulate sugar for commercial purposes, which not only revolutionized the sugar industry but provided a windfall for dentists everywhere. In 1871, a state agency bought part of the land for a public park, but nothing much happened here until 1884.

Landscape architect Frederick Law Olmsted, who designed New York's Central Park, had a hand in planning Audubon Park. It was named for naturalist John James Audubon, who spent a few years in this area working on his famed series *Birds of America*. Exactly 100 years before the 1984 World's Fair, the World's Industrial and Cotton Centennial Exhibition was held on this site. It featured, among other things, a 31-acre (13-hectare) exhibition center that sprawled over the site of the present 18-hole golf course. In addition to the golf course, the park has a lovely lagoon, a very pleasant 1½-mile (2.5-km) jogging path with 18 exercise stations (the path lopes along beneath a leafy canopy of oaks), a riding stable, and tennis courts.

Zoo time

Behind the park is the wonderful **Audubon Zoo** ⓱ (6500 Magazine St.; tel: 861-2537; open daily 9.30am–5pm, 9.30am–6pm summer weekends; fee). Wooden walkways provide scenic viewing of the more than 1,500 critters who roam about in natural-habitat settings. Among the major attractions are the Louisiana Swamp Exhibit (which includes rare white alligators); the Australian Exhibit, with its kangaroos and wallabies; the Reptile Encounter, which needs no explanation; and the African Savannah, through which runs the Mombassa miniature train. In 1998,

Maps on p202–03 & p206

the user-friendly zoo opened the $2.2 million Jaguar Jungle, which replicates an ancient Mayan civilisation, with stone temples and gods, and real spider monkeys, a sloth, and scarlet ibis, along with the eponymous jaguars. At the Zootique gift shop, you can buy souvenirs. This is one of the best places in town for biking and hiking. There are also ample grounds for picnicking, lolling about, and doing absolutely nothing.

Irish Channel

No one quite agrees on the actual boundaries of the neighborhood known as the **Irish Channel ⓲**. It undoubtedly lies between Magazine Street and the Mississippi river, but the uptown and downtown borders depend upon whom you ask. We side with those who say it extends from Howard Avenue to Louisiana Avenue.

This area, like the Garden District, was once a part of the Livaudais Plantation and the City of Lafayette. However, because of its proximity to the wharves along the river, it has always been a tough, working-class neighborhood. The Irish immigrants who flooded into New Orleans in the 1840s settled around **Adele Street**, which is still central to the Channel. About the same time, there were also large numbers of Germans who moved into this neighborhood, but for some reason the Channel remained "Irish." The Irish and Germans have since left, and the neighborhood is now predominantly black and Cuban.

The spirit of revitalization that swept through the Warehouse District is gradually seeping into the Channel, and in a few years thngs might be entirely different; various plans have been proposed and rejected for the redevelopment of the notorious St Thomas Housing Project, an extremely dangerous federal project at the heart of the Irish Channel, and until certain elements are resolved, *visitors should avoid this area entirely, and visit other sites of interest in the Irish Channel by taxi.* Just past the interstate underpass, at the point where Camp, Prytania, and Clio streets converge, is a small park called **Margaret Place**. The park's statue, unveiled in 1884, honors Margaret Gaffney Haughery, an Irish woman much loved for her charitable deeds. Three blocks up from Margaret Place, the triangular park between Camp and Coliseum streets is **Coliseum Place**. The original, somewhat grandiose plan called for the area to be modeled after villages in ancient Greece, each of which had a coliseum. At 1729 Coliseum Street is the **Goodrich-Stanley House**, the boyhood home of that intrepid explorer of Africa, Sir Henry Morton Stanley. Also worth noting is the baroque Roman Catholic church of **St Mary's Assumption** (2030 Constance Street).

Algiers

From the foot of Canal Street, a ferry glides across the Mississippi to **Algiers** on the West Bank. It's a short journey, but crossing Ol' Man River is a treat at any time, and this ride is free. (Algiers is also accessible via the Crescent City Connection bridge.) Although Algiers is part of the city of New Orleans, the area has the appearance and ambience of a small, 19th-century town. You somehow have the feeling that Algiers is peering over the levee at the huge skyscrapers of the Central Business District and wondering what life might be like in the

BELOW: defying death and dogs.

Algiers architecture: the Court House is clearly visible across the river in the French Quarter.

modern age. This little district is also called **Algiers Point**, the name by which the great, difficult-to-navigate bend in the river is known to ship captains.

Algiers dates from 1719, when Jean Baptiste le Moyne, Sieur de Bienville, was granted the West Bank tract. When African slaves were brought to this area in the early 18th century they were held in pens before being taken across the river and put on the auction block in New Orleans. The name Algiers perhaps comes from the African slave-trading center.

Plantation courthouse

The Duverje Plantation served as the courthouse from 1866 until the Great Algiers Fire of 1895 destroyed it and some 200 other buildings. The present **Algiers Court House** ⓳ (tel: 368-7642), whose ornate crenellated turrets are clearly visible across the river in the French Quarter, was built in 1896 on the site of the plantation. Located on Morgan Street, in front of the ferry landing, this is a marvelous Moorish-style structure whose interior features tall, dark, and handsome wooden doors, high ceilings, and a musty, anachronistic ambience.

The main historical points of interest are in a small section bounded by **Opelousas Avenue**, **Belleville** and **Morgan streets**, and the river. This is an easily walkable area, but it is not advisable to stroll around here after dark. To be sure, much of Algiers is in a sad state of repair, but there are some delightful old restored homes. Because of the 1895 fire, most date from around the turn of the 20th century and reflect the ornate Victorian style.

Behind the Court House is Delaronde Street, where two blocks are lined with frilly gingerbread rowhouses. The Greek Revival **Seger-Rees House** ⓴ at 405 Delaronde, built in 1849, mercifully survived the Great Fire.

BELOW: Algiers is well known to ship captains as Algiers Point but the landing is very difficult to navigate.

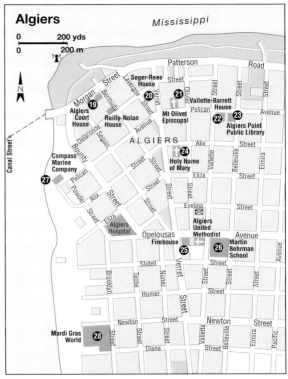

Another survivor of the conflagration is the **Mt Olivet Episcopal Church** ❹ (530 Pelican Avenue). The church was built around 1854, and is the oldest remaining church in Algiers. A block away, at 705 Pelican Street, is the plantation-style **Vallette-Barrett House** ❷, dating from around 1850. Next to it, on the corner, the **Algiers Point Public Library** ❸ is a small but eye-popping Italian Renaissance Revival building erected in 1910.

Town within a town

Olivier and Verret are two other streets that contain attractive buildings. The grand French Gothic-style **Holy Name of Mary Church** ❹ (tel: 362-5511) dominates the 400 block of Verret and was built in 1929 on the site of an older church. Two more blocks on Verret Street will bring you to Opelousas Avenue, a broad, once-grand boulevard with fine old trees and a mix of handsome mansions and nondescript shotgun houses.

The fiery red-brick **Firehouse** ❺, between Opelousas and Slidell, was built in 1925, and the very fussy Byzantine-style building next to the station is **Algiers United Methodist Church** (637 Opelousas Avenue). Across Vallette Street from the church, the Spanish Revival building with the red-tiled roof and bell tower is the **Martin Behrman School** ❻, built in the 1930s.

At Opelousas and Brooklyn, an intriguing complex of buildings makes up the **Compass Marine Company** ❼. The compound, built around a lawn, looks like a tiny town within a small town. Within it are several historic buildings that have been moved from other areas, restored and now house offices. Two blocks from Opelousas Street, at 223 Newton Street, is the razzle dazzle, very entertaining and highly colorful **Mardi Gras World** ❽ *(see box below)*. ❑

Map on page 206

TIP

Other New Orleans neighborhoods of note include the Lower Garden District and also the 9th Ward, where singer Fats Domino was born.

BELOW: shabby but interesting Algiers has several streets of Victorian and Greek Revival houses.

MARDI GRAS WORLD

For anyone unable to be in town for Carnival, a trip to Mardi Gras World is the next best thing. This is where many of the parade floats are designed, constructed and assembled, all in a series of enormous warehouses. It is the brainchild of entrepreneur Blaine Kern, who, growing up only a few blocks away in Algiers, worked hard, turned down a job offer with Disney, and went on to create what is now the largest float-building company in the world. As well as doing the floats for around 40 of the 60 major Mardi Gras organizations, Kern's clients include Universal Studios, Paramount Parks, Disney, Harrah's Casino and three of the most extravagant casinos in Las Vegas.

The first view inside a warehouse can be a shock. Gigantic heads rest on the floor and perch on top of shelves. Disembodied torsos lead against tables (*see photo on page 114*). The figures are huge, as they must be: once assembled, a float can be as tall as a small department store. Most of the figures are hollow inside, coated with fiberglass or papier-mâché. The painted figures are mounted on bases that, in turn, are mounted on or pulled by tractors during the parade itself. Tours of Mardi Gras World are held every day (fee); there's also a giftshop on the premises. Tel: 504-361 7821 for details.

SEASONAL CELEBRATIONS

Every day's a party in Louisiana – it's just that some are more organized than others. Urban or rural, most of them involve a great deal of food

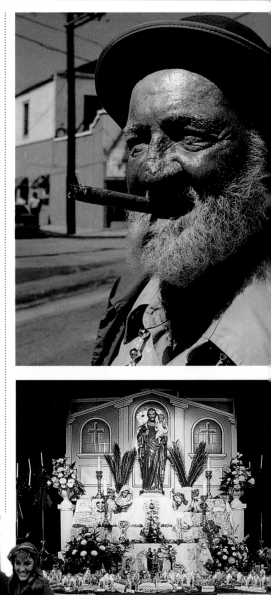

With more than 100 festivals from which to choose, Louisiana could hardly be called a party-pooper state. Christmas in New Orleans, for instance, lasts the entire month of December, with Dickens carolers in Jackson Square, teas, parades and eggnog parties at historic homes not normally open to the public. Although everyone dresses up for the occasion, City Park wins the top prize; its ancient oak trees are illuminated by over one million lights (*see photo on following page*).

Many celebrations are influenced by Mardi Gras. St Patrick's Day, for example, has not only parades, but floats. And whereas in Mardi Gras trinkets are thrown from the floats, St Patrick's revelers also throw cabbage and potatoes. This fascination with food is evident in almost all local festivals, like the Great French Market Tomato Festival in June, which turns the old streets of the Vieux Carré into a sea of red. Orange and black are the celebratory colors of Halloween, highly feted in the town of vampire queen and writer Anne Rice. There is much masking (aka Mardi Gras), drop-dead costumes, plus a Witches Run and tours of some of the city's many haunted houses. After all the sinning of Halloween in October, there's All Saints Day (Nov 1); Christmas; and then – before you can kick off your dancing shoes – it's time for Mardi Gras.

A list of festivals can be found in Travel Tips.

◁ **THICK SKINNED**
Shellfish "dressed,"
Crawfish Fest, Breaux
Bridge, Cajun
Country.

△ **ST JOSEPH'S DAY**
In mid-March, the Italian
community decorates altars
with food and the Mardi Gras
Indians make an appearance.

◁ **EAT ALLIGATOR HERE**
Summer's Wine and Food Experience has restaurant samplings along 7 blocks of the French Quarter – in art galleries and antique shops.

▽ **BELLES ON WHEELS**
A carriage parade in the Quarter and open house at some of the private homes in the Garden District are Spring Fiesta highlights.

◁ **ST PATRICK'S DAY**
There's two parades, with activity centered around the Irish Channel and Parasol's Bar, 2533 Constance Street.

△ **PARASOLS ON PARADE**
April's French Quarter Fest in the streets of the Vieux Carré is a weekend of parades, parties, and the largest pralines in the world.

△ **BOATS AFLOAT**
Blessing of the fleet near the Cajun Country town of Chauvin, south of Houma. Houma celebrates "Downtown on the Bayou" during the month of October.

CELEBRATIONS OUT OF TOWN

Although it's the Big Easy's Mardi Gras that brings in the big bucks, generating over $500,000,000 each year (*above, float detail*), anyone seeking a less frenzied Fat Tuesday can seek out Mardi Gras celebrations all over Louisiana. Madisonville and Slidell, both near Lake Pontchartrain, have boat parades. Monroe and Shreveport have lighted float parades. Lake Charles celebrates "Motor Gras" with antique and classic vehicles. And in Church Point near Eunice in Cajun Country, costumed young men on horseback roam the countryside begging for ingredients for their communal gumbo. In fact, Cajun Country is host to some of the best festivals in the US. A sampling from the Lafayette area alone includes the Festival Internationale de Louisiane in April; the Zydeco Festival in September; and the Festivals Acadiens in the fall. Not surprising in a state that throws organized parties to celebrate the wonders of watermelons (Franklinton), catfish (Des Allemands), alligators (Boutte), oysters (Amite) and frogs (Rayne).

CITY PARK AND LAKE PONTCHARTRAIN

Map
on page
214

When is a casino not a casino? Why did the Choctaw Indians call the lake the "wide water?" And where did William Makepeace Thackeray and Oscar Wilde stay?

Conventional images of New Orleans play on the narrow streets and filigree balconies of the French Quarter or on steamboats chugging down the Mighty Mississippi. What local people already know, and what visitors are delighted to find out, is that the city has a romantically landscaped park – almost twice the size of New York's Central Park – in addition to Lake Pontchartrain, whose shores contain some of the best seafood restaurants in town.

Occupying 1,500 lush, fertile acres (600 hectares), **City Park** (1 Palm Drive; tel: 482-4888) is bordered on the north by Robert E. Lee Boulevard, on the east by Bayou St John, on the south by City Park Avenue, and on the west by Orleans Avenue. The easiest way to reach City Park from the French Quarter is on Esplanade Avenue, which leads right to the entrance.

PRECEDING PAGES:
City Park at Xmas.
LEFT: NOMA.
BELOW: carousel,
circa 1900.

Land of dreamy dreams

City Park is the fifth-largest urban park in the nation. Lying on the site of the old Louis Allard plantation, which accounts for its dreamy appearance, the park contains an art museum, botanical gardens, an amusement park, four golf courses, several baseball diamonds, a soccer stadium, and lagoons for fishing and boating. It contains more than 2,000 stately live oak trees, dressed with frilly Spanish moss, which are among the loveliest in the South. Arched bridges over streams full of ducks complete the antebellum picture.

The large **equestrian statue** standing smack in the middle of Esplanade Avenue at the entrance to the park is of Confederate General Pierre Gustave Toutant Beauregard, a Creole who was one of the South's four-star generals. Lelong Drive extends from the park entrance to the **New Orleans Museum of Art** (NOMA) ❶ (1 Collins-Diboll Circle; tel: 488-2631; open Tues–Sun; fee), a white neoclassical building that has hosted international traveling exhibits such as "The Treasures of King Tutankhamun." The museum displays its entire collection, which includes pre-Columbian, African, and local art; Fabergé treasures; and early American furnishings. As well as staging an exhibition in 1999 of the works by French Impressionist painter Edgar Degas, the City Park area has its own Degas connections: Edgar's mother was from New Orleans, and a house in which he stayed is a B&B (*see page 196 and Travel Tips*).

One of the most stunning sights in the park is the **Dueling Oaks**; the gnarled boughs of the live oak trees sweep right down and touch the ground. Hot-blooded Creoles are said to have fought duels beneath these trees, hence the name and legends surrounding them.

*The University of
New Orleans, near
Lake Pontchartrain,
is on the site of a
former World War II
Naval Air Station.*

The park is laced with broad paved streets. Behind the museum, Victory Avenue leads past the 10-acre (4-hectare) **Botanical Garden** (tel: 483-9386; open Tues–Sun; fee), with a lovely conservatory and parterre garden. Nearby are **Storyland** (tel: 483-9382), a children's park replete with Mother Goose characters and storytelling, and the **City Park Tennis Center** (tel: 483-9383), which has 39 courts lit for night play.

Casino-less Casino

The **Casino Building ②** (1 Dreyfous Avenue; tel: 483-937; open daily; charge for rentals) – which has no casino – is the place to get a permit to fish within the park (the lagoons are well-stocked with bass and bream), and to enquire about boat rentals. Canoes and paddle boats are available for drifting out among the swans. There is also an inexpensive snack bar in the Casino. During the summer, a miniature train runs from the Casino to the **amusement park** (tel: 483-9356; seasonal hours; fee), whose rides include the magnificent turn-of-

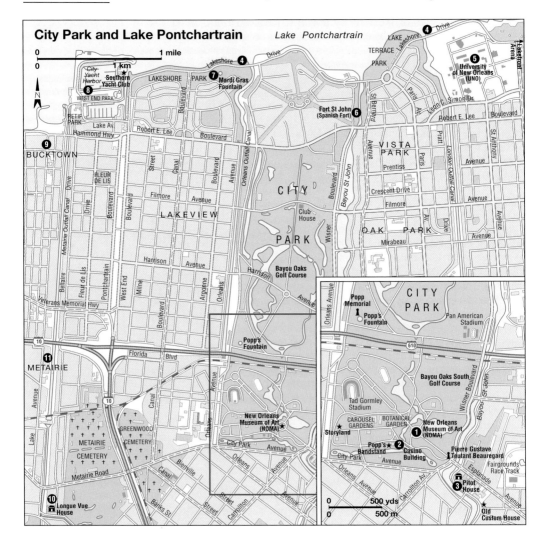

City Park and Lake Pontchartrain

the-century **Last Carousel**. Opposite the Casino, concerts are held regularly in summer at Popp's Bandstand. The Bayou Oaks Golf Facility (tel: 483-9397), with four 18-hole courses, is in the northern section of the park.

Bayou St John forms the eastern border of the park and curves down to the south. Moss Street, which intersects Esplanade Avenue, drifts alongside the bayou, and at No. 1440 is the **Pitot House** ❸ (tel: 482-0312; open Wed–Sat 10am–3pm; fee), a West Indies-style house built in 1799 (*see page 158*). An excellent example of homes that were built by the early planters, the house is named for mayor James Pitot, who bought it in 1810 and used it as a country home. Restored by the Louisiana Landmarks Society, it is now a museum.

Lakeshore rites

Cutting a wide swath across the northern border of New Orleans is sparkling **Lake Pontchartrain**. Now the pleasure-boating playground of New Orleanians, Lake Pontchartrain was once a major "highway" of the Choctaw Indians. When Pierre le Moyne, Sieur d'Iberville arrived in these watery parts in the late 17th century and launched the settlement of Louisiana, he named the lake after Count Pontchartrain, the French Minister of Marine.

The Choctaw had a much more appropriate name for it. They called it "Okwata," which means wide water. The shallow lake is 25 miles (40 km) wide and 40 miles (64 km) long; the toll causeway that crosses it, connecting New Orleans with St Tammany parish, is one of the longest bridges in the world.

In warm weather, New Orleanians flock to this area for boating and fishing. Just before sunset, the lake has a lovely silvery cast, and the picture-postcard look is replete with trim sailboats drifting on the waters. The terraced concrete seawall steps right down to the lake, but, unfortunately, the polluted water is unsuitable for swimming. All along Lakeshore Drive are ample parking bays, as well as rest rooms, sandwich stands, and broad expanses of tree-shaded lawn.

Accessible from downtown, via Elysian Fields Avenue or Canal Boulevard (an extension of Canal Street), **Lakeshore Drive** ❹ breezes along the lake for 5½ miles (9 km). The drive is anchored, roughly, to the east by the **New Orleans Lakefront Airport** (for private planes) and to the west by West End Park. Languidly docked near the Lakefront Airport is **Bally's Casino/Lakefront Resort** (1 Stars & Stripes Blvd; tel: 248-3200; open 24 hours daily), a double-decker riverboat with a whole raft of gambling tables, one-armed bandits, video poker, and entertainment.

West of the airport, Lakeshore Drive skims past the campus of the **University of New Orleans** (UNO) ❺, which was established in 1958 on the site of an old World War II Naval Air Station. UNO is the state's second largest university, after Louisiana State University in Baton Rouge. The large, modern structure hunkering to the left is the UNO **Lakefront Arena**, a 10,000-seat venue for top-name entertainers as well as sporting events.

Bayou St John flows alongside City Park, which lies to the south of Lakeshore Drive, and empties into Lake Pontchartrain. A small band of Frenchmen

TIP

Lake Pontchartrain's Lakeshore Drive is closed to car traffic from 10pm to 6am. The lake is named for Count Pontchartrain, the 17th-century Minister of Marine in France.

BELOW: angling for a catch in Lake Pontchartrain.

Map on page 214

camped along the bayou as early as 1708, 10 years before the founding of New Orleans. On the banks of the bayou, near the intersection of Robert E. Lee Boulevard and Beauregard Avenue, are the remnants of **Fort St John** ❻, also known as **Spanish Fort**. This was one of several outposts – all since demolished – built by the colonial French in the early 1700s.

Early protection

Fort St John was meant to protect the city from attack by way of Lake Pontchartrain. It was enlarged by the Spanish in 1779, restored by the Americans in 1808, and garrisoned during the War of 1812. In 1823, the Pontchartrain Hotel, an elaborate resort surrounded by botanical gardens, was built on this site and flourished until the 1920s. William Makepeace Thackeray and Oscar Wilde were among the hotel's guests. In truth, there is little to see here now except piles of old bricks, but the trees are lovely and the grounds pleasant for picnics.

Back on Lakeshore Drive, a few yards east of the intersection with Canal Boulevard, is the **Mardi Gras Fountain** ❼. Erected in 1962 by the New Orleans Levee Board, the fountain sprays to a height of 60 feet (18.5 meters) and is surrounded by plaques bearing the coat of arms of all the Carnival krewes. When it's fully operational (which is not all of the time due to maintenance costs), the fountain is illuminated in the Mardi Gras colors of purple, gold, and green. All around the fountain there are picnic grounds, pretty trees, and places in which to relax and enjoy the city's fine warm summer evenings.

West End Park ❽, the city's pleasure boating center, is awash with marinas, yacht clubs, and things of a nautical nature. Southern Yacht Club, established in 1849, is the nation's second oldest yacht club. It's a private club, but the drive to the entrance, along a broad boulevard with handsome trees, is well worth seeing. From West End Boulevard you can drive out and park on the yacht club's breakwater to enjoy a breathtaking view of the lake.

West End Park and the little village of **Bucktown** ❾ just to the west are filled with excellent seafood restaurants. Most of them are quite informal, but what they may lack in decor they more than make up for in the high quality of the food they produce. West End Park is right at the border between Jefferson and Orleans parishes. Also straddling the parish borders is the beautiful plantation **Longue Vue House** ❿ (7 Bamboo Rd.; tel: 488-5488; open Mon–Sat and Sun pm, fee). This classic estate, with its 8 acres (3.2 hectares) of grounds, is modeled after the great country houses of England. The interior is filled with antiques and fine paintings, while the gardens are for a cooling stroll on a hot day.

Sprawling to the west of West End Park is the old suburb of **Metairie** ⓫. The southern end of the impressive **Lake Pontchartrain Causeway** lies west of Bucktown in Metairie. The causeway is one of the longest bridges in the world built entirely over water. Birdwatchers should note that beneath this bridge is a major nesting place for purple martins, which stop off here en route farther south. At sunset during July, an estimated 200,000 birds can be seen swooping around the bridge's underpinnings, and negotiating for a position for the night. There is a viewing area near the toll booth. ❏

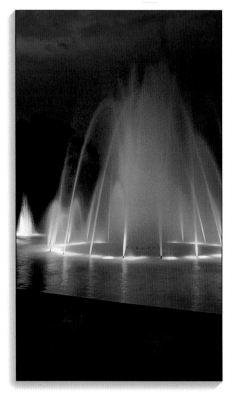

BELOW: the Mardi Gras Fountain is illuminated by the distinctive Carnival colors of purple, gold and green. **RIGHT:** the Lake Pontchartrain Causeway is almost 24 miles long.

LEVEL
5

THE MIGHTY MISSISSIPPI

*The Spanish called it Rio del Espirito – the
River of the Holy Spirit. Native Americans called it, simply,
the Great River. What makes it so special?*

Map on page 232

Noted for his withering sarcasm, sharp tongue, and caustic wit, Mark Twain waxed almost mushy when it came to his favorite river: "I still kept in mind a certain wonderful sunset which I witnessed when steamboating was new to me. A broad expanse of the river was turned to blood; in the middle distance the red hue brightened into gold… the dissolving lights drifted steadily, enriching its every passing moment with new marvels of coloring."

Many New Orleanians feel the same way, even though they may cross the river several times a day. Some use the little Canal Street ferry, which chugs between downtown and the old neighborhood of Algiers. Others use bridges, like the Huey P. Long bridge upriver near Harahan, or the heavily traveled Crescent City Connection, which links West Bank parishes with the Central Business District. Visitors and locals alike enjoy the Moonwalk promenade, the riverfront area of the French Quarter, where a saxophone solo may provide the soundtrack to Twain's drifting "dissolving lights." That Ol' Man just keeps on rolling along.

Mile-wide tide

This great mile-wide tide – North America's longest river – begins in northern Minnesota as little streams so small you can step across them. It widens into miles as it washes through America's heartland, then narrows again as it sidles through New Orleans and surges down toward the Gulf of Mexico. By itself, the Mississippi River is about 2,350 miles (3,760 km) long. Combined with its largest tributary, the Missouri River, which flows from the Rocky Mountains and into the Mississippi just north of St Louis, it is more than 3,700 miles (5,920 km) long. Only the Nile and the Amazon are longer.

Other rivers going with the flow include the Ohio, the Red, the Arkansas, the Tensas, and the Yazoo. The great river and its tributaries drain 1,245,000 sq. miles (3,225,000 sq. km) of the central part of the United States, including all or part of 31 states, as well as 13,000 sq. miles (33,670 sq. km) of Alberta and Saskatchewan in Canada.

In addition to bordering metropolises, the Mississippi flows through places with quaint names like Prairie du Chien in Wisconsin, where in a bygone era French fur traders bargained with the Winnebago Indians; Cave-In-Rock, Illinois, where an 18th-century man lured passing flatboaters into a big hole in a limestock rock and robbed them blind; Vicksburg, Mississippi, with its vast Civil War battlefield, where Southerners withstood General Ulysses S. Grant's siege for 47 days and nights; and, of course, Hannibal, the small Missouri town that was the boyhood home of Samuel Clemens, the future Mark Twain.

PRECEDING PAGES: paddle power on the Father of Waters; the river, 2,350 miles long, meanders through much of Louisiana. **LEFT:** riverboats are part of the appeal. **BELOW:** rolling dice on the rolling river.

New Orleans is located where it is because of one and only one reason – the river. John Law, the man who conceived of the City of New Orleans, knew that in order to control the economics of the Mississippi Valley, it was necessary to control the river traffic. With this worldly view, he convinced the Duke of Orleans to establish a city in the south, overturning the view of French engineers who wanted to locate it at what is now present-day Baton Rouge. Law knew that the closer to the Gulf of Mexico the settlement was, the smoother would be the sailing of the trading ships.

Fiddling where the river flows. Each day the rapidly flowing Mississippi dumps near its mouth enough sand, mud and gravel to fill a freight train 150 miles long.

Father of Waters

Legends abound about the Father of Waters, many of them having to do with steamboating. The first steamboat, the *New Orleans*, sailed into the Crescent City in 1811 and ushered in a whole new era. Forerunners of the phone and the fax, the steamboats brought news and gossip, as well as goods, to eager people on the river banks. In time, they also brought entertainment. The 1830s saw the beginning of the showboat era, which roared through the 19th century only to fizzle out in the early 20th century.

What wonderful images the word showboat conjures up! Floating palaces, they were called, with huge paddle wheels stirring up frothy Mississippi surf; salons decked out with gilt, scarlet velvet, and bright white paneling; plunkety-de-plunking banjos, fancy dance-hall girls, flamboyant magicians, and silly vaudeville slapstick; cheroot-smoking riverboat gamblers in crisp white suits with slick tricks up their sleeves. Numerous films have depicted the excitement with which showboats were greeted. The cry of "Steamboat's a-comin'" and the jubilant songs of the calliope attracted folks down to the river to see the show.

BELOW: the first steamboat sailed into New Orleans in 1811.

One of the great legends of the Mississippi, celebrated in song, is of the Great Steamboat Race of 1870, between the *Natchez* and the *Robert E. Lee*. Cheered on by massive crowds along the levee all the way from New Orleans to St Louis, the two steamboats raced upriver at the dizzying pace of 17 miles (27 km) an hour. (The *Robert E. Lee* eventually won the race by more than six hours.)

Fortunately, for those of us who live in a fast-paced age of frenzied high-speed travel, sightseeing boats in river cities up and down the Mississippi take passengers back in time for an outing that's taken at a leisurely 19th-century pace. New Orleans, St Louis, and Louisville are but three of the cities that provide homes for great white paddle streamers, embellished with all the trimmings.

Whatever the theme or destination, the steamboats depart from New Orleans in grand fasion amid a flurry of parasols, antebellum gowns, and a calliope whistlin' *Dixie*. The steamboat **Natchez** (tel: 586-8777), based in New Orleans, is a 1,600-passenger four-decker that hosts possibly the world's most enthusiastic calliope concerts to alert the whole wide world that she's in town and ready to roll. The five-deck side-wheeler **President**, which plys the river's northern waters, is another great sight.

New Orleans is also home port for the Delta Queen Steamboat Company (30 Robin St. Wharf; tel: 586-

0631) whose three paddlewheelers make excursions to river cities. The *Delta Queen*, the *Mississippi Queen*, and the *American Queen* ease up and down river the year round, making trips that last from three to 14 nights. The three boats (no, they're not ships) are done up with teakwood trim, Tiffany stained glass, and all imaginable steamboat accoutrements. Of the three, the *Delta Queen* – the eldest and smallest, as well as a National Historic Landmark – is cozier and somehow more evocative of the steamboat era.

The steamboat agenda includes everything from bingo, raffles, and lectures to a zany Floozie Parade, talent contests, and ear-shattering cabarets. (One of the great challenges of the river-boat ride is finding a place for a bit of peace and quiet.) A "riverlorean" presents talks about port cities and life on the water, and there's an observation deck affording great views. The annual re-enactment of the race between the *Natchez* and the *Robert E. Lee* is a popular event, usually sold out far in advance. A cannon roars, balloons fly skywards, and Dixieland music blares as the two boats stream upriver for the 11-day excursion. Along the way, the crews of both boats compete in foot races and other games for the benefit of those on board.

Steamboats a-coming

Between New Orleans and the town of **Baton Rouge**, the view is mostly of belching chemical and industrial plants; upriver of the Louisiana capital things improve considerably. Along the way, the steamboat slides by high yellow-gold bluffs; navy-blue oxbow lakes left behind when the Mississippi grew fickle and changed its course; elegant plantation mansions glimpsed beyond alley-ways of moss-draped oak trees; and patchworks of green in the tall grass

Map on page 232

The young Samuel Langhorne Clemens took his pen name from the riverboat lingo that means "safe clearance." When danger was no longer a concern, crewmen would call out "Mark Twain."

BELOW: that Ol' Man River keeps on rollin' along.

Map on page 232

prairies, not to mention a profusion of colorful flowers, trees, and shrubs that are green all year round. Another popular voyage calls at the beautiful town of **Natchez** during that town's annual Spring Pilgrimage. Shore excursions take you on tours of grand old mansions, where hoop-skirted Southern belles tell romantic tales having to do with saving the house and the silver from the cussed Yankee invaders. (Walker Percy was once asked why there were so many good Southern writers. He replied: "Because we lost the war.")

Into the heartland

In late 1998, competition came to the Delta Queen Steamboat Company in the form of the RiverBarge Excursion Lines (201 Opelousas Avenue; tel: 365-0022). The company operates the United State's first luxury riverbarge called the *River Explorer,* which plies the waterways from New Orleans into the heartland. Designed as a resort hotel and a touring vehicle, the vessel comprises two river-barges propelled by a 3,000-ton (2,720-metric ton) towboat. The aft barge has 100 double staterooms; on the forward barge are the Pilothouse Lounge (equipped, just like the navigation bridge, with radar, radio, and river navigation charts); a 200-seat dining room; and a two-story entertainment complex.

BELOW: light and shade.
RIGHT: floating casino. Confined to legend for more than a century, in 1994 a ruling came into effect that allowed riverboat gambling on New Orleans waterways, including Lake Pontchartrain.

The primary "theme" of the *Explorer* is – well, exploring. Churning up the waters of the Atchafalaya, the Mississippi, the Missouri, and Ohio rivers, to name but a few, the riverbarge calls in at cities and towns around, for example, Louisiana's Cajun Country, and Ohio's Amish Country. This gives passengers the opportunity to explore some of the diverse cultures of this country in a suitable mode of transport.

In 1994, with great hoopla, riverboat gambling returned to New Orleans after more than a century. This revival saw several floating casinos on Crescent City waterways. Of these, the *Boomtown Belle,* one of the original floating casinos, is all duded out in Wild West decor and docks on the West Bank's Harvey Canal. The enormously successful *Treasure Chest,* which has a dockside entertainment complex, sits on Lake Pontchartrain in the suburb of Kenner. Bally's *Casino/Lakefront Resort,* also moored on Lake Pontchartrain, occupies a berth adjacent to the Lakefront Airport.

Over the millennia, the river has changed its course many times. From Minnesota to Louisiana, there are lakes and marshes left behind as mementoes of the Mississippi. It is somberly predicted that the Ol' Man is itching to change course again, this time to divert through the Atchafalaya river – and bypass New Orleans entirely. The social and economic consequences of such a cataclysmic shift are unthinkable. The 15-mile (24-km) long Port of New Orleans is still one of the largest ports in the world, in terms of tonnage. Imagine the havoc if the river just drifted away.

For the present, anyway, there is comfort and a sense of vast eternity in these words of Mark Twain: "League after league, it still pours its chocolate tide along, between its sold forest walls… and so the day goes, the night comes, and again the day – and still the same – majestic, unchanging sameness of serenity, repose, tranquility." ❏

PLANTATION COUNTRY

Built along the river to escape the steamy summer heat,
Louisiana's plantation homes were really
colonies in miniature

Map
on page
232

The Southern plantation, with its vast acres of cotton fields and hundreds of slaves, ruled by a kindly ol' marse or a mean-eyed monster, is the stuff of novelists and scriptwriters. Descriptions are always similar: a massive white-columned mansion shaded by moss-draped trees and sweetened with the scent of honeysuckle. Sweet (or sultry) young belles with milk-white skin, a three-inch waistline, and teasing eyes, gotten up in miles of hoops and tons of crinoline. Handsome, though sometimes a mite sinister, cavaliers with stunning tans and bright white teeth, dashing off to the "wah" or wherever they must go in order to fight for love or honor, or preferably both.

New Orleans is surrounded by such plantations, some with wistful names like Rosedown, some old and crumbling, some dolled up and fit for overnight guests. All, however, offer the requisite degree of romance, and a few even add in a mystery or two.

PRECEDING PAGES:
Louisiana
Philharmonic plays
at Destrehan.
LEFT: verandas to
catch the cooling
summer breezes.
BELOW: Laura
Plantation.

A little village

Although scholars still argue about the causes and social structure of the plantation system, they are agreed on certain characteristics and the physical layout of the homes. Whether a result of demographics or economics, and whether large or small, the plantation was essentially a colony, a village-like complex with a "big house," small slave cabins, and outbuildings for the blacksmith's shop, milkhouse, barn, doctor's offices, store, and other necessities. For obvious reasons, plantations were generally situated on or near a waterway; they were dependent on the cities for marketing their products, and also for purchasing supplies that could not be grown, sewn, or manufactured on the grounds.

Distances between plantations were not far by contemporary standards; however, a 15-mile (24-km) jaunt by horse-and-buggy over rough dirt roads did take all day. Each plantation had accommodation for guests, who might stay for days or even weeks at a time. In Creole south Louisiana homes, there was always a separate quarter, called the *garçonnière*, where young unmarried men of the house lived, and where visiting gentlemen callers stayed.

As for crops, King Cotton is the most celebrated in legend. Other products included rice, indigo, hemp, tobacco, sorghum, corn, peanuts, potatoes, and sugar – not necessarily in that order.

Plantation Row

Louisiana's plantation country follows the Mississippi River from above Baton Rouge, and ends about 23 miles (37 km) west of New Orleans. There are more than a dozen antebellum homes on the Great River

Sweet dreams are made of this. Some of Louisiana's great plantations offer accommodation. For more information read on; for a list, contact the Louisiana tourist office, tel: 504-342 8119.

Road (built to escape the dripping summer heat) that are regularly open for touring, and it makes no sense at all to try to see them all in one fell swoop. Several of the plantations are also bed-and-breakfasts, and it's far better to plan on overnight pampering in a stately mansion, or two, to take advantage of real Southern hospitality. Many visitors to New Orleans make day trips to the plantations that lie between the city and Baton Rouge, 80 miles (129 km) northwest of the Crescent City; another pleasant outing is to St Francisville, 115 miles (185 km) north of New Orleans, to see the many plantation homes in that area.

Although the term 'Great River Road" conjures up wonderful images, the road is, sadly, neither great nor in river's view. Actually, since there are two riverbanks, there are two roads that meander alongside the Mississippi between New Orleans and Baton Rouge. In addition to US 61, the route is known variously as highways 1, 18, 75, 405, and 942 – to name but a few. Worse, the drive is lined with sprawling chemical and industrial plants.

Destrehan and San Francisco

The closest plantation to New Orleans lies 8 miles (13 km) west of the New Orleans International Airport, so about 23 miles (37 km) from the city. To reach **Destrehan ❶** (13034 River Road, Destrehan, tel: 764-9315; open daily, fee), drive west on US 61 or I–10, take exit 310, and follow the signs to Destrehan Plantation. The oldest plantation still on its feet in the Lower Mississippi Valley, Destrehan is typical of the homes built by the earliest planters, who derived a style of architecture prevalent in the West Indies. A two-story house with double galleries, white columns, and high-pitched roof pierced by tall chimneys, Destrehan was built in 1787 by a free man of colour; the Greek Revival touches

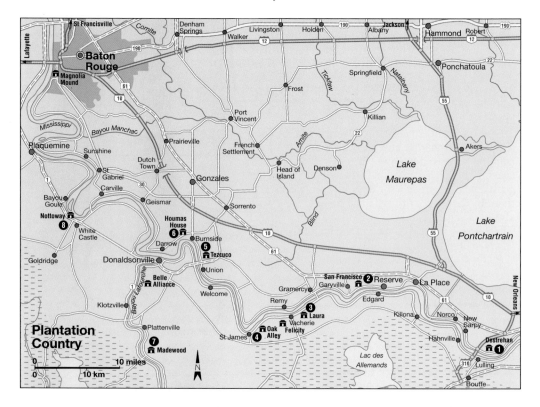

were added later in the 1800s. The house is somewhat simply furnished, although with period antiques.

If you've seen one plantation you've by no means seen them all. Gorgeous **San Francisco ②** (LA 44, tel: 535-2341; open daily, fee), about 5 miles (8 km) west of Destrehan, is entirely different. This ornate "Steamboat Gothic" house (Frances Parkinson Keyes used it as the setting for her novel of that title) was built in 1856 by Edmond Bozonier Marmillion. Gussied up with elaborate exterior ornamentation, it is noted for its stunning ceiling frescoes and intricate millwork. San Francisco sits in the shadow of a giant oil refinery, but it's worth remembering that the oil company pays for the upkeep of the house.

On the west bank

The next two plantations – Laura and its neighbor, Oak Alley – are on the west bank of the Mississippi, accessible via the Veterans Memorial Bridge.

Laura ③ (2247 LA 18, tel: 265-7690; open daily, fee), like San Franciso, is a Creole plantation. While the Americans built lavish white plantation mansions, Creole plantations are painted in vivid colours, as is evident in both these houses. Laura was built in 1805, and was for many years managed by women. It was to this plantation that Senegalese slaves brought the Br'er Rabbit stories. In 1896, Joel Chandler Harris translated them from Creole into English; the tales of Br'er Rabbit are known to every Southern schoolchild.

The restoration of the house is based on 100 pages of a diary written by Laura Locoul, the great-granddaughter of Guillaume DuParc, the Spanish commandant who built the plantation. Restoration work, which is expected to finish in 2005, involves 12 buildings, including two manor houses and several B&B cottages.

Map on page 232

The cost of building this "Steamboat Gothic" was so high that it prompted the owner's son to christen the house San Frusquin – French slang for, loosely, "without a penny in my pocket." The name San Frusquin became San Francisco.

BELOW: the parlor of San Francisco.

The subtropical greenery of The Myrtles.

Perhaps the most photographed of the Louisiana plantations, and a frequent movie set, is **Oak Alley** ❹ (3645 LA 18, tel: 265-2151 or 800/44ALLE; open daily, fee), 3 miles (5 km) upriver of Laura. The white-columned house, built in 1837, is set well back from the road beyond a stately avenue of 28 live oak trees (*see picture on page 112*). In fact, the grounds and exterior are somewhat grander than the interior. According to legend, the plantation was called Bon Sejour by its original owner, but awestruck steamboat passengers on the river referred to is as Oak Alley, and so it has long been known. Bed and breakfast rooms are in small cabins, and there is a restaurant serving Cajun and Creole fare.

Tezcuco and Houmas

On the Mississippi's east bank, 25 miles (40 km) upriver of Oak Alley, **Tezcuco** ❺ (3138 LA 44, near Burnside, tel: 562-3929; open daily, fee) is a lovely Greek Revival cottage in a glamorous subtropical setting and with a gallery festooned with fanciful ironwork. There are two bed and breakfast rooms in the main house, but most are in restored slave cabins furnished with 19th-century antiques, including brass and canopied beds; some have open wood-burning fireplaces. A full breakfast is brought to each cottage, and there is a restaurant on the grounds (lunch only). You could also try out **The Cabin**, at the intersection of LA 22 and LA 44 (I–10 exit 182, open daily). Housed in a cluster of 150-year-old slave cabins and serving gumbo, seafood, and Cajun food, this restaurant could have been the inspiration for the word "rustic."

Tezcuco is also home to the **River Road African-American Museum and Gallery** (tel: 504/562-7703, open Sat–Sun 1–5pm, Mon–Fri by appointment), where art and artifacts trace the history of African-Americans in Louisiana.

Just over 2 miles (3 km) from Tezcuco, a half mile off LA 44 near Burnside, **Houmas House** ❻ (40136 LA 942, tel: 473-7841; open daily, fee) is one of the most elegant of the River Road plantations, and a regular film "star." Among the movies filmed here was *Hush, Hush, Sweet Charlotte*, Robert Aldrich's 1965 Gothic thriller starring Bette Davis and Olivia De Havilland.

The mansion actually comprises two houses. A two-story house built in the 1700s is connected by a carriageway to the handsome white Greek Revival home that was completed in 1840. Tastefully furnished with antiques, the house has a graceful spiral staircase. The front lawn rolls up to the levee, and a fine view of the Mississippi River.

Madewood and Nottoway

Another beautifully restored Greek Revival mansion lies 20 miles (32 km) southeast of Houmas House, on the west bank, via the Sunshine Bridge, LA 70, and LA 308. **Madewood** ❼ (4250 LA 308, tel: 369-7151; open daily, fee) also boasts film credits. Cicely Tyson's *A Woman Called Moses* was filmed here in 1978, and this house, too, is open for B&B guests. Painted a pristine white (and so-named because it was "made of wood"), the house dates from 1846, when it was designed by noted architect Henry Howard and built for Colonel Thomas Push. The Colonel's family is buried in Madewood's small, picturesque cemetery.

Map on page 232

The mansion's 21 rooms are furnished with American and English antiques, and there are several outbuildings scattered throughout the grounds that reflect different styles of Louisiana architecture.

The South's largest plantation home is on the west bank, 33 miles (53 km) northwest of Madewood, via LA 1. **Nottoway** ❽ (30907 LA 405, near White Castle, tel: 545-2730, open daily, fee) is, quite simply, a knockout.

The house, completed in 1859, was designed by Henry Howard, architect of Madewood. The statistics are staggering: Nottoway contains 64 rooms, 200 windows, and 22 columns. It bears some resemblance to a gigantic wedding cake. The grounds are lush, and the river rolls by just across the road. Thirteen rooms are let to overnight guests, and there is an excellent restaurant.

Nottoway was completed two years before the War of Northern Aggression in 1861. A Yankee soldier who had once been a house guest asked that it be spared from demolition.

Beyond Baton Rouge

Heading north of Baton Rouge on US 61, about 15 miles (24 km) north of the city you sweep by the **Port Hudson State Commemorative Area** (756 W. Plains-Port Hudson Rd, tel: 654-3775; open daily, fee). It seems fitting that a visit to plantation country should include the site of a famous Civil War Site. The 643-acre (260-hectare) site commemorates an 1863 battle, when 6,800 Rebs held off 30,000 Yankees for 48 days and nights – the longest siege in US military history. The Southerners surrendered only after word came to them that Vicksburg had fallen. A boardwalk winds through an area that saw some of the fiercest fighting, and there are 6 miles (10 km) of trails.

Four miles (6 km) north of Port Hudson, turn right off US 61 onto LA 965 to see the house where, in 1821, naturalist John James Audubon completed 80 of his famous Birds of America. Within the **Audubon State Commemorative**

BELOW: Nottoway has 64 rooms and 200 windows.

Map on page 232

Area (LA 965, tel: 635-3739; open Wed–Sun 9am to 5pm, fee) is Oakley Plantation, a West Indies-style house in which Audubon, when not bird-watching or painting, tutored Eliza Pirrie, daughter of the plantation owner. The house is furnished with federal-era antiques, and decorated with prints from Audubon's folio of elephants.

Three miles (5 km) to the north, about 35 miles (56 km) from Baton Rouge, is **St Francisville**. This utterly charming little town, dressed with magnificent live oak trees, has been described as a town 2 miles long and 2 yards wide. Louisiana is shaped rather like a boot, and this part of the state is the instep of the boot. Entirely different from Cajun Country, or French Louisiana, to the west, the Feliciana parishes, in which St Francisville sits, were settled by the English. Culturally, this area has more in common with North Louisiana and other Southern states than with French Louisiana.

One of the most impressive mansions in the state is at the juncture of US 61 and LA 10, not far from the center of St. Francisville. **Rosedown Plantation and Gardens** (12501 LA 10, tel: 635-3332; open daily, fee) is a stunning museum house, whose extensive grounds include centuries-old camellias and azaleas. Built in 1835, the restored house has most of the original furnishings and elegant objets d'art. A separate house on the estate offers bed and breakfast, with canopied beds and private baths, plus a pool and tennis courts.

BELOW AND RIGHT: plantation scenes. Other mansions worth seeing include Felicity, Belle Alliance, and Magnolia Mound.

North of St Francisville

Several elegant homes line US 61 north of St Francisville, most of them planted among huge live oaks, magnolia trees, and subtropical greenery. **The Myrtles** (7747 US 61, tel: 635-6277; open daily, fee) bills itself as "America's Most Haunted House," and is said to be on the site of an ancient Indian burial ground. It has a sweeping veranda lavishly covered with lacy blue ironwork, elegant period antiques, and splendid chandeliers. B&B accommodations are in outbuildings behind the main house, and there is an excellent restaurant (open for dinner Wed–Sun). As well as daily tours, mystery tours of the house are conducted on weekends.

Not far from the Myrtles, **Butler-Greenwood** (8345 US 61, tel: 635-6312; open daily, fee) is a 1790s plantation, still working and operated by descendants of its builder. The 18th-century formal Victorian parlor is among the finest in the state. B&B guests stay in their own private cottage, each elegantly furnished and equipped with kitchenettes and the makings for a continental breakfast.

A little farther along, off US 61, is **The Cottage** (10528 Cottage Lane, tel: 365-3674; open daily, fee), one of the few plantations whose original outbuildings still remain. Nestled in grounds punctuated by live oak trees dripping in Spanish moss, the main house, built in 1795, is appropriately elegant – while the outbuildings are properly rustic and weathered. Following his triumph in the Battle of New Orleans, General Andrew Jackson was a house guest of the original owner. The Cottage, too, is a bed-and-breakfast, and Matty's Restaurant in the grounds serves good South Louisiana food. ❑

CAJUN COUNTRY

Foot-stompin' music and down-home cooking are two of the attractions in what might be America's most distinctive region, but there's also gardens, good yarns and grand houses

Map on pages 242–43

New Orleans was founded by French Creoles – that is, the descendants of French people who were born "in the colonies" – and the vast area to the west of the Crescent City was also settled by the French. However, the French of Cajun Country (which is also called Acadiana, or French Louisiana) have a different heritage from that of the Creoles.

From Canada to Cajun Country

In the early 17th century, the French colonized parts of Canada that were at the time called New France, and are now the provinces callded New Brunswick and Nova Scotia. Farmers and fur trappers for the most part, the colonists established a settlement called *l'Acadie*, or Acadia, and referred to themselves as *Acadiens*. In the mid-18th century, when the British took control of the region, the *Acadiens* – or "Cajuns," the anglicized version of the word – were expelled because of their refusal to forsake their Catholic faith and swear allegiance to the British crown.

The Cajuns' expulsion, which came to be known as *Le Grand Dérangement*, was immortalized, as well as highly romanticized, by Henry Wadsworth Longfellow in his epic poem, *Evangeline (see page 248).*

At the time of the exile, Louisiana was a Spanish colony, and the Spaniards – also Catholic and therefore sympathetic to the problem – welcomed the Cajuns to this region. The Creoles of New Orleans, however, viewed the Cajuns as peasants, while for their part the Cajuns thought the Creoles were snobs. On the whole, the new arrivals settled along the bayous and in the prairies to the west of New Orleans. And there they have flourished, ever since about 1764, imbuing this region with a marvelous *joie de vivre*. Cajuns tend to be hard-working and deeply religious, as well as friendly and fun-loving, so visitors should find a warm welcome in store whenever they choose to explore this part of the state.

Because the Acadians had long been separated from Mother France, their language developed differently, too. Today, Cajun French still varies from standard French in much the same way that Shakespearian English differs from standard English; it is a 17th-century form of the language. English, of course, is also spoken everywhere, and most Acadians can respond to standard French.

Several radio stations in the region broadcast regular programs in French. (A few years ago, an anonymous linguist in Acadiana translated Chaucer's *Canterbury Tales* from Middle English into Cajun French, and sent it to a local radio station – a feat that could be described as "no mean," indeed.)

PRECEDING PAGES: paddling a Cajun *pirogue* (canoe) at Vermilionville. **LEFT:** foot-stompin' music at Mulate's, Breaux Bridge. **BELOW:** alligator on Bayou Black.

If your feet are itching to dance, check out the clubs mentioned in this chapter. Other great places include Grant Street Dance Hall in Lafayette; Slim's Yi-Ki-Ki in Opelousas, and Richard's (Ree-shars) in Lawtell.

The swiftest route from New Orleans into the heart of Cajun Country is via Interstate-10. The proud "capital" of French Louisiana is Lafayette, which lies 128 miles (205 km) west of New Orleans (*see page 249*). But it's fun to take the longer, more scenic route, in order to savor as much of the Acadian flavor as possible. (Alternatively, of course, you can make a beeline for Lafayette and use it as a base for exploring.)

Houma and Morgan City

To opt for the scenic route, drive south on US 90, which dips down to **Houma ❶**, 57 miles (92 km) below New Orleans. Named for the Houmas Indians who inhabited this area, Houma is a lazy little town snuggled in among marshlands and bayous. This is an excellent departure point for swamp tours, and even an airplane tour of these wetlands. The Houma/Terrebonne Tourist Commission (1702 S. St Charles St, tel: 800 688-2732, www.houmatourism.com; open daily) has a wealth of information about the area. Among the attractions is **Southdown Plantation** (A311 at St Charles St, tel: 504 851-0154, www.southdown.org; open Tues–Sat, fee), a small but colorful Victorian house, replete with turrets and galleries as well as artifacts pertaining to Houma and Terrebonne Parish. Fourteen miles (22 km) west of Houma, via US 90, is the **Wildlife Gardens**, offering walking and boat tours through the swamp as well as simple bed and breakfast (*see page 261*).

Sprawled on the banks of the Atchafalaya River 37 miles (60 km) northwest of Houma via US 90, **Morgan City ❷** has a couple of claims to fame. These Amazon-like environs served as the set for the very first Tarzan movie, filmed in 1917. To see a video of the movie, inquire at the Morgan City Information

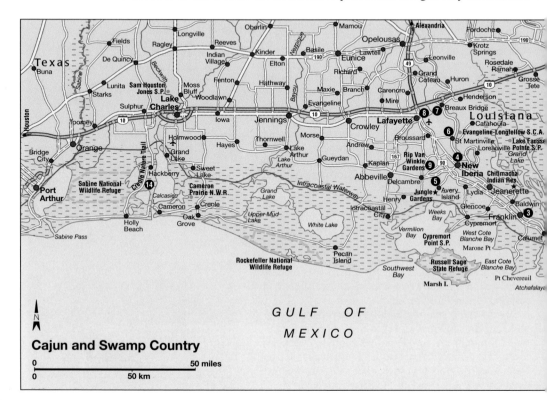

Cajun and Swamp Country

GULF OF MEXICO

Center (725 Myrtle St, tel: 504 384-3343; open daily). Right across from the information center, you can take a guided tour of the **Swamp Gardens** (tours daily, call information center for hours; fee).

In addition to movie credits, the town saw the beginning of the "Black Gold Rush," when the Kerr-McGee Rig No. 16 struck oil offshore of Morgan City on November 14, 1947. Regrettably, it also saw the boom go bust in the 1980s; only in the late 1990s has the state's oil industry begun to make a comeback.

Moonwalk, atop the Great Wall – a flood wall that runs 22 miles (35 km) alongside Front Street – is a fine observation deck for viewing the Atchafalaya, and for examining the historical displays that pertain to the town and environs.

In the town of Patterson, a few miles west of Morgan City on US 90, pop into the **St Mary Parish Tourist Commission** (112 Main St., Patterson, tel: 504 395-4905, open Mon–Fri) to fill up your tote-bag with maps and brochures about the "Cajun coast" on the Old Spanish Trail (US 90/LA 182).

A serpentine route to Franklin

Just past Patterson, detour to LA 182 to follow **Bayou Teche**. *Teche* is an Indian word meaning "snake." According to an ancient legend, the death throes of a snake were responsible for carving out the bayou. The snake would have to have been a pretty good-sized fellow, and a mighty miffed one to boot, as the Teche is the state's largest bayou. Its brackish, bottle-green waters are still and sluggish, but its contorted contours do seem to have been thrashed out in a fit of pique. Mercifully, the highway does not thrash about in like fashion.

Both US 90 and LA 182 lead to the pretty little town of **Franklin** ❸, approached from the east beneath an arch of handsome live oak trees. Unique

Map on pages 242–43

St Mary's parish. The tourist office is a good place for maps and brochures.

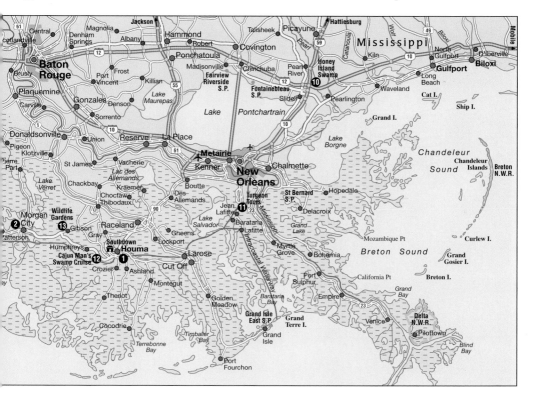

Crawfish pie at the Café des Amis, Breaux Bridge.

BELOW: good Cajun music depends on spoons and a washboard.

in this part of the gallic *bois*, Franklin was settled not by Frenchmen, but by the English, and the town has a wealth of beautiful white mansions – several of which are open for tours and some of which are, inevitably bed-and-breakfasts.

Among Franklin's "must-sees" is **Grevemberg House** (407 Sterling Rd, tel: 318 828-2092; open daily, fee), an 1851 Greek Revival townhouse furnished with period antiques. The house contains displays of Civil War artifacts, and charming antique toys. **Oaklawn Manor** (3296 E. Oaklawn Drive, tel: 318 828-0434; open daily, fee), the home of Louisiana Governor and Mrs Mike Foster, is a Greek Revival mansion, built around 1837, furnished with European antiques, and decorated with original Audubons.

And don't fail to take a few minutes to stroll around the enchanting **Franklin Historic District** (bounded by Main, Willow, Morris, and Second streets), but be prepared for an attack of nostalgia. Franklin is a Main Street USA town, designated by the National Trust for Historic Preservation, and its historic district is on the National Register of Historic Places.

Chitimacha Indian Reservation

Three miles (5 km) north of Franklin, in the town of Charenton, via LA 326, you can visit the **Chitimacha Indian Reservation** (tel: 318 923-4830, open daily). The Chitimacha roamed freely in Lower Teche country for centuries before the arrival of the White Eye. Theirs was the first tribe in Louisiana to be federally recognized; the reservation was established in 1925, after the tribe, which had numbered in the thousands, was reduced to 50.

The Chitimacha were famed for their handsome woven baskets, and some are still made on the reservation. However, the reservation's biggest attraction is the

FAIS-DO-DO AND OTHER FACTS

The Cajun motto is, "*Laissez les bons temps rouler,*" which means: Let the good times roll! You'll never hear anyone in Louisiana actually *say* that, of course, but you do see it on signs all over the region.

Cajun food could be thought of as a country cousin to French Creole cuisine. It is hearty and robust, often shellfish mixed up with whatever's around in the pantry.

Cajun music, and its zippy cousin, zydeco – which was developed by black Creoles – accompanies chank-a-chanking at *fais-do-dos* throughout the area. For the uninitiated, a *fais-do-do* is a dance, as performed in a dance hall, and "chank-a-chanking" is the dancing done at the dance. Cajun evenings are traditionally family affairs, and the expression *"fais-do-do,"* meaning "go to sleep," is an admonishment to children, so that the big folks can get on down and kick up their heels.

Cajun bands almost always feature a little iron triangle that makes a chank-a-chank sound when tapped – thus, the chank-a-chank is, essentially, the rhythm of the dance. It's all exuberant, foot-stomping good fun, and should not be missed while you're in Cajun Country. Cajun and zydeco music are wildly popular in New Orleans nightclubs and Jazz Fest, too.

Map on pages 242–43

ever-expanding **Cypress Bayou Casino** (832 Martin Luther King Rd, tel: 800 284-4386), which is open 24 hours, seven days a week, and is invariably packed. Gaming tables abound, vying with video poker and slot machines, ever ready and distressingly able to relieve you of your money.

Iberian outpost

The Spaniards who founded **New Iberia** ❹, 25 miles (40 km) northwest of Franklin, named it for the Iberian Peninsula of their homeland, but you'll see much more of the Acadian influence than Spanish. New Iberia is a pretty little town, smack on the banks of the Teche. Information and friendly advice about touring the town and environs is available at the Iberia Parish Tourist Commission (2690 Centre St, tel: 318 365-1540; open daily).

New Iberia's outstanding attraction is **Shadows on the Teche** (317 E. Main St, tel: 318 369-6446; open daily, fee), Louisiana's only National Trust Historic House Museum & Gardens. With Bayou Teche in its backyard and giant live oaks to shade it, the Shadows was built in 1834 for sugar planter David Weeks, and is magnificently restored. Furnishings are authentic 19th-century Louisiana and European antiques.

Across the street from the Shadows, with an ancient rose garden, is the **Inn at leRosier** (314 Main St, tel: 318 367-5306/888 804-7673, www.lerosier.com), an enchanting bed-and-breakfast with six rooms for overnighters and an award-winning dining room under Chef Hallman Woods III. Other B&Bs include the **Estorge-Norton House B&B**, **La Maison du Teche**, and **Chez Hebert**.

New Iberia is home to the oldest rice mill in America. Tours are conducted of the **Conrad Rice Mill** (307 Ann St, tel: 318 364-7242 or 800 551-3245; closed

TIP

One block from le Rosier, Al and Elaine Landry's Lagniappe Too (204 E. Main St, tel: 318 365-9419) is a delightful and reasonably priced bistro that features Elaine's cooking and Al's paintings on the walls.

BELOW: Franklin Historic District.

Sun, fee), while the on-site **Konriko Country Store** sells Cajun food baskets, crafts, and and other collectible gifts.

New Iberia is just a short detour away from one of South Louisiana's stellar attractions, **Avery Island ❺**, which is about 7 miles (11 km) southwest of town. To reach it, go north on US 90 from New Iberia, take the LA 14 exit and turn left, then turn right on LA 329. There are no bridges or pontoons on the approach to Avery Island, and were it not for the signs you would not know that you'd even reached an island.

A hot island

In South Louisiana, Avery Island is synonymous with Tabasco sauce, the hot-hot condiment that gives a whole new meaning to the term Bloody Mary, since this is where the sauce originated. Edmund McIlhenny concocted the first Tabasco sauce in the 1880s, and today a fourth generation of McIlhennys run the **Tabasco Factory** (tel: 800 634-9599, www.tabasco.com; open Mon–Fri 9–4pm, Sat 9–noon; tours are free). This is a major operation, given that Tabasco graces kitchens and cafes the world over.

It was also a McIlhenny – Edward Avery McIlhenny, to be precise – who developed the adjacent 200-acre (80-hectare) **Jungle Gardens** (tel: 318 369-6243; open daily, fee), which is Avery Island's most spectacular attraction. The gardens are ablaze with camellias, azaleas, and tropical flowers and plants – something is in bloom, whatever the time of year. The Chinese Gardens area contain a Buddha that dates from AD 1,000. In the spring and summer, the bird sanctuary is a-flutter with white egrets and herons, while in wintertime hordes of ducks come quacking in.

Islands in this area are not really islands; the domes of the salt mines that dot the coastline are covered with sub-tropical vegetation, and since the domes rise above the terrain they are called "islands."

BELOW:
fishing boats,
Bayou Lafourche.

St Martinville: home of Evangeline

Ten miles (26 km) north of New Iberia lies **St Martinville ❻**, virtually the heart and soul of the Evangeline Legend (*see page 248*). And no one defends the legend more fiercely than the local tourism people, since it was Evangeline that put the town on the map. The **St Martinville Tourist Information Center** (127 N. Market St, tel: 318 394-2233; open daily) sits on the banks of the Teche, in the shadow of the fabled Evangeline Oak. While there are those who declare this to be the third live oak in the past century to bear that name, it is nevertheless an awesome old tree. Almost as legendary as Evangeline, the Romero brothers are a pair of flesh-and-blood elderly gentlemen who can usually be found sitting in the shade the tree, playing the accordion and singing Cajun and French songs. It is utterly delightful. Needless to say, this is a superb place in which to practice your French.

In the shadow of the oak, the **Old Castillo Hotel/La Place d'Evangeline** (220 Evangeline Blvd, tel: 318 394-4010 or 800/621-3017) is a bed & breakfast and restaurant in an historic 18th-century building that has served as an inn for steamboat passengers and a haven for French Royalists.

Just a block away, on the square, is the mother church of the Acadians, known as **St Martin de Tours**; a statue of Evangeline stands in the churchyard behind. The neighboring **Petit Paris Museum** (103 S. Main St, tel: 318 394-7334; open daily, fee) is quite small, but is nevertheless filled to the rafters with artifacts and memorabilia about St Martinville and the environs. One of the exhibits pertains to an 1870 wedding that took place just outside of town. When two daughters of Charles Durand wanted a double wedding, the father of the brides pulled out all the stops. He ordered that, prior to the wedding, giant spiders be set

Map on pages 242–43

The St Martinville Acadian Memorial contains a mural depicting the arrival of the Acadians, as well as a Wall of Names of the exiles. At the back, beside the Teche, a small eternal flame burns.

BELOW: Tabasco sauce factory on Avery Island.

Seafood and live Cajun bands are the top attractions at Mulate's in Breaux Bridge. The portions and dance floor are both ample, and the crowd is friendly.

loose in a mile-long alley leading to the house. On the big day the spiders' webs were sprayed with silver and gold dust to create a glittering archway for the bridal party. All of this is gone with the wind, of course, and only the site remains, 2 miles (3 km) outside of town on LA 96.

Just outside the city limits, on LA 31, the star-crossed Acadian exile is remembered in the **Evangeline-Longfellow State Commemorative Area** (tel: 318 394-3754; open daily, fee). Within the lovely 157-acre (63-hecatre) park there is an interpretative center sited in a raised cottage, picnic grounds and barbecue grills, a craft shop, and a boat launch on Bayou Teche.

A feast in Breaux Bridge

Breaux Bridge ❼, 10 miles (16 km) farther along US 31, is famous for two reasons – firstly, for its **Crawfish Festival** held on the first weekend in May, when the resident population of less than 7,000 swells to over 100,000 hungry visitors. The second reason is that it is the home of **Mulate's** (325 Mills Ave, tel: 318 332-4648 or 800 424-2586), a family restaurant-cum-dance hall which swings all year round. Do note, however, that Mulate's can be overrun with badge-wearing crowds disgorged from tour buses originating in New Orleans or Baton Rouge. Breaux Bridge also has a charming restaurant and bed-and-breakfast, called, respectively, **Café des Amis** and **Maison des Amis** (140 Bridge St, tel: 318 332-5273), as well as yet another legendary Cajun dance hall, this one called **La Poussiere** (1712 Grand Point Rd, tel: 318 332-1721).

Five miles (8 km) east of Breaux Bridge, via LA 94 and I-10, is the awesome **Atchafalaya Basin**, an 800,000-acre (324,000-hectare) swampland replete with bald cypresses standing in murky waters, knee-deep and naked save for

BELOW:
St Martinville.

THE ROMANCE OF EVANGELINE

In recent years the Evangeline story has been hotly disputed, but it remains a charming tale. Henry Wadsworth Longfellow's poem *Evangeline* was based on the true story of Emmeline Labiche ("Evangeline") and Louis Arceneaux ("Gabriel"), sweethearts in Acadia who were separated for long years during Le Grand Dérangement (*see page 241*). Gabriel arrived in St Martinville many years before Evangeline. When finally she did arrive, she stepped ashore beside the Evangeline Oak, and there she and Gabriel were reunited. In Longfellow's poem, Gabriel's face turns white when he sees his former lover. He turns and disappears into the mists of myths, leaving in his wake the heartbroken Evangeline, for, having despaired of ever seeing her again, he had married another.

Based on Longfellow's tale, the movie *The Romance of Evangeline* was filmed in St Martinville in 1929, starring Dolores del Rio, who posed for the statue of Evangeline that the film cast and crew presented to the city and which stands in the grounds behind the church of St Martin de Tours. Parts of this movie were spliced into the Acadian film that is shown at the Jean Lafitte Acadian Cultural Center in Lafayette.

shawls of Spanish moss, as well as exotic plants and water-fowl. Guided boat tours are from **McGee's Landing** and **Angelle's Whiskey River Landing**; the boat landings are on the levee, along with cafes and restaurants.

Map on pages 242–43

Lafayette: the big cheese

Lafayette ❽, 10 miles (16 km) west of Breaux Bridge on LA 94, is the big cheese in Cajun Country, with the region's greatest concentration of sites, sights, museums, restaurants, nightclubs, and lodging. It is also ground zero for the wonderful Cajun Mardi Gras, a celebration that runs a close second to its elder sibling in New Orleans. In the surrounding countryside, the *Courir de Mardi Gras*, or Mardi Gras Run – which has no rival and no equal – is a wild affair during which masked riders thunder through the countryside on horseback, stopping at farmhouses to gather up food for one big fete in the town square.

The logical first stop after arriving is the Lafayette Convention & Visitors Bureau (1400 N.W. Evangeline Thruway, tel: 318 232-3808 or 800 346-1958, www.lafayettetravel.com. open daily). After that, high on a list of priorities should be the **Acadian Cultural Center** (Jean Lafitte Historical Park, 501 Fisher Rd, tel: 318 232-0789, open daily, admission free), where the informative and fun exhibits thoroughly examine Cajun culture. Visitors are shown a well-made introductory film, in which parts of the 1929 *Romance of Evangeline* Hollywood movie are incorporated.

Across the street from the Acadian Cultural Center, **Vermilionville** (1600 Surrey St, tel: 318 233-4077 or 800 992-2968; open daily, fee) is an enormous theme park cum living history museum which focuses on Lafayette's early Creole and Cajun culture. (Lafayette's original name was Vermilionville.)

BELOW: the words "crawfish" and "Cajun" are almost synonymous.

Costumed folk in more than twenty 19th-century houses demonstrate arts, crafts, and cooking; live Cajun music is played in the music hall; and good fare is served in rustic *La Cuisine de Mama*. The **Acadian Village** (200 Green Leaf Drive, tel: 318 981-2364 or 800 962-3133; open daily, fee), smaller and somewhat more user-friendly than Vermilionville, is a folk-life museum that re-creates an early 19th-century Cajun village. The banks of a lazy, slow-moving bayou are dotted with several authentic houses, each with a different exhibit. There is also an enchanting little chapel.

Saturday night fever

It would be a shame to leave these parts without going 35 miles (56 km) northwest to the town of **Eunice**. As well as being a typical Cajun town, Eunice on a Saturday night is host of the ***Rendez-Vous des Cajuns*** (Liberty Center, tel: 813 457-8577; 6pm Sat, fee). This is a two-hour radio show, broadcast mostly in French (trust us, you don't have to know the language), with story-telling and plenty of music and dancing. Not to be missed.

Likewise, another indigenous delight is in **Mamou**, about 45 miles (72 km) from Lafayette. **Fred's Lounge** (420 Sixth St, tel: 318 468-5411) really zings on Saturday mornings when it is the venue for radio station KVPI-Ville Platte's live music/news/gossip show between 8am and 1pm. Despite big signs proclaiming that this is NOT a dance hall, and pleading, please, do NOT stand on top of the jukebox, Fred's gets extremely lively, with customers chank-a-chanking like crazy and hanging off the jukebox.

One thing is certain: you will not go hungry in and around Lafayette. Eating places are ubiquitous, and portions are downright portly. Among the variety of

BELOW: the 1870s Jefferson House stands in Rip Van Winkle Gardens.

eateries on offer are **Café Vermilionville** (1304 W. Pinhook Drive, Lafayette, tel: 318 237-0100); **Enola Prudhomme's Cajun Café** (4676 N.E. Evangeline Thruway, tel: 318 896-3646); **Prejean's** (3480 I-49 North, Lafayette, tel: 318 896-3247); and **Randol's Restaurant** and Cajun Dance Hall (2320 Kaliste Saloom Rd, Lafayette, tel: 800/YO–CAJUN).

Lafayette and surrounding towns also have a host of B&Bs, hotels, and chain motels. In the former category, recommended places include **Bois des Chiens** (338 N. Sterling, Lafayette, tel: 318 233-7816); **T'Frere's House** (1905 Verot School Rd, Lafayette, tel: 318 984-9347); **Chretien Point Plantation** (665 Chretien Point Rd, Sunset, tel: 318 662-5876 or 800 880/7050); and **Seale Guest House** (125 Seale Lane, Eunice, tel: 318 457-3753).

Rip Van Winkle Gardens

US 90 and LA 675 travel 15 miles (24 km) south of Lafayette to a veritable Eden, in the form of **Rip Van Winkle Gardens** ❾ (5505 Rip Van Winkle Road, tel: 318 365-3332 or 800 375-3332, www.ripvanwinkle.com; open daily, fee), which sit atop a typical South Louisiana "island."

In the 1870s, American actor Joseph Jefferson gained great fame by touring the country portraying Rip Van Winkle. He made frequent hunting trips to South Louisiana, and in 1870 purchased 5,000 acres (2,000 hectares) here and built a splendid three-story Gothic/Moorish house. The present gardens comprise 25 acres (10 hectares) of Jefferson's estate; they are quite sumptuous, and annuals keep the grounds in bloom the year round. Besides touring the gardens and house, there are boat rides on the lake, a cafe, and a B&B cottage, which makes a pleasant overnight stay before a leisurely journey back to The Big Easy. ❑

Map on pages 242–43

TIP

The Cajun motto translated as "Let the Good Times Roll!" certainly extends to local celebrations. For information about Cajun festivals, see *Travel Tips* and page 209 of this book.

BELOW: an actor created the semi-tropical Rip Van Winkle Gardens.

TOURING THE SWAMPS

A swamp tour is not merely a swamp tour: it can be ecological, educational, or just plain entertaining. Here's a first-hand report on five very different kinds of tours

Map on pages 242–43

N ew Orleans is an island in a vast wetlands that laps northward in varying stages of salt, brackish and fresh water marsh. For almost 300 years, people in the Crescent City have fought the Mississippi with levees, while simultaneously exploiting the delta's rich resources of food, fur and oil, as well as its natural convenience for water transportation. The water has also contributed to the city's tourism industry, particularly in boat excursions and sport fishing charters. More recently, environmental tourism has spawned a proliferation of swamp tours. Most tours focus on wildlife and wetland ecology; most tourists want to see alligators, and most times they do, especially in the hot months that dominate the southern Louisiana calendar.

Honey Island Swamp tour

A blanket of morning mist lifts off the West Pearl River, revealing a weathered dock jutting out into a primordial scene of steaming marsh grass and tropical foliage, disappearing into fog. **Crawford Landing** sits at the edge of Honey Island Swamp, near Slidell on the north shore of Lake Pontchartrain. It is a 45-minute drive northeast of New Orleans, but seems far, far removed from the city.

At 400 sq. miles (1,000 sq. km), **Honey Island Swamp ❿** is the second largest swamp in Louisiana. Around 70,000 acres (28,000 hectares) of the swamp are a protected wildlife area, making Honey Island one of the wildest and most pristine areas in the US. It is a fresh-water swamp named after the honey bees that once nested here, and is a 40-mile (64-km) long rectangular flood plain of the Pearl River, which defines the border between Louisiana and Mississippi. It is a place where alligators, snakes, feral hogs, otters, deer, raccoons, turtles, great egrets, blue herons, white ibis and many other creatures and birds abound.

A dozen butterflies dance in the air among a group of people gathering on the veranda of a neat cabin, headquarters of **Honey Island Swamp Tours**. We separate into two boats and disappear into the swamp, trusting the savvy of the khaki-suited guides, one of whom is Dr Paul Wagner.

Wagner, a wetland ecologist and environmental consultant who has lived all his life at the edge of the swamp, founded his tour operation in 1982. He is also the preserve manager in the **White Kitchen Natural Area**, a part of Honey Island Swamp considered to be the premier cypress-tupelo gum swamp in Louisiana. The area is named after an old gambling house, restaurant and bar that once thrived in the southwest corner of the swamp.

"At this time of year you're more likely to see deer and hogs than alligators," says Wagner, perhaps

PRECEDING PAGES: be a Cajun for a night, Wildlife Gardens B&B. **LEFT:** Joe Provost with friend. **BELOW:** vultures.

Honey Island Swamp is named for the bees that nested in the overhanging trees.

preparing everyone for a no-show by the star attraction. Alligators grow progressively dormant in the fall and winter, closeting themselves in the swamp's deeper reaches. "In the spring the swamp becomes like the Amazon again," he adds. Nevertheless, a 6-foot (2-meter) alligator is spotted on a mud bank, awash in sunlight that has threaded the canopy. The primeval creature lies rigid, relying on his natural camouflage for cover. "Alligators eat fish, frogs, turtles, snakes, dogs, but not people," says Wagner.

He then launches into his theory, that man-made levees have contributed greatly to the disappearance of 80 percent of the Mississippi delta's wetlands. "That's a pine ridge," he explains, pointing to a line of trees protruding above the gum, tupelo and cypress trees. Pine ridges form natural levees that allow the free flow of water over them in times of flood. This natural occurence is important to the life of a swamp because it assures the widespread deposit of sediments. "The Louisiana coast is a skeleton of what it used to be. This swamp is in good shape because it gets to flood."

Cypress knees

Defining the high-water mark is a perfectly level line on all the trees, making them seem as if they were painted dark below and silver-gray above. The bulbous mass at the base of cypress trees, called a buttress, is the swollen result of impregnating water. Dozens of gnarls, a foot or so long, called cypress knees, are aerial roots protruding from the murky water surrounding the tree. They could well be called cypress noses as they are believed to be a breathing apparatus. Cypress roots are resistant to disease and decay, and all of the trees in the swamp live in soaking water up to 95 percent of the year.

Retracing the path out of **Gum Bayou**, the canvas of the swamp reveals another layer: palmetto and black gum trees, swamp maples and live oaks draped in Spanish moss. The boat passes blue herons, white ibis, great egrets, a red-eared slider turtle sunning on a log, and a raccoon waiting for a handout. All manner of life is nourished by the rich soup of the swamp.

Wagner talks about growing up half Cajun, half German. But he is all swamp. The Walt Disney company consulted him, using Honey Island as a blueprint, for their "Model Swamp" exhibit at Walt Disney World. Wagner also scouted out the remote cabin used in the 1986 movie starring Tom Waits, *Down By Law*.

"People think it is dangerous to live or be in the swamp," says Wagner. "It's not. It's a lot more dangerous going out to get your morning paper in New Orleans." He expresses his preference for frogs' legs and crawfish, "... the two best things to eat in the swamp. Everything in the swamp eats crawfish. Even Yankees eat crawfish. They probably don't eat the heads like we do, but they eat 'em."

The boat turns into the 600-acre (240-hectare) White Kitchen Natural Area, which was purchased by the Nature Conservancy in 1988 and which Wagner presides over as the preserve steward. "This is about as pretty as it gets." he says.

Pretty indeed. The bayou starts out fairly wide, and several turtles, herons, egrets, and another alligator are spotted. The trees close in as the channel narrows into picture-book swamp. We pass a huge cypress tree over 500 years old. The trees give way to giant cut grass, and we stop at a dead end in a pond covered in lily pads, surrounded by an expanse of marsh grass. The view is punctuated by live oaks, silhouetted against the golden grass and blue sky like huge black cutouts.

Zipping back along the **Pearl River**, so named for the valuable pearls cultured in the river's fresh-water mussels, everyone's hair is blowing straight back in an exuberant style to fit the mood. At Crawford Landing one of the guests shakes the hand of Dr Wagner as he steps from the boat to the dock. "You did a great job," the visitor says. "And you didn't rush it."

Map on pages 242–43

A tour with Captain Turgeon

On a bright sunny morning, Captain Dave Fleming Turgeon edges his boat out of **Cochiara Marina**, where **Goose Bayou** joins Bayou Barataria on its course to the Gulf of Mexico. The confluence is the sight of the Cajun fishing village of **Jean Lafitte ⓫**, 23 miles (37 km) south of New Orleans, on Highway 45.

Captain Turgeon conducts two types of tours for up to eight people: one travels the bayous and marshes surrounding the islands of Jean Lafitte and Barataria, and the other journeys south to the barrier islands of Grand Isle and Grand Terre, where brown pelicans nest, shore birds abound and dolphins play in the Gulf of Mexico. Today, we are headed into the brackish marsh near to **Jean Lafitte National Historical Park** to learn a bit about the wetlands, the birds, and possibly spot an alligator or two braving the cool weather.

Turgeon begins with a lament over the proliferation of levees and canals. "The levees block the distributary waters like **Bayou Barataria**," he says. "The

BELOW: Honey Island's Dr Paul Wagner, ecologist and swamp guide.

Since trafficking in the plumes of herons (above) is prohibited, these birds – once hunted to the brink of extinction – thrive in the labyrinth of Louisiana's bayous.

BELOW: Turgeon Tours edges past Jean Lafitte National Park.

canals – usually leading to an oil pumping station – are cut as straight shots from point to point. They form unobstructed waterways that allow the tides to bring salt-water farther into the estuary, and change the character of the marsh. Natural channels, or bayous, have bends and snags in them which retard the encroachment of salt in the water. We are losing 25 square miles of good marsh a year."

A stately blue heron, over 3 feet (1-meter) tall, patient and solitary, grows nervous at our approach. The heron is a wary bird, with a long sharp beak that strikes fish and frogs like a rapier. Uttering a squawk, it rises, waving its 70-inch (178-cm) wingspan into a rhythm of effortless grace. Birds love Louisiana. They like the temperature, the canopy of cover, and the abundant food. For the migratory ducks and geese of the **Mississippi flyway**, this state is Grand Central Station. We come upon a 7-foot (2-meter) alligator, straddling an old piece of driftwood cypress. The reptile waits, appearing larger and larger in the camera lenses as we drift near. Splash! And lightning quick, the 'gator is gone.

Merging and meandering

The bayous merge and meander. The boat noses up to a wall of cypress trees reaching from their waterlogged roots into a web of twisted limbs and Spanish moss. Later, we slip under a long canopy of outstretched live oak limbs draped in fibrous moss. The light sprinkles down, shimmering off the black water like sparklers from a wand, creating a dazzling tunnel. After a few miles the channel widens and we pass a large weathered cypress, where a dozen or more black vultures perch, waiting for a meal to float by.

We pass by the town of Jean Lafitte. Everything in a Cajun's world seems to collect between his house and his dock, where his boat is moored. The boats are

TOUR INFORMATION

Below is a list of some of the main companies offering tours through Louisiana's swamps:
● **Honey Island Swamp Tours:** Dr Paul or Sue Wagner, Crawford Landing at West Pearl River, Slidell, LA 70461, tel: (504) 242-5877 (New Orleans), tel: (504) 641-1769 (Slidell). Hotel pick up: (504) 242-5877.
E-mail: swamp@cmq.com
● **Turgeon Tours and Charters:** Captain Dave Fleming Turgeon, Rt 1 Box 527-A, Lafitte, LA 70067, tel: 1 800-737-9267 or (504) 689-2911. Bus pick up: Commodore Transportation: (504) 328-4110.
Website: http://www.labirding.com
● **Cajun Man's Swamp Cruise:** Black Guidry, Hwy 90, Houma, LA 70360. Reservations: (504) 868-4625.
Website: http://www.cajunman.com
E-mail: rjguidry@cajunman.com
● **Wildlife Gardens:** Winter Gardens: Betty Provost; 5306 North Bayou Black Drive, Gibson, LA 70356. Reservations: tel: (504) 575-3676. Tours all year, closed Sun and Mon.
● **Creole Nature Trail:** Sabine National Wildlife Refuge, 3000 Holly Beach Highway, Hackberry, LA 70645, tel: (318) 762-3816. Website: http://www.fws.gov/~r4eao. E-mail: r4rw_la.sbn@fws.gov

predominantly spoon-stern Lafitte skiffs, elegant and fast fishing vessels aptly named for the town – and the legendary pirate, who presumably needed a very fast boat indeed. Interspersed along the bank are shrimp shacks and boatyards; in Lafitte everything happens on the water. In the words of Captain Turgeon "Lafitte was settled by the French, Haitians, Canary Islanders, English, Irish, and Spanish – the whole gumbo, in fact."

Map on pages 242–43

A Cajun Man's Swamp Cruise

Black Guidry, the Cajun Man, straddles an old weathered bench, playing Cajun tunes on his homemade accordion, while his trusty dog named Gator Bait howls a discordant harmony. Behind the two, Guidry's large pontoon boat waits on Bayou Black, a stretch of water cutting through an expanse of forest reaching out of the swamp. A **Cajun Man's Swamp Cruise** ⓬ departs from deep-water **Bayou Black** marina, a 90-minute drive from New Orleans, on Highway 90, 10 miles (16 km) west of the Tourist Information Center in **Houma**.

"I'm used to answering every question at least three times," Black says to the guests arriving for his down home-style swamp tour. "If I don't know the answer I'll make it up. You won't know the difference, and we'll all pass a good time."

Guidry slips the boat's mooring and launches into a Cajun banter. "All us Guidrys were kicked out of Nova Scotia by the English," he comments to a group of German tourists. "When I get an Englishman way out in the deepest part of the swamp, I slow down the boat, stare him in the eye and say 'Guess what? Do you English remember when you kicked us out of Nova Scotia?'" For added emphasis, he reminds everyone that the price of this tour is for one way only, not return. And, as if he needs to drive home the point even farther, our first

A bayou is a natural canal, the result of the overflowing of a river or the draining of a marsh. It has no current. A slough (pronounced slew) is a shallow, dead-end bayou. A pirogue (pronounced pee-roh) is a Cajun canoe.

BELOW: alligator in the sun, Bayou Barataria.

stop is in a little side bay where the long nose and intense eyes of a huge alligator pierce the green layer of floating duckweed. Guidry summons the alligator in a guttural call, "umph, umph, umph," while Gaiter Bait snarls and paces.

After stabbing a big chunk of chicken, Guidry holds the long, baited stick over the port side, about 3 feet (1 meter) off the water. The tranquil looking alligator suddenly thrusts through the surface, stretches half of its body clear of the water, then opens its jaws to display a jagged array of threatening teeth. Snapping its prey between huge molars, it slinks back into the water.

Consummate entertainer

Black Guidry is a consummate entertainer who couches a good deal of knowledge in his stories. He points to the strands of Spanish moss that proliferate on the bald cypress and live oak trees. The plant is mistakenly called moss and mistakenly thought to be a parasite. It is in fact an epiphyte, feeding from the air, not the tree. It was used as a substitute for straw in mud-building materials, and for bedding by the Indians and Acadian settlers. Dried moss was also used as a stuffing for upholstery – most notably in Model T car seats.

"We call those little yellow flowers, little yellow flowers," Guidry chortles, nosing the boat into a spongy bank fronting a carpet of bur marigold. Then, pulling out his Cajun accordion, its box made from an old cedar chest, its buttons from 44 caliber bullet caps, and its other parts from welder's rods, a bicycle sprocket, trophy blanks, chair glides, diaper pins and other household items, Guidry straps it on his shoulder with a man's belt, and launches into "Good-bye Joe, we gotta go, down the bayou." Gaiter Bait hits the deck howling, everyone laughs and sways to the music, and we all pass a good time.

ABOVE AND BELOW:
swamp scenes.
According to some
sources, man-made
levees along the
Mississippi River
have diminished
wetlands by up
to 80 percent.

Wildlife Gardens tour

Sitting on the porch of a cabin perched on pilings driven deep into the swamp, it is not hard to conjure up a Cajun's evening: listening to the sound of the swamp creatures after a hard day of fishing, hunting or trapping. In fact, anyone can do it: there are four bed-and-breakfast cabins at **Wildlife Gardens ⓲**, with rooms so close to the water you can feed a 'gator from the porch. Wildlife Gardens is a 33-acre (13-hectare) swamp park filled with native flora and fauna, located on Highway 90 near **Gibson**, 16 miles (26 km) west of the Tourist Information Center in Houma. Thirteen years ago, Betty Provost and her late husband James, converted their bird sanctuary hobby into a business. Since then, the inhabitants of Wildlife Gardens have multiplied into a collection of over 300 native birds and animals thriving in the fertile environment. Bobcats, nutria, red fox, wild boar, whitetailed deer, otters, owls, peacocks, pheasants, ducks and more ducks, geese, turtles and alligators coexist in the sanctuary.

"Tourists do not come to see peacocks or pheasants," says Betty Provost, over a hearty Cajun breakfast of coffee, orange juice, eggs, turkey ham, grits and biscuits. "They would ask. 'Do you have alligators?' When we said no, they left. So, we started the alligator farm."

Living with the alligators

Troy, a 13-ft (4-meter) alligator, languishes in an enclosed pond. Leaving the giant to his nap, Betty's son, Joe, grabs a 2-ft gator by its tail, slides his forearm under its belly and cradles its neck in his open palm. At the same instant, and with his other hand, he snaps the jaws closed, pointing out that alligators have no significant strength with which to open their jaws, but can develop up to 2,500 pounds (1,130 kg) of pressure when closing it.

Joe handles the big animals. He has been bitten by alligators, snapped by turtles and scratched by bobcats. Grasping a 110-pound (50-kg) alligator turtle by the shell and hoisting it out of the pond, he explains that it is important to grab the shell of the turtle right behind the head, out of range of the mouth. Alligator turtles grow to 300 pounds (135 kg) and have a closing jaw pressure of 1,500 pounds (680 kg).

Betty conducts the daily **walking tours** along a path that encounters all of the animals and birds. There's Leroy, the great horned owl, grounded because of an accident in his youth. There is a nutria named Newt, his grouchy character perhaps a reaction to the local view of these small beaver-like rodents, who are not natives and considered by some to be a nuisance. Bozo and Elsie, a wild boar couple, have their front hooves on the top rail of the fence as they root into the pail of mash that Joe has replenished. "Bozo doesn't know he's supposed to be a ferocious animal,"

Joe has picked up where his father left off; currently he is fashioning a small memorial island to James Provost. James was an accomplished carver, sculpting waterfowl from tupelo wood. Though not for sale, they grace the shelves in the gift shop. Wildlife Gardens includes an authentic trapper's cabin that has been converted into a **trapper's museum**. "Our generation will be the last to remember the trapping and

Map on pages 242–43

TIP

The rustic cabins at Wildlife Gardens have heat, air conditioning, clean sheets and good reading lamps. Rides in a Cajun canoe and twilight boat tours can also be arranged.

BELOW: Cajun man Black Guidry with dog Gaiter Bait.

No homemade sausages today – this café "broke" while being moved to a nearby location.

BELOW: white ibis, called "be-croche-crooked-beak" in Louisiana.

fishing era, so it is our duty to keep this memory alive in our children's minds," says Betty Provost. "Then we realized people loved the idea of staying in the cabin, so that's when we started the bed-and-breakfast."

Creole Nature Trail

"It broke," said the woman behind the counter at a Sweet Lake gas station. Referring to a Cajun restaurant on the **Creole Nature Trail** ⓮, she adds, "They were trying to move it." The building looks as if it had been picked up by a crane and dropped from a height of 20 ft (6 meters). With stomachs grumbling but humor intact, we continue the **driving tour** of the 100-mile (160-km) lap around **Calcasieu Lake** and its surrounding marshland.

The trail begins at **Sulphur**, 10 miles (16 km) west of Lake Charles, over three hours' drive west from New Orleans. Plunging south in a counter clockwise direction on Highway 27, the trail crosses the **Intracoastal Waterway**, runs through the town of **Hackberry** – the "Crab Capital of the South" – to the Sabine National Wildlife Refuge. Continuing south, the trail then turns due east onto Route 82 at **Holly Beach**, on the shores of the Gulf of Mexico. Dubbed the "Cajun Riviera," Holly Beach consists of a cluster of ramshackle camps and motels that hosts the annual **Cajun Riviera Festival** in the second week of August. The festival is, a beery, sun-drenched rodeo and carnival that features popular Cajun and zydeco bands. From Holly Beach continue east on Route 82 (the "Hug the Coast Highway") across **Calcasieu Pass** on a 50-car ferry, which runs every 20 minutes, 24 hours a day, to **Cameron**. At Our Lady Star of the Sea Church, in this fishing and petroleum industry town, there is a shrine to the 525 victims of Hurricane Audrey, which cut a swath of destruction through

Cameron Parish in 1957. East of Cameron, the trail forks left on Highway 27 to the town of **Creole**, where Highway 27 veers north toward the Gibbstown Bridge across the Intracoastal Waterway, forming the eastern leg of the trail. At the **Cameron Prairie Wildlife Refuge**, a 2-mile (3-km) drive yields good views of birds and alligators in the slough. At the crumpled remains of the Boudin Factory in Sweet Lake, the trail heads west on Highway 383 and then north on Highway 385 to **Lake Charles**. Accommodation and good food are available in both Sulpher and Lake Charles.

 Map on pages 242–43

Refuge for wildlife

The Creole Nature Trail is a magnificent trip through vast wetlands, highlighted by the **Sabine National Wildlife Refuge**, 125,000 acres (50,000 hectares) of salt and fresh-water marsh. In the fall, the refuge is full of migratory birds using the Mississippi flyway. In the hotter months alligators are on review. **Marsh Trail**, an elevated boardwalk, offers excellent views of the waterfowl and wildlife, and terminates at an observation tower. A pamphlet at the **Sabine Visitor's Center** lists 250 species of birds that have been observed, from the common moorhen to the rarely seen roseate spoonbill.

There is a sudden shock of pink on the left. Five, spooked, roseate spoonbills take flight against an overcast sky. They lift in a long sweeping arc, landing a few hundred yards away, their brilliant plumage set off by hundreds of dark-colored waterfowl in the gun-metal gray water. The spoonbill is a large, pink bird that was hunted relentlessly for its stunning plumage; in 1915, there were a mere 20 birds left in Cameron Parish. Numbers have increased, and although sightings are still rare, the prospect of seeing a shy spoonbill is exhilarating. ❏

BELOW: cypress trees and cypress knees along Bayou Black.

INSIGHT GUIDES

Travel Tips

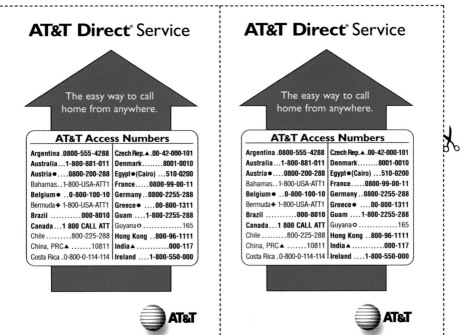

Global
connection
with the AT&T
Network

AT&T
direct
service

The best way to keep in touch when you're traveling overseas is with **AT&T Direct®** Service. It's the easy way to call your loved ones back home from just about anywhere in the world. Just cut out the wallet card below and use it wherever your travels take you.

For a list of AT&T Access Numbers, cut out the attached wallet guide.

AT&T

Israel 1-800-94-94-949	Portugal ▲ 800-800-128
Italy ● 172-1011	Saudi Arabia ▲ 1-800-10
Jamaica ● 1-800-USA-ATT1	Singapore 800-0111-111
Japan ● ▲ 005-39-111	South Africa 0800-99-0123
Korea , Republic ● ...0072-911	Spain 900-99-00-11
Mexico ▽ ● ..01-800-288-2872	Sweden..............020-799-111
Netherlands ● ..0800-022-9111	Switzerland ● 0800-89-0011
Neth.Ant. ▲⊕001-800-USA-ATT1	Taiwan 0080-10288-0
New Zealand ● 000-911	Thailand ⟨....001-999-111-11
Norway.............800-190-11	Turkey ● 00-800-12277
Panama 00-800-001-0109	U.A. Emirates ● 800-121
Philippines ● 105-11	U.K. 0800-89-0011
Poland ● ▲..00-800-111-1111	Venezuela 800-11-120

FOR EASY CALLING WORLDWIDE
1. Just dial the AT&T Access Number for the country you are calling from.
2. Dial the phone number you're calling. 3. Dial your card number*

For access numbers not listed ask any operator for **AT&T Direct®** Service.
In the U.S. call 1-800-222-0300 for **AT&T Direct** Service information.
Visit our Web site at: **www.att.com/traveler**
Bold-faced countries permit country-to-country calling outside the U.S.
- ● Public phones require coin or card deposit to place call.
- ✚ Public phones and select hotels.
- ▲ May not be available from every phone/payphone.
- ○ Collect calling only.
- ▽ Includes "Ladatel" public phones; if call does not complete, use 001-800-462-4240.
- ⊕ From St. Maarten or phones at Bobby's Marina, use 1-800-USA-ATT1.
- ⟨ When calling from public phones, use phones marked Lenso.
- * AT&T Calling Card, AT&T Corporate, AT&T Universal, MasterCard®, Diners Club®, American Express®, or Discover® cards accepted.

When placing an international call *from* the U.S., dial 1-800-CALL ATT.
WW   © 6/00 AT&T

Israel 1-800-94-94-949	Portugal ▲ 800-800-128
Italy ● 172-1011	Saudi Arabia ▲ 1-800-10
Jamaica ● 1-800-USA-ATT1	Singapore 800-0111-111
Japan ● ▲ 005-39-111	South Africa 0800-99-0123
Korea , Republic ● ...0072-911	Spain 900-99-00-11
Mexico ▽ ● ..01-800-288-2872	Sweden..............020-799-111
Netherlands ● ..0800-022-9111	Switzerland ● 0800-89-0011
Neth.Ant. ▲⊕001-800-USA-ATT1	Taiwan 0080-10288-0
New Zealand ● 000-911	Thailand ⟨....001-999-111-11
Norway.............800-190-11	Turkey ● 00-800-12277
Panama 00-800-001-0109	U.A. Emirates ● 800-121
Philippines ● 105-11	U.K. 0800-89-0011
Poland ● ▲..00-800-111-1111	Venezuela 800-11-120

FOR EASY CALLING WORLDWIDE
1. Just dial the AT&T Access Number for the country you are calling from.
2. Dial the phone number you're calling. 3. Dial your card number*

For access numbers not listed ask any operator for **AT&T Direct®** Service.
In the U.S. call 1-800-222-0300 for **AT&T Direct** Service information.
Visit our Web site at: **www.att.com/traveler**
Bold-faced countries permit country-to-country calling outside the U.S.
- ● Public phones require coin or card deposit to place call.
- ✚ Public phones and select hotels.
- ▲ May not be available from every phone/payphone.
- ○ Collect calling only.
- ▽ Includes "Ladatel" public phones; if call does not complete, use 001-800-462-4240.
- ⊕ From St. Maarten or phones at Bobby's Marina, use 1-800-USA-ATT1.
- ⟨ When calling from public phones, use phones marked Lenso.
- * AT&T Calling Card, AT&T Corporate, AT&T Universal, MasterCard®, Diners Club®, American Express®, or Discover® cards accepted.

When placing an international call *from* the U.S., dial 1-800-CALL ATT.
WW   © 6/00 AT&T

CONTENTS

Getting Acquainted

The Place

Population 1.2 million.
Language English, spoken in the speedy and guttural Southern accent. A form of French patois is spoken by a few in the city, but is more common in Cajun Country.
Religion Roman Catholic (60 percent), others (40 percent).
Time Zone Central Time Zone (GMT minus six hours).
Currency US dollar (US$).
Weights and Measures
The Imperial system is used throughout the US. Metric is rarely used. Below is an imperial/metric conversion chart.

1 inch = 2.54 centimeters
1 foot = 30.48 centimeters
1 mile = 1.609 kilometers
1 quart = 1.136 liters
1 ounce = 28.34 grams
1 pound = 0.453 kilograms
1 yard = 0.9144 meters
Electricity 110 volts.
Direct Dialing 1 (for the United States). The local dialing code is **504** – all telephone numbers in this book are preceded by this code, unless otherwise stated.

The Climate

The sultry, subtropical *City That Care Forgot* has an annual average temperature of 70°F (20°C). A profusion of blossoms bursts forth in mid-March with the arrival of the warm weather, which often lingers on through October. Ideal times to visit are early spring or fall, when the city is decked out with flowers and greenery.

The hottest months are June, July, and August. The mercury shoots up above 90°F (32°C) and remains there for weeks at a stretch. The humidity makes for a sticky atmosphere. Thunderstorms and lightning are frequent, and vanish as quickly as they appear. It is not unusual for the sun to shine brightly throughout a summer shower.

Hurricane season begins in June and extends through November. New Orleans, being so far inland, has rarely been hit with the full force of a hurricane, but high winds and torrential rains do occur.

Winters are far less predictable than the hot, sticky summers. December, for example, can be a balmy 85°F (30°C), but has been known to reach a chilly 35°F (2°C). As a general rule, January and February are the only months in which the weather is really cold. The temperature during these months rarely dips below 40°F (5°C), but the high humidity encourages a bitterly cold chill.

Government and Economy

New Orleans is governed by a mayor and a seven-member city council, all of whom are elected for a period of four years. Like many US oil-producing states, Louisiana in recent years suffered heavy losses in revenue; however, since 1988 there has been a slow but steady recovery. Louisiana handles over 60 percent of US offshore oil production, and New Orleans serves as the offshore administrative oil center. The Port of New Orleans and port-related activities represent a key industry for the New Orleans region. The New Orleans port area is the largest in the US in terms of total cargo tonnage handled. The economic impact of the port and maritime activities in the six-parish metropolitan New Orleans region is in excess of $3 billion.

Tourism is a $2 billion industry in New Orleans; Mardi Gras alone brings close to $500 million annually. With more than one million square feet of convention space and more than 25,000 hotel rooms, the city is ranked number six in the nation for conventions. As the largest city within 350 miles, New Orleans is a regional center for surrounding states. The addition of such shopping malls as the Jackson Brewery Corporation developments, Riverwalk, Canal Place, and the New Orleans Centre has established the city as a major shopping area.

Culture and Customs

The famous **jazz funerals** of New Orleans are still alive and well. In fact, there will probably be more of these remembrance services than usual in the years around the millennium, as veteran musicians reach the age where the Pearly Gates begin to beckon. What happens to the tradition after this generation has departed is anyone's guess – one social chronicler observes that the jazz fraternity has so widely embraced the talents of young, up-and-coming artists that the continuation of this tradition is practically ensured.

You may be lucky enough to witness a **brass marching band** while walking down the street. These bands tend to pop up out of nowhere and parade around town. A marching band usually picks up 'second-liners,' or parade followers, along the way. The term '**second-liners**' comes from jazz funerals, in which the 'second line' follows along behind the musicians, singing, dancing, and pumping parasols in the air in a joyous celebration of the release of the soul of the departed. Second-lining is as much a tradition in New Orleans as Mardi Gras and good food.

Planning the Trip

What to Bring

Whatever time of year you come to New Orleans, bring sunglasses and an umbrella; believe it or not, there will be instances when you'll need both on the same day. A small tote bag is useful for carrying brochures, maps, and so on. Mosquito repellent is useful in the summer months. Don't forget to bring plenty of good sunscreen and, of course, a camera and film.

Clothing

Street wear is quite casual, especially in the French Quarter where a standard summertime outfit for women is short shorts, a halter or tee-shirt, and sandals. Clothing in all but the finest restaurants is informal, although shorts and cutoffs cannot be worn in some establishments. Several of the more elegant restaurants require men to wear jackets and ties. Although cottons do not pack as well as synthetic fabrics, they are considerably cooler and more comfortable in the sticky daytime heat, and summer nights are also hot and sultry. Air-conditioning is widely used, so a light sweater or jacket may come in handy.

Winter weather is unpredictable; it is best to bring clothing that can be layered. A good bet is an all-weather coat that has a zip-out wool or pile lining. Even when the temperature hovers around 40°F, it seems much cooler due to the extreme humidity. The wind can be bitterly cold. Comfortable walking shoes are essential for maneuvering along the French Quarter's cracked sidewalks and flagstone passageways. Shoes with non-skid soles are recommended for river-boat rides; you may also want to tuck in a scarf and sweater to guard against river breezes.

Entry Regulations, Visas and Passports

A valid passport is required for citizens of Great Britain and Canada who are visiting the US for up to 90 days with a return ticket. Citizens of all other countries must have a valid passport, a visa, and a return or ongoing ticket.

Regulations at city gateways vary regarding transit stops, and a visa may be required for re-entry after a visit outside the US. Vaccinations are not required.

Customs Formalities

Aboard ship or on the airplane you will be given a Customs declaration form. Fill out the identification part (the upper portion) of the form and, upon arrival, present it to the Immigration and Customs Inspector. Visitors arriving by land borders must identify themselves during their oral declaration. All articles brought into the US, including gifts for other persons, must be declared to US Customs at the time you enter. If all the articles are entitled to free entry under the exemptions allowed, you need not fill in the reverse side of the declaration form. Instead, you should declare them orally to the Customs Inspector. (If an inspector deems it necessary, you may be required to make a written declaration.

Visitors to the US are allowed to bring into the country items of a personal nature, plus 200 cigarettes or 100 cigars or 3 pounds (1.3 kg) of smoking tobacco (or proportionate amounts of each), and vehicles (e.g. automobiles, trailers, airplanes, motorcycles, and boats) for personal use if imported in connection with your arrival. Adult nonresidents may also bring in 1 liter (33.8 fl. oz.) of alcoholic beverage. The state of Louisiana has a lengthy list of restrictions on liquor imported from other states. In addition to the above restrictions, articles up to US$50 in total value for use as bona fide gifts to other persons may be brought in free of duty and tax, if you will be in the US for at least 72 hours and have not claimed this gift exemption in the past six months. You may include in this exemption up to 100 cigars. There is no limit on the amount of money (US or foreign currency), travelers checks, money orders, or negotiable instruments in bearer form that you may bring into, or take out of the US. However, a report must be filed with US Customs at the time of arrival or departure for amounts that exceed $10,000 or the equivalent in foreign currency. A form will be provided for this purpose.

The import of illegal drugs is a very serious offense.

Medical Alert

If you require medicine that contains habit-forming drugs, carry only the quantity normally needed and make sure it is properly identified. You should also have a prescription or written statement from your physician stating the medicine is necessary for your condition.

Certain items are expected to meet set specifications, require a license or permit, or may be prohibited entry. Among these are fruit, plants and endangered plant species, vegetables and their products; firearms and ammunition if not intended for legitimate hunting or lawful sporting purposes; hazardous articles (fireworks, dangerous toys, toxic or poisonous substances); lottery tickets; meats, poultry and their products (e.g. sausage and pâté); pets; pornographic articles and publications; switchblade knives; certain trademarked items (cameras, watches, perfumes, musical instruments, jewelry, and metal flatware); vehicles and motorcycles not equipped to comply with US safety or clean air emission standards; wildlife and endangered species, including any part or product of the animal (e.g. articles from made reptile skins, whalebone or ivory, mounted specimens and trophies, and feathers or skins of wild birds).

Extending your Stay
For recorded instructions regarding visas, contact the Immigration and Naturalization Service in New Orleans, tel: 589 6533. Applications must be made to the INS Southern Regional Service Center, P.O. Box 568808, Dallas, TX 75356-8808.

Animal Quarantine
All importations are subject to health, quarantine, agriculture, wildlife, and customs requirements and prohibitions. Pets taken out of the US and returned are subject to the same requirements as those entering for the first time. Pets excluded from entry into the US must be exported or else put down. The US Public Health Service requires that pets – particularly dogs, cats, and turtles – brought into the country be examined at the first port of entry for possible evidence of disease that can be transmitted to humans. Wild or domestic animals and birds must be free from contagious diseases.

The Animal Welfare Act requires that all birds and animals must be imported under humane, healthy conditions. Every imported pet container must be plainly marked, labeled or tagged on the outside with the names and addresses of the shipper and consignee, along with an accurate invoice statement specifying the number of each species contained in the shipment. Since the hours of service and availability of Customs inspectors vary from port to port, visitors who plan to bring animals or birds into the country are strongly advised to check with their anticipated port of arrival prior to importing a pet or other animal. Information from:
US Public Health Service
Center for Disease Control
Division of Quarantine
Atlanta, Georgia 30333
Tel: (404) 329 2574

Animal and Plant Health Inspection Service
US Department of Agriculture
Hyattsville, Maryland 20782
Tel: (301) 436 7786

Health

American medical services are extremely expensive. Always travel with comprehensive travel insurance to cover all emergencies.

Summers in New Orleans are very hot. Visitors should ensure they bring plenty of sunscreen to protect the skin against the sun.

Money

American visitors Most hotels, restaurants, and shops accept major credit cards (American Express, Diners Club, MasterCard, Visa, and En Route). Rather than carrying large amounts of cash around the city, it is better to withdraw small sums of money from local banks or ATMs (automatic teller machines) every couple of days. A small charge is made for these transactions. Travelers checks are widely accepted, although you may have to provide proof of identification when cashing the checks at banks. (This is not required by most stores.)
Overseas visitors: The best rates of exchange for travelers checks are in banks, which are open Monday–Friday 9am–3 or 4pm. Again, take your passport along for identification purposes. Foreign exchange offices include **Whitney Bank** (228 St Charles Ave, tel: 586 7272, and several branch locations, including **New Orleans International Airport**, tel: 838 6492). Whitney 24-hour information line, tel: 838 4450.

Reservations

Anyone who plans to visit during Mardi Gras or other events such as the Jazz Fest or Sugar Bowl, should make hotel and even restaurant reservations about a year in advance. The busiest months in the city are between September and May. During the summer, many

Public Holidays

New Year's Day
Martin Luther King Day (January)
Inauguration Day (third Monday in January, every four years)
Mardi Gras Day (February or March)
Presidents' Day (February)
Good Friday
Memorial Day (last Monday in May)
Independence Day (July 4)
Labor Day (first Monday in September)
Columbus Day (second Monday in October)
All Saints' Day (November 1)
Veterans' Day (November 11)
Thanksgiving (fourth Thursday in November)
Christmas Day

Banks and most offices are closed on public holidays.

hotels offer special incentives (i.e. slashed prices and attractive packages) to encourage visitors to come. During this slow period, it is often possible to be seated in a good restaurant without a reservation – impossibile during the popular months of the year.

Getting There

By Air
New Orleans has two airports. The largest is **New Orleans International Airport** (also called **Moisant Field**). It is located roughly 15 miles west of the city and is served by AeroMexico, American, Continental, Delta, Lacsa, Northwest, Piedmont, Sasha, Southwest, Taca, TWA, United, and USAir. **Lakefront Airport** in the eastern part of town is used by small, local private and corporate planes.

By Sea
Celebrated in song and legend, the mighty Mississippi River is the scenic route to the city. The *Delta Queen* and her younger, larger sisters, the *Mississippi Queen* and the *American Queen*, all make the

trip downriver from Cincinnati, Pittsburgh, St Louis, and other northerly ports. All three boats are outfitted in nostalgic 19th-century style, and the sentimental journeys feature plenty of banjos, mint juleps and Dixieland bands. A wide variety of theme cruises are offered, including the annual Great Steamboat Race from New Orleans to St Louis in which the siblings recreate the famed 19th-century race between the *Natchez* and the *Robert E. Lee*.

For details, contact the **Delta Queen Steamboat**, 30 Robin Street Wharf, New Orleans, LA 70130, tel: toll-free (800) 543 1949, email: www.deltaqueen.com. This steamboat company – America's oldest – offers a range of packages that includes hotel stopovers in several city ports. Do note that steamboating down the Mississippi is neither swift nor inexpensive.

The nation's first luxury riverbarge, the *River Explorer*, is a recent addition to the Mississippi, making trips from New Orleans into the heartlands of Louisiana. Designed as a resort hotel and a touring vehicle, the vessel is comprised of two riverbarges propelled by a 3,000-ton towboat. For more information contact **River Barge Excursion Lines** at 201 Opelousas Ave. New Orleans, LA 70114, tel: 365 0022 or (888) 781 4158, fax: 362-6531, email: rel@riverbarge.com.

Two cruise lines operate out of New Orleans. The *Celebration*, one of the 'Fun Ships' of **Carnival Cruise Lines** (1031 Fern St, New Orleans, LA 70118, tel: 865 7260, (800) 327 7276; fax: 862 0190, www.carnival.com) sails every Sunday for a seven-day cruise to Jamaica, Grand Cayman, and Cozumel. The *Enchanted Isle* of **Commodore Cruise Line** (940 Royal St. New Orleans, LA 70116, tel: 367 9443, (800) 545 5609; fax: 367 8488, email: www.commodorecruise.com), embarks every Saturday on a seven-day cruise to the Western Caribbean and Mexico.

By Rail

New Orleans is served by Amtrak trains, connecting the city with Los Angeles, Chicago, New York, Miami and Washington DC among others. **Union Passenger Terminal** in the Central Business District is the arrival and departure point. For information, tel: (toll-free) (800) USA RAIL.

By Road

Union Passenger Terminal is also the station for national bus services. For further information, contact **Greyhound/Trailways**, tel: 525 6075 in New Orleans, (800) 231 2222, nationwide.

For those arriving by car, the major east-west artery is **Interstate 10 (I-10)**, which strings across the southern US from Florida to California and through downtown New Orleans. **Interstate 55 (I-55)** is a north-south highway that connects with I-10 just west of the city. Other major routes into town are **US 90** and **US 61**.

To drive in Louisiana, you must have a current driving license (an international license is not required), a vehicle registration document, and proof of automobile insurance. Non-citizens must also have a valid passport.

Special Information

Traveling with Children

Children love New Orleans. As well as its many appealing attractions (*see page 189*), the Children's Corner at Le Petit Théâtre du Vieux Carré presents children's productions during the season.

Apart from its more exotic aspects, Mardi Gras is a festival that is made for kids. In fact, it is a family event for locals. The entire clan is roped into planning and making costumes and family picnics along the parade routes are festive occasions. As the parades pass, parents hoist kids onto their shoulders for a better chance of grabbing the 'throws' tossed enthusiastically from the floats.

In addition to the attractions, the Greater New Orleans Tourist and Convention Commission publishes a special coloring book. The book, *New Orleans for Kids*, is available at the New Orleans Welcome Center in Jackson Square.

Gay Travelers

New Orleans' flamboyant gay population is centered largely in the lower French Quarter. Gay Pride Day (June), Pride Fest (fall) and Halloween (October) are celebrated with great panache, as participants parade around in eye-popping attire. Mardi Gras also looms large on the social calendar, centered around the 'adult Mardi Gras' in the French Quarter, and the gay Mystic Krewe of Barkus. On Fat Tuesday, the annual competition for best costume – held at St Anne and Burgundy streets – is one of the most popular events of Carnival. If you're in the vicinity and spot a man all dolled up like a Las Vegas showgirl, surrounded by an entourage, follow him to the nearest parade and be prepared.

For information on gay lodging, nightlife and activities go to: www.neworleans.com/rainbow

Senior Travelers

The **American Association of Retired Persons** (1909 K St NW, Washington, DC 20049, tel: (202) 662 4850) offers its members discounts on air fares, hotels, car rentals, and sightseeing attractions, as well as the AARP Motoring Plan. Members, who must be age 50 and over, pay a small annual fee.

The organization **Mature Outlook** (6001 N. Clark St, Chicago, IL 60660, tel: (800) 336 6330) also offers accommodation discounts as well as a bimonthly newsletter. On-the-spot membership is available at participating Holiday Inns. Mature Outlook is a subsidiary of Sears Roebuck & Co.

Saga International Holidays (120 Boylston St, Boston, MA 02116, tel: (800) 343 0273), an agency specializing in tours for people age 60 and over, offers a selection of package tours.

Student Travelers

The **Council on International Educational Exchange** (CIEE, 205 E. 42nd St, New York, NY 10017, tel: (212) 661 1414) issues an International Student Identity Card (ISIC) to full-time students, entitling the bearer to reduced fares on transportation, discounts at museums, theaters and sports events, student charter flights, and other reductions. The ISIC is available in Canada for $10 on application to the Association of Student Councils, 187 College St, Toronto, Ont, M5T 1P7.

Council Travel is a US student travel agency offering low-cost charter flights and tours. For information about the agency, contact the CIEE headquarters in New York.

The **Federation of International Youth Travel Organizations** (81 Islands Brugge, DK-2300 Copenhagen S, Denmark) offers the Youth International Educational Exchange Card (YIEE) to travelers under 26. The benefits are similar to those of the ISIC. It is available from the CIEE (*see above*); in Canada, from the Canadian Hostelling Association (333 River Rd, Vanier, Ottawa, Ont. KIL 8H9, tel: (613) 476 3844).

The **Educational Travel Center** (438 N. Frances St, Madison, WI 53703, tel: (608) 256 5551) is a student travel agency specializing in fares, bookings, and tours.

Disabled Travelers

The organization called **Mobility International USA** (Box 3551, Eugene, OR 97403, tel: (503) 343 1284) coordinates exchange programs for disabled people and provides useful information.

The **Information Center for Individuals with Disabilities** (Ft Point Place, 27–43 Wormwood St, Boston, MA 02210, tel: (617) 727 5540) holds a list of travel agents who deal in specialized tours.

Travel Industry and Disabled Exchange (5435 Donna Ave, Tarzana, CA 91356, tel: (818) 368 5648) publishes a newsletter and directory of specialized travel agents.

The **Society for the Advancement of Travel for the Handicapped** (26 Court St, Brooklyn, NY 11242, tel: (718) 858 5483) issues free-of-charge access guides written especially for disabled travelers.

Consulates

Britain: 321 St Charles Ave, tel: 524 4180.
Finland: 1100 Poydras St, tel: 523 6451.
France: 3305 St Charles Ave, tel: 897 6387.
Germany: 225 Baronne St, tel: 569 4289.
Italy: 630 Camp St, tel: 524-2271.
Netherlands: 643 Magazine St, tel: 596 2838.
Spain: World Trade Center, tel: 525 4951.
Sweden: 2640 Canal St, tel: 827 8600.

Tourist Offices

The **New Orleans Metropolitan Convention & Visitors Bureau** is in the Superdome (1520 Sugar Bowl Drive, New Orleans, LA 70112, tel: 566 5011, toll-free: (800) 672 6124, fax: 566 5021, email: www.neworleansvb.com.

The **New Orleans Welcome Center**, 529 St Ann St, in Jackson Square, which provides free maps, brochures, and advice, is operated by the tourist commission. There

is a desk at New Orleans International Airport, located by the customs desk, and also a tourist kiosk on N. Peters Street next to the Hard Rock Café.

Lafayette Convention & Visitors Bureau (1400 N.W. Evangeline Thruway, tel: (318) 232 3808 or 800/346-1958; fax: (318) 232 0161, is a good place for obtaining information about Cajun Country.

Practical Tips

Business Hours

Offices, as a rule, are open Monday–Friday 8 or 8.30am–5 or 5.30pm. Some are open on Saturday until noon. Banking hours are Monday–Friday 9am–3 or 4pm. In general, shops in the Central Business District open Monday–Saturday from 9.30 or 10am–5.30 or 6pm, but many of the mall shops stay open until 9 or 10pm. Opening and closing hours of French Quarter shops are whimsical, depending on how business is doing; some but not all are open on Sunday.

Opening hours for museums and art galleries vary greatly, depending on the premises and the season. It is best to check in advance the exact hours of those you wish to visit, but some of these, too, are open on Sundays.

Porter Services

Porters (called 'Skycaps') are readily available in the baggage claim area at New Orleans International Airport. If given your baggage receipt and a description of your suitcases, a porter will retrieve your luggage from the carousel and deliver it to the ground transportation area. Porters are also available at Union Passenger Terminal. All of the larger hotels have bellmen, but in many of the small, family-run guest houses, you may be responsible for getting your luggage from lobby to guestroom.

Tipping

Restaurants in New Orleans do not include a service charge in the bill. Note that it is customary to leave a 15–20 percent tip if the service has been satisfactory. The porters at the airport and the bus terminals are tipped per bag, as are the bellmen at hotels. The hotel maid should receive a tip based on the number of nights stayed at the hotel. The hotel doorman who calls a cab for you is also tipped a modest sum. Cab drivers expect a 10–15 percent tip.

Religious Services

Baptist Churches
First Baptist Church
4301 St Charles Ave,
tel: 895 8632
Lakeview Baptist Church
6100 Canal Blvd, tel: 482 3109
St Charles Avenue Baptist Church
7100 St Charles Ave, tel: 861 9514

Catholic Churches
St Louis Cathedral
Jackson Square, tel: 525 9585
St Patrick's Church
724 Camp St, tel: 525 4413
Our Lady of Guadalupe, 411
N. Rampart St, tel: 525 1551
Holy Name of Jesus
Loyola Campus, 6367 St Charles
Ave, tel: 865 2776
Jesuit Church of Immaculate Conception
130 Baronne St, tel: 529 1477

Episcopal Churches
Christ Church Cathedral
2919 St Charles Ave, tel: 895 6602
Grace Episcopal Church
3700 Canal St, tel: 482 5242
St George's Episcopal Church
4600 St Charles Ave, tel: 899 2811

Lutheran Churches
Grace Lutheran Church
5800 Canal Blvd, tel: 482 4994
Zion Lutheran Church
1924 St Charles Ave, tel: 524 1025

Methodist Churches
First United Methodist Church
3401 Canal St, tel: 488 0856
Rayne Memorial United Methodist Church
3900 St Charles Ave, tel: 899 3431
Wesley United Methodist Church
2517 Jackson Ave, tel: 524 8270

Presbyterian Churches
Covenant Presbyterian Church
4422 St Charles Ave, tel: 899 2481
St Charles Avenue Presbyterian Church
1545 State St, tel: 897 0101

Media

The city's only daily newspaper is the *Times-Picayune*. On Friday, the newspaper's 'Lagniappe' tabloid section carries information about weekend entertainment, as well as cultural and sporting events. *Gambit* is a free weekly newspaper, available in supermarkets and many bookstores, that provides listings of the local entertainment, notably the music clubs.

News to Go

The city's largest newsstand is Lenny's at 622 South Carrollton and 5420 Magazine Street, which is well-stocked with a good range of magazines and out-of-town newspapers. In the French Quarter, try Sidney's at 917 Decatur Street or the Matassas Grocery, 1001 Dauphine Street.

The well-written and glossy *New Orleans* magazine is a monthly publication that focuses on local stories, and also carries calendar listings of events. *Vignette*, a beautifully illustrated magazine, is published twice annually and is sold in many bookstores. Its interesting features focus on local history, lore, and entertainment. *Offbeat* is a free weekly magazine that is devoted exclusively to the local music scene. *GO*, *Where*, and *This Week in New Orleans* are all free publications aimed at the tourist. They are usually available in most hotels.

Most major hotels have TVs that show the Tourist Channel, which broadcasts packaged snippets about the city's history, nightlife, restaurants, and attractions.

The local television network affiliates are WWL (CBS, Channel 4), Fox (Channel 8); WDSU (NBC,

Channel 6), and ABC (Channel 26). Most of the major hotels and some of the guest houses can offer cable service.

Postal Services

The **Postal Answer Line** (tel: 589 1360) provides 24-hour recorded information about all US Postal Service facilities in the city. The Answer Line can be accessed from a Touch Tone phone.

The main branch of the US Postal Service is at 701 Loyola Avenue (tel: 589 1112). Windows are open Monday–Friday 9am–4.30pm, and Saturday 8am–1pm. Branch offices (which are closed on Saturday) include those at the World Trade Center (tel: 524 0033), the Vieux Carré (1022 Iberville St, tel: 524 0072), the Carrollton Station (3400 S. Carrollton Ave, tel: 484 6473), and the New Orleans International Aiport (tel: 589 1294). The French Quarter Postal Emporium (940 Royal St, tel: 525 6651) provides stamps, package-mailing, and other services at slightly higher prices.

Phones and Faxes

Public pay telephones can be found on the streets, as well as in bars. Listen for a dial tone, deposit coins, and dial the desired number. There is no charge for dialing **911**, the emergency number.

Western Union has a toll-free number – (800) 325 6000 – for sending mailgrams, telegrams, or cablegrams. Their toll-free number for telexes is (800) 527 5184. There are several Western Union stations where you can pick up or send money or messages, among them 334 Carondelet St, 2131 Canal St, 5500 Prytania St, and Royal Street A&P, 701 Royal St.

Kinko's Copies (762 St Charles Ave, tel: 581 2541) offers 24-hour facsimile services. American Express (158 Baronne St, tel: 586 8201) and the French Quarter Postal Emporium (940 Royal St, tel: 525 6651) also provide a speedy fax service.

Emergencies

Security and Crime

Pickpockets are at work while others play during major events such as Mardi Gras. It is unwise at any time to carry cash or to wear flashy, expensive jewelry. Always carry travelers checks. Don't leave money or valuables unattended in your hotel room; put them in the hotel's safety deposit box. Be sure to lock your car, with any luggage or valuables stashed out of sight. Avoid wandering alone on dark, deserted streets; stick to well-lit, areas. Do not walk through Armstrong Park, the Irish Channel or New Orleans' above-ground cemeteries when alone, even in daylight hours.

Loss of Belongings

If you think you've left belongings on a bus or streetcar, contact the Regional Transit Authority Lost and Found, 101 Dauphine St, tel: 569 2625. Otherwise, contact the police tel: 821 2222.

Medical Services

For emergency **ambulance** services, dial **911**. City **hospitals** with 24-hour emergency departments include the Tulane Medical Center (1415 Tulane Ave, tel: 588 5711) and Touro Infirmary (1401 Foucher, tel: 897 8250).

Pharmacies with branches lthroughout the city are Walgreen's, Rite-Aid, and Eckerd. Several local pharmacies are open 24 hours, among them Rite-Aid (3401 St Charles Ave, tel: 895 0344), both branches of Walgreen's (3311 Canal St, tel: 833 8073, and 3057 Gentilly Blvd, tel: 282 2621) and Eckerd store at 3400 Canal St (tel: 488 6661). There are Walgreen's stores in the CBD (900 Canal St, tel: 523 7201) and in the French Quarter (134 Royal St, tel: 522 2736), but the Royal store has no prescription service. In the CBD, there is a Rite-Aid at Lee Circle.

The **Aids Hotline** (929 Bourbon St, tel: 522 2437) provides counseling and assistance.

Getting Around

The heart and soul of New Orleans is the **French Quarter**, which was the original colony founded by French Creoles in 1718. Laid out in a perfect grid, the Quarter encompasses about a square mile and is bordered by Esplanade Avenue, the Mississippi River, and Canal and North Rampart Streets. Strung alongside the Mississippi, downriver of Esplanade Avenue, are the residential suburbs of **Faubourg Marigny, Bywater**, and **Arabi**. Six miles downriver lies **Chalmette Battlefield**, site of the 1815 Battle of New Orleans.

On the upriver side of the Quarter, the **Central Business District** (**CBD**) lies between the Mississippi River, Poydras Street, Howard Avenue, and Loyola Avenue. The **Warehouse District**, nestled in the Central Business District, is a residential and cultural center that is changing all the time.

St Charles Avenue, which stretches upriver from the Central Business District to the lovely **Garden District**, is known for stately and palatial mansions and splendid gardens, as well as some fine hotels, guest houses, and restaurants. Between the Garden District and the River, roughly within Howard Ave, Magazine St, Louisiana Ave, and the river, is the **Irish Channel**, a run-down neighborhood that is struggling for revitalization.

The **Uptown** area, beyond the Garden District, includes Audubon Park, Audubon Zoo and the University Section, home of Loyola and Tulane universities. **Mid-City** is a predominantly residential area that stretches from the Central Business District and the French Quarter to Lake Pontchartrain, City

Park, and the Fair Grounds. Several notable restaurants are located in the Mid-City area.

Lake Pontchartrain cuts a blue 40-mile swath across the northern border of the city. **West End Park**, at the western end of Lakeshore Drive, is home to yacht clubs, marinas, and outstanding seafood restaurants. On the north shore of Lake Pontchartrain are the pine woods and quiet towns of **St Tammany Parish**, one of the four parishes comprising the greater metropolitan area.

Algiers, due east of the French Quarter and across the river, on the **West Bank**, is an old, largely residential part of town. To the west of the city proper is **Jefferson Parish**, a vast area which was once sugar plantations. **Metairie**, an old suburb that occupies a large chunk of Jefferson Parish, has many good seafood restaurants. **Kenner**, home of New Orleans' only international airport, is also in Jefferson Parish, as is Jefferson Downs Race Track.

Recommended Maps

The Greater New Orleans Metropolitan Convention & Visitors Bureau publishes excellent self-guided walking and driving tour maps, available free at the New Orleans Welcome Center, 529 St Ann Street. Maps of the city produced commercially are available in most bookstores.

Orientation

First-time visitors often find New Orleans disorientating, as the terms 'north,' 'south,' 'east,' and 'west' mean very little in the Crescent City. (The meandering Mississippi wreaks havoc with such mundane designations.) Instead, directions are defined by the waterways: *riverside* is toward the Mississippi; *lakeside* toward Lake Pontchartrain; *downriver* is downtown; and *upriver* is uptown. As an example, the landmark bar called the Napoleon House is located on the downtown, riverside corner of Chartres Street.

From the Airport

The fastest way to reach the down-town area from the airport is by **taxi**. The fare is under $25 for one or two people, plus a sum for each additional passenger. The trip takes 20–30 minutes. The 14-passenger vans of the **Airport Shuttle** cost roughly $8 per person, one way. The vans drop passengers off at all hotels and guest houses; the length of the trip depends on whether your hotel is one of the first or the last along the route. **Express buses** are very reasonably priced and run between the airport and Elk Place in the Central Business District. The trip can take from 45 minutes to more than an hour.

Complaints

Streetcars and buses: Complaints about buses or streetcars should be made directly to the Regional Transit Authority, 101 Dauphine St, tel: 569 2625.
Taxis: To make a complaint about a taxi driver or service, contact the Taxicab Bureau, City Hall, tel: 565 6272.

Public Transportation

By Bus and Streetcar

The Regional Transport Authority (RTA) operates the city's buses and streetcars. Exact fare is required in all cases. Transfers cost a few cents extra, on top of the normal fare. For 24-hour information about the transit system, call the **RideLine** (tel: 242 2600). The RTA produces an excellent color-coded map of the bus and streetcar routes which is available free at the New Orleans Welcome Center in Jackson Square. One- and three-day VisiTour passes, allowing unlimited rides on buses and streetcars, are available from hotels and shopping areas.

By Ferry

A ferry which carries vehicles and pedestrians runs from Canal Street Wharf to Algiers on the West Bank every 20–30 minutes. There is no charge to Algiers, but there is a small fee for the return trip.

Private Transportation

By Car

Outlets for many of the car rental agencies can be found at the airport as well as in the Central Business District. Listed below are telephone numbers for some reputable agencies.

Avis
2024 Canal St
Tel: 523 4317 or (800) 331 1212
Budget
1317 Canal St
Tel: 467 2277 or (800) 527 0700
Thrifty
740 Baronne St
Tel: 523 0850 or (800) 367 2277
Hertz
901 Convention Center Blvd
Tel: 568 1645 or (800) 654 3131
National
324 S. Rampart St
Tel: 525 0416 or (800) 227 7368

Anyone planning to rent a car should note that driving, and especially parking, in the French Quarter is not an easy task. Streets are narrow and often congested; cars parked illegally are towed away swiftly, and it is an expensive to-do to retrieve them. There is a $100 fine for blocking a parade route during Mardi Gras.

While a car is useful to have for weekend excursions, you may find it convenient to leave it in a secured parking lot and forget about it until you need it.

On Foot

The French Quarter is easily (and best) explored on foot. The Garden District and much of the Central Business District are also easy to walk around. Apart from these areas, New Orleans is not a 'walking city.'

Hitchhiking

Hitchhiking is illegal in the state of Louisiana.

On Departure

Your hotel or guest house can make arrangements for taxi or shuttle transportation to the airport.

The cheapest (and slowest) way to get to the airport is to catch an express bus at the corner of Tulane Avenue and Elk Place.

Taxis

Taxis are reasonably priced in New Orleans. Some drivers are loquacious and charming, story-telling a mile a minute and sometimes even knocking a dollar or two off the fare if they find the passenger suitably entertaining. Taxis cruise the Riverwalk and French Quarter areas fairly regularly; it's not usually a problem finding a cab unless you're in a hurry or it's raining. The *Yellow Pages* carries a list of taxi firms if you prefer to book by phone, but be prepared to wait: the easy-going way of life for which the city is famous seems to be particularly prominent in cab firms, and there is no specific firm we can – hand on heart – recommend. Despite honey-drawled assurances that a ride is on its way, cabs are often very late, or never show up at all. If you plan to take many long-distance journeys, it's a good idea to strike up a relationship with a firm, or even better, a particular driver early on in your trip, and ask for a business card. Tip handsomely and they'll remember you when you come to book again.

Where to Stay

Choosing Accommodation

New Orleans offers a wide range of accommodation, from small, antique-filled guest houses to high-tech convention hotels complete with restaurants, bars, and health clubs. Local hotels are frequently part of a chain, and tend to be large, rather formal establishments favored by business travelers. Guest houses are smaller, often family-run, with fewer amenities but a cozier ambiance. Unless otherwise stated, hotels and guest houses have swimming pools and air-conditioning, and many have lush, subtropical courtyards.

The Americans with Disabilities Act requires that public buildings provide facilities for the disabled. *Federal law also requires that hotels set aside rooms for non-smokers, so be sure to specify at the time of booking.* All major hotels are in compliance with this act, except for facilities built in the 19th century or earlier (such as the majority of bed-and-breakfasts and guest houses), which were exempt from the laws at press time.

The greatest concentration of hotels and guest houses is in the French Quarter and the Central Business District.

Reservations

It is relatively easy to find accommodation in New Orleans during June, July, and August. However, New Orleans is a major convention city, so between the months of September and May, hotels in the French Quarter and Central Business District may be fully booked.

For events such as Mardi Gras and the Jazz Fest, reservations should be made up to a year in advance, and almost all hotels and guest houses require a three- to five-day minimum stay. Virtually all establishments raise their prices during these events. It is wise to check the cancellation policy at the time of reservation. Many hotels offer attractive package deals for stays during these events – be sure to ask your travel agent or hotel when booking. Almost all hotels and guest houses accept major credit cards, but this, too, should be ascertained in advance.

The following selection of accommodation is divided into hotels and motels, guest houses, and bed and breakfast. Within these divisions they are are categorized by price range (*see Price Guide, right*). However, note that several hotels have moderate rooms as well as deluxe suites. The chains (Hilton, Marriott, and Sheraton) are rather expensive, but frequently offer discounted rates that are very attractive to visitors.

Reservation Services

Accommodations Express is a nationwide hotel reservations service catering for individuals as well as groups. The service can often offer discounted rates for New Orleans hotels. Contact them at 801 Asbury Ave, Ocean City, NJ 08226-3625, tel: (609) 525 0800 or (800) 837 3822, fax: (609) 525 0111, email: www.accommodationsexpress.com

Room Finders USA (1112 N. Rampart St, New Orleans, LA 70116, tel: 522 9234 or (800) 478 7829, fax: 529 1948, email: www.roomfinders.com) has listings of hotels in all categories in the New Orleans metropolitan area.

Hotels and Motels

Deluxe
Bourbon Orleans
717 Orleans St, New Orleans, LA 70116
Tel: 523 2222 or (800) 521 5338
Fax: 525 8611
Email: www.bourbonorleans.com

Queen Anne furnishings and marble baths with phones and mini-TVs are among the amenities in this French Quarter hotel, which is built around an outdoor courtyard where cabanas encircle the pool. There are rooms with balconies overlooking Bourbon Street, but it is quieter on the courtyard side. The premier banquet room is the restored Quadroon Ballroom, which dates from the 19th century (the hotel itself was built in the 1970s). Crystal chandeliers shine over the white marble lobby, where armchairs and settees are well placed in conversational groupings. The hotel has a restaurant and lounge.
AE, D, DC, MC, V. **$$$$**

Chateau Sonesta
800 Iberville St, New Orleans, LA 70112-3143
Tel: 586 0800 or (800) SONESTA
Fax: 586 1987
Email: www.sonestano.com
In a landmark building that once housed the D.H. Holmes department store, this hotel is situated between Canal Street and the French Quarter – an ideal Mardi Gras location. The irregularly-shaped rooms are quite large, sometimes with huge windows or balconies overlooking Bourbon Street. Each room has a minibar, hair drier, and phone with voice mail and dataport. The hotel is built around two courtyards, one of which has an outdoor pool. There is also an exercise room. One of the restaurants is Ralph Brennan's Red Fish Grill, which is among the hot tickets in town.
AE, D, DC, MC, V. **$$$$**

Courtyard by Marriott
124 St Charles Ave, New Orleans, LA 70130

Tel: 581 9005 or (800) 321 2211
Fax: 591 6264
Email: www.marriott.com
This hotel is set in a renovated Central Business District office building at the corner of Canal and Carondelet streets – one of the best locations for Mardi Gras. The courtyard has large, well-lit rooms with desks, coffeemakers, cable TV, and phones with voice mail and dataports. Each weekday the morning paper is delivered to your door. The restaurant is open for breakfast only. There is a pool, a hot tub, and a well-outfitted exercise room.
AE, D, DC, MC, V. **$$$$**

Doubletree Hotel
300 Canal St, New Orleans,
LA 70130,
Tel: 581 1300 or (800) 222 8733
Fax: 523 6536
Email: www.doubletree.com
At the foot of Canal Street, across the street from the Canal Place mall, the French Quarter, and the Aquarium, this high-rise property is virtually at the front door of the Harrah's Casino. The signature chocolate-chip cookies await guests in the lobby. Rooms are light-filled and tastefully decorated; guests can also use the coin-operated laundry. There is a restaurant, deli, lounge, and health club.
AE, D, DC, MC, V. **$$$$**

Embassy Suites Hotel
315 Julia St, New Orleans,
LA 70130
Tel: 525 1993 or (800) 362 2779
Fax: 522 3044
Email: www.embassy-suites.com
Each suite in this Warehouse District hotel has a living room, separate bedroom, and kitchenette with microwave, coffeemaker, and mini-fridge. Rates include a full breakfast. The hotel is by Gallery Row, the Warehouse District's street of wall-to-wall contemporary art galleries. Good restaurants, Riverwalk and the Convention Center are all within a five-minute walk away.
AE, D, DC, MC, V. **$$$$**

Fairmont Hotel
123 Baronne St, New Orleans,
LA 70112-2355

Tel: 529 7111 or (800) 527 4727
Fax: 523 2303
Email: www.fairmont.com
This *grande dame* hotel, completely refurbished in 1998, is one of the city's finest. Beyond its baroque facade, the lobby, with its glittering pillars and chandeliers, runs to the length of a full block, from University Place to Baronne Street. Rooms here are exceptionally spacious, and each has large down pillows and terry-cloth robes. Weighing scales and clothes lines are provided in the bathrooms. Each suite has a fax machine. Some suites are large enough for cocktail and dinner parties. Among the restaurants and lounges are the svelte Sazerac restaurant and the Sazerac Bar, in which movie scenes have been filmed. There is a rooftop resort with tennis courts, a pool, and a fitness center.
AE, D, DC, MC, V. **$$$$**

Key to Credit Cards

Credit cards are abbreviated in these listings as follows:

AE	American Express
D	Discover
DC	Diners Club
MC	Mastercard
V	Visa

Grand Boutique Hotel
2003 St Charles Ave, New Orleans,
LA 70130
Tel: 558 9966 or (800) 976 1755
Fax: 571 6464
Email: www.grandboutique.com
In the Garden District, smack on the Mardi Gras parade route, this modern hotel has 44 suites, all done up in Art Deco style. Next door (and providing the room service) is the Straya restaurant, the eatery famously criticized by novelist Anne Rice. Each suite has a microwave, coffeemaker, and refrigerator.
AE, DC, MC, V. **$$$$**

Hotel Inter-Continental, 444 St Charles, New Orleans Ave, New Orleans, LA 70130-3171
Tel: 525 5566 or (800) 33-AGAIN or toll-free phone (800) 445 6563
Fax: (585 4376)

Email: www.neworleanshotel.com
This elegant hotel in the heart of the Central Business District has sunny, attractively decorated rooms and sumptuous suites. Geared toward the business traveler, it is equipped with the latest high-tech features, such as teleconferencing via satellite, which can be received through TV sets in individual rooms. Good location for shoppers, business travelers, and sightseers.
AE, D, DC, MC, V. **$$$$**

Hyatt Regency New Orleans
Poydras and Loyola streets, New Orleans, LA 70113-1805
Tel: 561 1234 or (800) 233 1234
Fax: 523 0488
Email: www.hyatt.com
Big and splashy, with lots of bars, lounges, and restaurants, the Hyatt is connected via a glass atrium to the Superdome and the New Orleans Centre shopping mall. With more than 1,000 rooms, the hotel offers a variety of choices. Lanai rooms, each with patio or balcony, are off the pool area; the Regency Club offers key access rooms and sundry perks, as does the Business Plan level. There are complimentary guest shuttles to the French Quarter and to the foot of Canal Street. The revolving top of the Dome steakhouse is the city's only revolving restaurant, from which you can gain some spectacular views.
AE, D, DC, MC, V. **$$$$**

International House
221 Camp St, New Orleans,
LA 70130
Tel: 553 9550 or (800) 633 5770
Fax: 553 9560
Email: www.ihhotel.com.
The IH is in a renovated Beaux Arts office building in the Central Business District, two blocks from the French Quarter. In contrast to the old-world ambiance of many, the tone here is contemporary, which can be seen in the metal sculptures and modern lighting in the lobby, as well as the rooms that feature natural fibers, trim lines, and monochromatic colors. Rooms have 12-foot ceilings, minibars, cable TV, stereos with CD players and CDs of local musicians, and baths with Aveda amenities. Pent-

house suites have Jacuzzi baths, and huge windows that open onto landscaped terraces. The Lemon Grass restaurant is off the lobby, and there is also a lobby lounge.
AE, D, DC, MC, V. **$$$$**

New Orleans Hilton Riverside
2 Poydras St, New Orleans, LA 70140-1600
Tel: 561 0500 or (800) HILTONS
Fax: 568 1721)
Email: www.hiltonhotels.com
This hotel has more than 1,600 rooms. Standard rooms are quite cushy, and concierge level suites come with fax machines. The Hilton is one of the largest hotels in the Gulf South. Located next to Riverwalk, a short walking distance to the Convention Center, this big convention hotel has a whole raft of restaurants and lounges, including Pete Fountain's Club. From both the Tower and the Riverside sections of the multilevel hotel there are excellent views of the Mississippi River. The rooftop health club is among the finest in this part of the world, with tennis, racquetball, squash courts, a jogging track, putting green and resident golf pro, plus massages and an outdoor hot tub.
AE, D, DC, MC, V. **$$$$**

New Orleans Marriott
555 Canal St, New Orleans, LA 70140,
Tel: 581 1000 or (800) 228 9290
Fax: 581 5749
Email: www.marriott.com
The Marriott's lobby, only slightly smaller than a football field, is almost always crowded with conventioneers and tour groups. The backdoor of the huge high-rise is a few steps away from the French Quarter, and the attractions at the foot of Canal Street, including the Harrah's Casino, are just four blocks away. The Marriott is awash with restaurants, bars, and lounges, including a lobby lounge with nightly live entertainment. The restaurant is the Riverview, which has stunning views as well as nightly entertainment and a Sunday jazz brunch. In addition to the outdoor pool there is a sauna and health club.
AE, D, DC, MC, V. **$$$$**

Omni Royal Crescent Hotel
535 Gravier St, New Orleans, LA 70130
Tel: 527 0006 or (800) THE-OMNI
Fax: 571 7575
Email: www.omnihotels.com
This classy, business-oriented boutique hotel is sister to the Royal O (*see below*). Amenities include robes and slippers, Egyptian sheets, minibars and fax machines in each room, with music and a telephone in each bathroom. Some rooms have hot tubs. A rooftop outdoor pool, with sauna and fitness center, is fashioned after a Roman bath.
AE, D, DC, MC, V. **$$$$**

Omni Royal Orleans

Key to Credit Cards

Credit cards are abbreviated in these listings as follows:

AE	American Express
D	Discover
DC	Diners Club
MC	Mastercard
V	Visa

621 St Louis St, New Orleans, LA 70140
Tel: 529 5333 or (800) THE-OMN
Fax: 529 7016
Email: www.omnihotels.com
Situated near Jackson Square, this stunning French Quarter property has vast marbled halls, oriental rugs, exotic statuary, and crystal chandeliers. Rooms are average size, but some large, individually decorated suites have canopy beds and Jacuzzis. The Rib Room stands out among the hotel's several restaurants, and is popular with local business men and women and politicians, too.
AE, D, DC, MC, V **$$$$**

Parc St. Charles
500 St. Charles Ave, New Orleans, LA 70130
Tel: 522 9000 or (888) 211 3447
Fax: 569 0460
Email: www.neworleanscollection.com
This recent addition to the Central Business District hotel scene is on the streetcar line. It is near the Superdome and the New Orleans

Centre shopping mall and a short walk from the Convention Center and Riverwalk. Standard to each room are terry-cloth robes, minibars, hair driers, and irons.
AE, D, DC, MC, V. **$$$$**

Pelham Hotel
444 Common St, New Orleans, LA 70130
Tel: 522 4444 or (888) 211 3447
Fax: 569 0640
Email: www.neworleanscollection.com
This quiet alternative to the flashy Central Business District hotels is in a four-story restored building. Rooms have a mix of four-poster and brass beds; each has a marble bath with terry-cloth robe, hair drier, and English toiletries. Interior rooms have no windows. The Metro Bistro provides room service; guests have use of the health club and pool of a nearby hotel.
AE, D, DC, MC, V. **$$$$**

Ritz Carlton New Orleans
921 Canal St, New Orleans, LA 70112
Tel: 524 1331 or (800) 241 3333
Fax: 524 7233
Email: www.ritzcarlton.com
Opened in 1999, this deluxe Central Business District hotel is set in the former home of the Maison Blanche department store. It is one minute's walk from Bourbon Street, and a couple of blocks from the St Charles Streetcar line.
AE, D, DC, MC, V. **$$$$**

Royal Sonesta
300 Bourbon St, New Orleans, LA 70140
Tel: 586 0300 or (800) 766 3782
Fax: 586 0335
Email: www.sonestano.com
This French Quarter hotel is a serene spot on boisterous Bourbon Street. The hotel has a French country flavor. There are tiny dormer rooms, as well as spacious, luxuriously decorated rooms and suites, some with canopy beds, parquet floors, oriental rugs, and Jacuzzis. Many rooms and suites have balconies overlooking Bourbon Street – these should be avoided by those who sleep lightly.
AE, D, DC, MC, V. **$$$$**

Westin Canal Place

100 Iberville St, New Orleans,
LA 70130-1159
Tel: 566 7006 or (800) 228 3000
Fax: 553-5120
Email: www.westinhotels.com
Located at the corner of the Central Business District and the French Quarter, this glamourous luxury hotel has a glass elevator that sweeps up through the Canal Place atrium to the 11th-floor lobby, which is resplendent with rose Carrara marble, period furnishings, oriental carpeting, and large windows with a commanding view of the river and the Quarter. Extensive use of marble, artwork, and antiques throughout the hotel adds to the appeal of the place.
AE, D, DC, MC, V. **$$$$**

Windsor Court

300 Gravier St, New Orleans,
LA 70130
Tel: 523 6000 or (800) 262 2662
Fax: 596 4513
Email: www.windsorcourt.com.
The city's most luxurious hotel, built around a $5 million private art collection, is thoroughly British in flavor. Located in the Central Business District, near Canal Place and Riverwalk, it has a stunning lobby and elegantly appointed suites. Afternoon tea, served daily to the tune of chamber music, features scones, finger sandwiches, and chocolates, and is enormously popular. The names of celebrity and royal guests can be spotted in the guest register
AE, D, DC, MC. **$$$$**

Wyndham Riverfront Hotel

701 Convention Center Blvd,
New Orleans, LA 70130-1655
Tel: 524 8200 or (800) WYNDHAM
Fax: 524 0600
Email: www.wyndham.com
In the Warehouse District, across the street from Riverwalk and the Convention Center, a circular drive replete with trickling fountain leads to the entrance of this handsome 19th century property. Rooms, varying in size, all have coffeemakers and modems. The restaurant serves three meals and provides room service. There is a business center and exercise room.
AE, D, DC, MC, V. **$$$$**

Expensive

Ambassador Hotel

535 Tchoupitoulas St, New Orleans,
LA 70130
Tel: 527 5271 or (888) 527 5271
Fax: 599 2110
Email: www.neworleans.com/
ambassador
Iron beds and large executive desks are among the features at this small and chic boutique hotel. Standard rooms all have coffeemakers, hair driers, and phones with dataports. The hotel is in the Warehouse District, across the street from Riverwalk and the Convention Center, near shops, restaurants, and art galleries.
AE, D, DC, MC, V. **$$$**

Avenue Plaza Hotel & Spa

2111 St. Charles Ave, New Orleans,
LA 70130
Tel: 566 1212 or (800) 535 9575
Fax: 525 6899
Email: www.neworleanscvb.com
In the Garden District, on the streetcar line and Mardi Gras parade route, the Avenue Plaza is an all-suites hotel. Each unit has a separate and spacious dressing area, and a kitchenette with full-size refrigerator. The exercise facilities and spa of internationally-known sports trainer Mackie Shilstone are located here; hotel guests may use them at a discount. There is a rooftop sundeck and hot tub.
AE, D, DC, MC, V. **$$$**

Price Guide

Prices are for a standard double room (not suites), exclusive of 11% hotel tax and a $1–$3 per diem surcharge, depending on the size of the hotel.

$$$$ More than $150 (deluxe)
$$$ $125–150 (expensive)
$$ $100–125 (moderate)
$ Under $100 (inexpensive)

Holiday Inn Select

881 Convention Center Blvd,
New Orleans, LA 70130
Tel: 524 1881 or (888) 524 1881
Fax: 528 1005
Email: www.HISelect.com
A small hotel, catering to business travelers, the HI Select is in the Warehouse District, directly across the street from the Convention Center. Restaurants and art galleries, among other attractions, are nearby. Rooms are spacious, and equipped with desk, dataport, two phones with voice mail, hair drier, iron and ironing board, and cable TV. Suites have speaker phones and call waiting. The hotel has a restaurant, bar, coin-operated laundry, pool, and health club.
AE, D, DC, MC, V. **$$$**

Lafayette Hotel

600 St Charles Ave, New Orleans,
LA 70130
Tel: 524 4441 or (800) 451 6536
Fax: 523 7326
Email: www.neworleans.
collection.com
A small gem, the very Gallic Lafayette is on the cusp of the Central Business District and the Warehouse District, on the streetcar line. Just off the tiny white marble lobby, with its lovely concierge and attractive millwork, is Mike's on the Avenue, one of the city's 'hot-ticket' restaurants. The beautiful rooms have minibars, ottomans and easy chairs, plus bookshelves lined with reading material. Many rooms have four-posters, and some on St Charles Avenue have floor-length windows that open onto balconies – great during the Carnival season. Guests use the pool and health club at a nearby hotel.
AE, D, DC, MC, V. **$$$**

Le Meridien

614 Canal St, New Orleans,
LA 70130-9946
Tel: 525 6500 or (800) 543 4300
Fax: 586 1543
Email: www.meridien-hotel.com
This modern high-rise property, located in the Central Business District, across the street from the French Quarter, has average-sized rooms with monochromatic decor, but corner rooms are split-level with two-story windows that have exciting views. There are also exquisite penthouse suites. A popular convention hotel
AE, D, DC, MC, V. **$$$**

Le Pavillon
833 Poydras St, New Orleans,
LA 70140
Tel: 581 3111 or (800) 535 9095
Fax: 522 5043
Email: www.lepavillon.com
Le Pavillon, a European-style hotel, has occupied the corner of Baronne and Poydras streets since 1905. It is a member of both Historic Hotels of America and Preferred Hotels & Resorts. The stunning chandelier in the lobby was imported from Czechoslovakia, and a marble railing in the lounge came from the Grand Hotel in Paris. Rooms are above average in size, and are identical in decor, with traditional mahogany furnishings. The suites are opulent. There is a restaurant, lounge, pool, hot tub, spa, and health club.
AE, D, DC, MC, V. **$$$**

Oldest Hotel

Monteleone is the French Quarter's oldest hotel and is still operated by the Monteleone family; it celebrated its 100th anniversary in 1986. This elegant 600-room hotel has a baroque facade, a large lobby with chandeliers and handsome rooms and suites. An ideal location for shopping as well as sightseeing.
214 Royal Street, New Orleans, LA 70140. Tel: 523 3341 or (800) 535 9595. Fax: 528 1019. Email: www.neworleanscvb.com
AE, D, DC, MC, V. **$$$**

New Orleans Airport Hilton & Conference Center
901 Airline Dr, Kenner, New Orleans, LA 70062
Tel: 469 5000 or (800) HILTONS
Fax: 466 5473
This $32 million soundproof property, across the street from New Orleans International Airport, is an ultramodern hotel. All rooms are identical. Former US president Ronald Reagan features on the guest list. The location of the hotel is 20–30 minutes from the French Quarter and the Central Business

District from the airport area by car.
AE, D, DC, MC V. **$$$**
New Orleans Sheraton
500 Canal St, New Orleans, LA 70130
Tel: 525- 2500 or (800) 325 3535
Fax: 561 0178
Email: www.sheraton.com
In the Central Business District, across the street from the Marriott, this major convention hotel has an inviting lobby with a spiral staircase, and attractive rooms and suites. Service is excellent. There are several restaurants and lounges and music is played nightly in the lobby. A branch of the wildly popular Starbucks coffeehouse is in the lobby, overlooking Canal Street.
AE, D, DC, MC, V. **$$$**
Pontchartrain Hotel
2031 St Charles Ave, New Orleans, LA 70140
Tel: 524 0581 or (800) 777 6193
Fax: (504) 524 7828
Email: www.neworleanscvb.com
This charming 'old-world' hotel in the Garden District offers a range of accommodation, from small rooms to some of the most exquisite suites in town, several named after celebrities who made this their home-away-from-home, such as Mary Martin and Richard Burton. It has neither pool nor health club, but does feature the appealing Caribbean Room restaurant. The hotel is situated right along the St Charles Streetcar line, about 10 minutes from the Central Business District and French Quarter.
AE, D, DC, MC, V. **$$$**
Queen & Crescent Hotel
344 Camp St, Central Business District, New Orleans, LA 70130
Tel: 587 9700 or (800) 975 6652
Fax: 670 6309
Email: www.queenandcrescent.com
This new and chic charmer is in a renovated office building not far from Riverwalk. Amenities include minibars, hairdryers, complimentary Continental breakfast, ironing boards, and an exercise room.
AE, DC, MC, V. **$$$**

Moderate
Comfort Suites
346 Baronne St. New Orleans, LA 70112-1627
Tel: 524 1140 or (800) 524 1140
Fax: 524-523 4444
Housed in a renovated office building, the Comfort Suites does indeed offer comfort to the budget traveler. Just ignore the dubious-looking lobby – the suites, each actually a large room, are outfitted with hair driers, microwave, mini-fridge, coffeemaker, and safe. The more expensive suites have whirlpools. Guests receive a complimentary morning paper. The first five local calls are free. The hotel also has a sauna, hot tub, spa, and exercise room.
AE, D, DC, MC, V. **$$**
Dauphine Orleans
415 Dauphine St, New Orleans, LA 70112-3405
Tel: 586 1800 or (800) 521 7111
Fax: 586 1409
Email: www.dauphineorleans.com
A 1994 renovation of this property revealed that parts of the building date from the late 1700s; the restored section has been transformed into luxury Jacuzzi suites in which the ancient 'brick-between-posts' wall construction is exposed. These suites, as well as the Patio Suites across the street, have a romantic ambiance. Rates include a Continental breakfast; afternoon tea is available, and there is a guest library. On-site parking is a plus, and a free jitney scoots guests around the area.
AE, D, DC, MC, V. **$$**
Hampton Inn Downtown
226 Carondelet St, New Orleans, LA 70130
Tel: 529 9990 or (800) HAMPTON
Fax: 529 9996
Email: www.hampton-inn.com
Located just two blocks from Bourbon Street, this chain hotel was once an office building – the UNO Downtown Center is still here. Great for budget travelers, it offers such rare frills as free local phone calls, as well as complimentary Continental breakfast. There is a coffee shop and exercise room.
AE, D, DC, MC, V. **$$**

Hotel De la Poste
316 Chartres St, New Orleans,
LA 70130
Tel: 581 1200 or (800) 448 4927
Fax: 523 2910
Email: hoteldelaposte@worldnet.
att.net
Located in the French Quarter, this
upmarket motel has a splendid
courtyard and large, sunny,
tastefully decorated rooms. The
rooms on the front of the building
are noisy, however. Carriage house
suites on the courtyard are large
bedsitting rooms with private
patios. Room service is provided by
Bacco, an on-site Brennan's Italian
restaurant.
AE, DC, MC, V. **$$**

Le Richelieu
1234 Chartres St, New Orleans,
LA 70116-2507
Tel: 529- 2492 or (800) 535 9653
Fax: 524 8179
This lovely 88-room hotel,
considered by many to be the best
bargain in town, is situated in a
restored macaroni factory and 19th-
century rowhouses in the
residential Lower Quarter. Large
rooms are individually decorated,
and have balconies, brass ceiling
fans, and small refrigerators. Paul
McCartney stayed in one of the
suites for several weeks while in
the city cutting an album.
AE, D, DC, MC, V. **$$**

Provincial Hotel
1024 Chartres St, New Orleans,
LA 70116-3298
Tel: 581 4995 or (800) 621 5295
or (800) 535 7922
Fax: 581 1018
Email: www.hotelprovincial.com
Also in the Lower Quarter, near the
French Market, this hotel comprises
four-balconied units built around
five lush patios. Large rooms are
furnished with antiques and period
reproductions. The staff are friendly. The hotel has a charming little
restaurant and on-site parking.
AE, D, DC, MC, V. **$$**

Prytania Park Hotel
1525 Prytania St, New Orleans,
LA 70130
Tel: 524 0427 or (800) 862 1984
Fax: 522 2977
Email: www.prytaniaparkhotel.com

Popular with European travelers,
this small, intimate hotel is located
in the Lower Garden District, one
block from the St Charles Streetcar
line. There are two sections of the
hotel; some rooms are in an
historic 1834 house; others are in
a more modern building. Rooms in
the latter have microwaves and
refrigerators. A Continental
breakfast is included in the rate.
Note that walking around in this
area at night is not advised.
AE, D, DC, MC, V. **$$**

Price Guide

Prices are for a standard double
room (not suites), exclusive of
11% hotel tax and a $1–$3 per
diem surcharge, depending on
the size of the hotel.
$$$$ More than $150 (deluxe)
$$$ $125–150 (expensive)
$$ $100–125 (moderate)
$ Under $100 (inexpensive)

Quality Inn Maison St Charles
1319 St Charles Ave, New Orleans,
LA 70130
Tel: 522 0187 or (800) 831 1783
Fax: 528 2993
Email: QIMSC.@aol.com
An eye-catching mural is painted
on the wall of the tunnel-like
driveway of this comfortable motel.
Six restored townhouses, set
among courtyards, house the large,
rooms, each with voice mail and
dataport. A Continental breakfast is
included in the rate. One of the well-
known restaurants of Emeril
Lagasse, Delmonico's, is just
across the street. The St Charles
Streetcar stops in front of the hotel.
AE, D, DC, MC, V. **$$**

Inexpensive
Chateau Hotel
1001 Chartres St, New Orleans,
LA 70130
Tel: 524 9636
Fax: 524 9636
A small, tastefully furnished motel
with a charming courtyard, located
in the residential Lower Quarter – a
good choice for budget travelers.
AE, DC, MC, V. **$**

St. Charles Inn
3636 St Charles Ave, New Orleans,
LA 70115-4690
Tel: 899 8888 or (800) 489 9908
Fax: 899 8892
Being the cheapest hotel on St
Charles Avenue, this hotel is not
luxurious, but it is comfortable.
A complimentary Continental
breakfast is delivered daily to your
room, along with the morning paper.
The streetcar stops practically at
the front door, and a Mexican
restaurant, is smack next door.
AE, DC, MC, V. **$**

YMCA International Hotel
920 St. Charles Ave, New Orleans,
LA 70130
Tel: 558 9622
Fax: 523 7174
Spartan and clean, the Y has
accommodations for both men and
women. All rooms have color TV
with shared bathrooms. Rooms
sleep from one to four people.
There is a restaurant, and guests
may use the health club – one of
the city's best – with an indoor half-
Olympic-size pool, a gym, and a
track. The Y is located at Lee Circle,
so if you book early enough for
Carnival season, you may be able to
snag a room overlooking St Charles
for Mardi Gras parades.
MC, V. **$**

Guest Houses

Deluxe
Maison de Ville
727 Toulouse St, New Orleans, LA
70130-2188
Tel: 561 5858 or (800) 634 1600
Fax: 528 9939
Email: www.maisondeville.com
This small hotel in the French
Quarter is exquisitely furnished with
antiques. Rooms in the main house
and adjoining slave quarters are
small and can be quite noisy (the
guest house is near Bourbon
Street).The exclusive Audubon
Cottages that surround a serene
courtyard and pool have spacious
apartments with full kitchens and
many amenities. Complimentary
Continental breakfast is served in
the rooms on silver trays.
AE, D, DC, MC, V. **$$$$**

Expensive
Olivier House Hotel
828 Toulouse St, New Orleans,
LA 70112
Tel: 525 8456
Fax 529 2006
This small, friendly family-run guest house, set in the French Quarter, was built in 1836 as a Creole townhouse. It is popular with Europeans and casts of touring shows that play at the Saenger Center. Some rooms are furnished with antiques – others are contemporary in decor. There are a few split-level suites with canopy beds and fireplaces, and a swimming pool, but no restaurant.
AE, DC, MC, V **$$$**

Terrell House
1441 Magazine St, New Orleans,
LA 70130
Tel: 524 9859 or (800) 878 9859
Fax: 529 9771
Email: www.lacajun.com/
terrellhouse.html
This guest house, set in a Greek Revival mansion with filigreed iron galleries, contains an excellent collection of antiques. Guest rooms are in the main mansion, carriage house, and old servants' quarters. A full breakfast and afternoon cocktails are served daily. There is no restaurant or pool, but there is
a hot tub in courtyard.
AE, MC, V. **$$$**

Soniat House
1133 Chartres St, New Orleans,
LA 70116
Tel: 522 0570 or (800) 544 8808
Fax: 522 7208
Email: www.soniathouse.com
Built as a townhouse in 1830, this charming French Quarter guest house is a pleasant alternative to splashy convention hotels. Furnished throughout with antiques, it is located in the quiet, mostly residential Lower Quarter. Although it has neither restaurant nor pool, it has many amenities one normally associates with a full-service hotel. In addition, the guest house also lets six comfortable apartments on Esplanade Avenue.
AE, MC, V. **$$$**

Moderate
Cornstalk Hotel
915 Royal St, New Orleans,
LA 70116
Tel: 523 1515
Fax: 522 5558
This Victorian Gothic mansion, with crystal chandeliers, canopy beds, four-poster beds, has 14 rooms, some of which have fireplaces. A complimentary Continental breakfast is provided. There is no restaurant or pool. The guest house is conveniently located for Jackson Square and other Quarter sights.
V, MC, AE **$$**

Key to Credit Cards

Credit cards are abbreviated in these listings as follows:
AE	American Express
D	Discover
DC	Diners Club
MC	Mastercard
V	Visa

Villa Convento
616 Ursulines St, New Orleans,
LA 70116
Tel: 522 1793
Fax: 524 1902
A simply furnished, 24-room guest house, family owned and operated, the Villa Convento is located in a 19th-century townhouse in a secluded section of the French Quarter. A complimentary Continental breakfast is served in a pretty courtyard. There is no pool or restaurant.
AE, D, DC, MC, V **$$**

Inexpensive
St Charles Guest House
1748 Prytania St, New Orleans,
LA 70130)
Tel: 523 6556
Fax: 522 6340
Simple and charming, this guest house, which has friendly, helpful hosts, is frequented by writers, artists and other visitors on a budget. Small 'backpacker' rooms are not air-conditioned, and bathrooms are shared. Amenities include complimentary breakfast and afternoon tea. The building is located in the Lower Garden District, so be careful at night. It is, however, only a block from the St Charles Streetcar line. There is a pool, but no restaurant.
AE, MC, V. **$**

Bed and Breakfast

Although the categories for B&B's are the same as those for guest houses, prices might be slightly lower. Be sure to check whether smoking is allowed.

There are two organizations that arrange accommodations in private homes with friendly, knowledgeable hosts. Contact **New Orleans Bed & Breakfast**, P.O. Box 8163, New Orleans, LA 70182, tel: 838 0071/2 or **Bed & Breakfast, Inc**, 1021 Moss St, Box 52257, New Orleans, LA 70152, tel: 488 4640 or (800) 749 4640.

Deluxe
Claiborne Mansion
2111 Dauphine St, New Orleans,
LA 70116
Tel: 949 7327 or (800) 449 7327
Fax: 949 0388
This sumptuous B&B is in an historic house on Washington Square Park in Faubourg Marigny, that dates from the 1850s. It has sky-high ceilings, polished hardwood floors, and tasteful furnishings upholstered in rich fabrics. Rooms and suites are in the main house and in the rear carriagehouse, which overlooks the lush gardens and pool. Each room has cable TV and a VCR, and each phone has voice mail. Cocktails are served in the evening, and a gourmet breakfast, each morning.
AE, MC, V. **$$$$**

House on Bayou Road
2275 Bayou Rd, New Orleans,
LA 70119
Tel: 945 992 or (800) 882 2968
Fax: 934 0993
Email: www.houseonbayouroad.com
House on Bayou Road is on two beautifully landscaped acres near the Fair Grounds and City Park – a country setting in the city. The main house, a West Indies-style plantation home, was built in the

late 1790s; beautifully restored, it contains a collection of antiques and handsome family heirlooms. Behind the house is an outdoor hot tub, and a pool around which guests gather for breakfast in pleasant weather. Guest rooms and suites are in the main house and separate cottages. Among the latter is a private cottage, with a huge four-poster beneath a skylight, a wet bar, and a Jacuzzi bath. A hands-on cooking school is conducted here the year round. Breakfast is a full gourmet feast, and on weekends a Champagne brunch is served.

AE, MC, V. **$$$$**

Melrose Mansion
937 Esplanade Ave, New Orleans, LA 70116
Tel: 944 2255
Fax: 945 1794
Email: www.melrosemansion.com
This luxurious nine-room guest house is in a Victorian mansion on the fringe of the French Quarter. Rooms and suites, each individually decorated with period antiques, have hardwood floors, high ceilings, and old-world charm. As the location is not central, there is a complimentary chauffeured limo for guests' use. There are frequent soirées, at which an astonishing array of foods is served, as is a complimentary Continental breakfast by the pool each morning. Expect to be pampered.

AE, D, DC, MC, V **$$$$**

Expensive

B&B Courtyards
2425 Chartres St, New Orleans, LA 70117
Tel: 945 9418 or (800) 585 5731
Fax: 949 3483
Email: faubourg@aol.com
Winner of an award for architectural restoration, this B&B is comprised of three 1850s cottages which are joined by two courtyards. Terra cotta tile floors, lovely stained-glass windows, and a mixture of antique and reproduction artwork are very welcoming. Four rooms are let to overnighters, each with private bath and separate entrance. There is a whirlpool in one of the courtyards,

and in another, a guests' fridge stocked with soft drinks. Over a breakfast of pastries, homemade granola, and fruit, innkeepers Rob Boyd and Kevin Wu chat with their guests and give tips about things to do in the city.

AE, D, MC, V. **$$$**

Lanaux Mansion
547 Esplanade Ave, New Orleans, LA 70116
Tel: 488 4640 or (800) 729 4640
Fax: 488 4639
The Lanaux is a striking Italianate mansion that sits on tree-lined Esplanade Avenue, which borders the Quarter. Built in 1879, the house has some of the original wallpaper, cornice and ceiling medallions, 14-foot ceilings up- and downstairs, and a drawing room with regal Renaissance-revival furniture. There are four guest suites, each with a kitchenette with mini-fridge, microwave, coffeemaker, and the makings of a continental breakfast. Each suite has a phone and answering machine, iron and ironing board, hair drier, and TV. Two suites are decorated in enchanting Victoriana, while the Library Suite and the Weiland Suite, with its big open fireplace, were, respectively, the original library and kitchen. Credit cards are not accepted. **$$$**

Moderate

The Chimes
Constantinople and Coliseum Streets, New Orleans, LA 70115
Tel: 488 4640 or (800) 729 4640
Fax: 488 4639
The home of Charles and Jill Abbyad is on a pretty Uptown residential street, three blocks from the streetcar line. The five guest rooms, each different in size and decor, are situated in cottages off the rear courtyard. Some rooms have a four-poster, others have twin beds. The largest room is a loft, which has slate floors and a large, white iron bed. All rooms come with a TV, stereo, phone, coffeemaker and teapot, and have a private bath. Guests may use a full-size refrigerator, an iron and ironing board, which are tucked in a closet

off the courtyard. A full breakfast is served in the Abbyad home.

AE, D, MC, V. **$$**

The Columns
3811 St Charles Ave, New Orleans, LA 70118
Tel: 899 9308 or (800) 445 9308
Fax: 899 8170
Built in 1883, this gorgeous white mansion is listed on the National Register of Historic Places. It is famous locally, having been the setting for the Brooke Shields film *Pretty Baby*. Beyond the veranda, where guests often gather for breakfast and cocktails, is a hall which has a stunning staircase with a stained glass window and high ceilings. Off this hall is the Victorian Lounge, a favorite watering hole for Uptown Orleanians, especially on Tuesday and Thursday jazz nights. (There is also a jazz brunch every Sunday). Most guest rooms are large and sunny. The least expensive rooms share a bathroom. The rate includes a Continental

Art for Breakfast

Degas House bed and breakfast is a tall, Greek-Revival building constructed in 1852. It is situated near the Museum of Art, which contains a portrait of Estelle Musson painted by Edgar Degas (*see page 289*). The French Impressionist made the painting in the 1870s, while staying in this house with his aunt and uncle; Estelle was not only his cousin but also his sister-in-law. The largest rooms in the house, with 14-ft ceilings and chandeliers, are on the second floor and individually decorated. There is a mix of four-poster and canopied beds, one with access to a balcony on which there are rocking chairs; another with a whirlpool bath. Degas prints are scattered throughout the house. 2306 Esplanade Ave, New Orleans, LA 70119. Tel: 821 5009 or (800) 755 6730. Fax: 821 0870. Email: www.degashouse.com
AE, MC, V, $$

breakfast and the morning paper.
AE, MC, V. **$$**

Josephine Guest House

1450 Josephine St, New Orleans,
Tel: 524 6361 or (800) 779 6361
In the Garden District, a block away
from the St Charles Streetcar line,
this Italianate mansion displays an
elaborate collection of antiques.
Each of six rooms is individually
decorated. Complimentary
Continental breakfast is served on
Wedgwood china. There is no pool
or restaurant.
AE, D, DC, MC, V **$$**

McKendrick-Breaux House

1474 Magazine St, New Orleans,
LA 70130
Tel: 586 1700 or (888) 570 1700
Fax: 522 7138
This B&B is set in a stately three-
story Greek Revival house with high
ceilings, polished hardwood floors,
and an uncluttered ambiance. The
downstairs double parlor is divided
into a formal sitting room, furnished
with Victorian antiques, and a dining
area, where, in the mornings, the
table is set with a Continental
breakfast. Affable proprietor Eddie
Breaux says guests may eat at the
table, take their breakfast to their
rooms, or repair to the broad
sundeck. Guest rooms, decorated
with custom-made fabrics, are on
the second and third floors (up very
steep steps) and in a separate
building across the back lawn.
Baths are quite large, with clawfoot
tub/shower, big thirsty towels, terry
cloth robes, and Lord & Mayfair
toiletries. There is a phone in each
guest room with modem and voice
mail; guests may borrow a VCR.
AE, MC, V. **$$**

Inexpensive

**Depot House at Madame Julia's
Boarding House**

941 Julia St, New Orleans,
LA 70113
Tel: 529 2952
Fax: 522 2908
Email:www.bestofneworleans.com
/depot
This modest hostelry was opened
recently to provide an inexpensive
alternative in a fairly pricey
neighborhood. The Depot is a

compound of 19th-century houses.
Accommodations are pretty basic –
14 rooms share two bathrooms.
The rate includes a Continental
breakfast. Guests may use the pool
at the St Charles Guest House.
AE, MC, V. **$**

Campgrounds

Jude Travel Park of New Orleans

7400 Chef Menteur Hwy, New
Orleans, LA 70126
Tel: 241 0632 or (800) 523 2196
Fax: 245 8070
Located in the eastern part of the
city, with a shuttle bus to the
French Quarter, this camping
ground has 43 sites with full hook-
ups, showers, restrooms, laundry,
pool, and playground.
MC, V. **$**

Youth Hostels

**Hostelling International–Marquette
New Orleans**

2253 Carondelet St, New Orleans,
LA 70130
Tel: 523 3014
Fax: 529 5933
This, the nation's fourth largest
youth hostel, is set in a complex of
century-old buildings one block from
St Charles Avenue. There are
dormitory rooms with bunk beds,
private rooms and apartments.
MC and V. **$**

**Marquette New Orleans Interna-
tional Hostel**

2253 Carondelet St
Tel: 523 3014
Both apartments and dormitory
rooms rooms are available in this
hostel. The kitchen, dining area,
reading room and patio are
communal. The Marquette can be
found near the Garden District, a
block away from the St Charles
Streetcar line. **$**

Where to Eat

Where to Eat

New Orleans' extraordinary range of
food includes everything from haute
cuisine and Bananas Foster to
blacked catfish and Creole soul.
Unless otherwise noted in the
description with words like 'casual'
or 'informal,' men are requested to
wear a jacket and tie in the
restaurants listed.
*When booking, be sure to check
whether smoking is allowed.*

Price Guide

$$$$ Over $35 (deluxe)
$$$ $25 –35 (expensive)
$$ $20–25 (moderate)
$ Under $20 (inexpensive)
Price categories are for one
three-course dinner, not including
beverages, gratuities, and a
9.5 percent tax.

Deluxe

Antoine's

713 St Louis St, French Quarter
Tel: 581 4422
Fax: 581 3003
This well-known French Creole
restaurant, which celebrated its
150th anniversary in 1990, has
been run by the same family
continuously since opening. Famous
dishes such as Oysters Rockefeller
originated at Antoine's. Many
dishes are sensational, especially
the Baked Alaska. Stroll around
after dinner to take in the many
dining rooms, including the Rex
Room, with its glittering display of
Mardi Gras memorabilia, or the
50,000-bottle wine cellar.
Reservations are essential during
peak periods. Closed on Sunday.
AE, D, DC, MC, V. **$$$$**

Arnaud's
813 Bienville St, French Quarter
Tel: 523 5433
Fax: 581 7908
A large, handsome restaurant with mosaic tile floors and etched glass windows, Arnaud's has been a local favorite since its opening in 1918. Specialties are French and Creole dishes. Don't miss the jazz brunch each Sunday. The Richelieu Room is open for late night live jazz, supper, and dancing. Reservations are essential during peak periods.
AE, D, DC, MC, V. **$$$$**

Bayona
430 Dauphine St, French Quarter
Tel: 525 4455
Fax: 522 0589
Small, chic, noisy, and popular, the Bayona offers creative nouvelle cuisine with a Mediterranean flavor. Jackets are suggested, and reservations are essential. Closed on Sunday.
AE, DC, MC, V. **$$$$**

Brennan's
417 Royal St
Tel: 525 9711
Fax: 525 2302
Although lunch and dinner at Brennan's are always culinary delights, it is breakfast that the restaurant is famous for, and justifiably so, with Eggs Benedict, Eggs Houssarde, and Eggs Sardou as typical fare. Bananas Foster, a traditional breakfast dessert, originated here. Seating is in 12 dining rooms and a courtyard. Make reservations during peak periods.
AE, D, DC, MC, V. **$$$$**

Commander's Palace
1403 Washington Ave,
Garden District
Tel: 899 8221
Fax: 891 3242
A first-rate restaurant in a Victorian mansion, serving Creole and American dishes. The Garden Room overlooks a courtyard. The jazz brunch, which originated here, is the city's finest, and sometimes occurs on Saturdays as well as Sundays. The house dessert creation – bread pudding soufflé with sauce – is divine. Reservations are essential during peak periods.
AE, D, DC, MC, V. **$$$$**

Delmonico
1300 St Charles Ave
Tel: 525 4937
Fax: 525 0506
This restaurant, which has been on the New Orleans' culinary scene for more than a century, was recently purchased and renovated by superchef Emeril Lagasse of Food Network fame. The flashy, noisy bistro, with a waitstaff that seems to number in the thousands, serves traditional New Orleans favorites, such as sherry-spiked turtle soup and lip-smacking barbecue shrimp. The menu also includes yummy chicken Cordon Bleu and juicy filet mignon. Make sure you visit the men's and ladies' rooms before or after the meal to view the impressive decor.
AE, D, DC, MC, V. **$$$$**

Emeril's
800 Tchoupitoulas St,
Warehouse District
Tel: 528 9393
Fax: 558 3925
This restaurant is the first of three opened in New Orleans by TV chef Emeril Lagasse, and is one of the best tickets in town. The cuisine is nouvelle, and virtually everything is homemade. Dress is upscale casual. Reservations are required.
AE, D, DC, MC, V. **$$$$**

Galatoire's
209 Bourbon St, French Quarter
Tel: 525 2021
Fax: 525 5900
Long lines form outside this intimate, mirror-panelled French Creole restaurant, with an extensive menu and 140 seats. Sunday afternoons take on a salon atmosphere, with locals table-hopping to chat with friends. The long wait can be avoided by arriving for lunch about

11.30am or around 1 or 2pm in the afternoon. Closed on Monday. Reservations are not accepted.
AE, MC, V. **$$$$**

Grill Room
Windsor Court Hotel, 300 Gravier St, Central Business District
Tel: 522 1992
The Austrian drapes and marbled floors of this hotel dining room create the backdrop for, as the name of the restaurant suggests, the specialties that come mostly from the grill. Among the standouts are the grilled salmon, the grilled sirloin and the grilled marinated rack of lamb. A harp player entertains during Sunday brunch. Reservations are recommended.
AE, D, DC, MC, V. **$$$$**

Red Room
2040 St Charles Ave
Tel: 528 9759
Fax: 528 9766
Shades of the 1940s! Seven shades of red, to be more precise, decorate this very posh supper club, where steaks, foie gras, and whole Maine lobster top the menu. Even one of the desserts is a luscious Red Velvet chocolate cake. Dancing is to live jazz, and for those who'd rather listen than dine, there is a bar (where cigars are welcome) that opens at 5pm. The restaurant is in the structure that was built to house the ill-fated Eiffel Tower Restaurant, which was transported to these shores in the 1980s. Dinner only. Closed on Sunday.
AE, D, DC, MC, V. **$$$$**

Sazerac
Fairmont Hotel, 129 Baronne St
Tel: 529 4733
Things are quite *haute* in the main dining room of the Fairmont Hotel, elegance that comes from the fine crystal and silver, impressive oil

Spoiled for Choice

New Orleans has over 1500 restaurants. These are recommended for their good food or great views, but it's hard to go wrong when choosing in a town where eating is as important as love-making or Mardi Gras.

portraits and the sculpted and illuminated ice-swans in which sorbet is served Intermezzo – between appetizers and entrees. Appetizers include cold lobster tails and turtle soup. Renowned for its lobster bisque, the kitchen also turns out a stunning Caesar salad for two, prepared tableside. Oven-baked chicken Sazerac is served in a Creole sauce. The steak Diane and filet mignon are especially good here. Jackets are required. Reservations are recommended.
AE, D, DC, MC, V. **$$$$**

Smith & Wolensky's
1009 Poydras St
Tel: 561 0770
S&W's slogan is "A steakhouse to end all arguments." No argument here. Carnivorous Orleanians were delighted when this branch of the New York steakhouse came to the Crescent City in 1998. The large 400-seat restaurant focuses on red meat, and lots of it. If meat is not your dish you can opt for a whole lobster. Wollensky's Grill is an annex to the main event. It is casual but not funky. Reservations are recommended.
AE, D, DC, MC, V. **$$$$**

Expensive

Andrea's
3100 19th St, Metairie
Tel: 834 8583
Fax: 834 6698
Although the dress is casual, this restaurant is a rather smart venue that serves northern Italian and Continental cuisine. The pasta is homemade, and there is a tempting antipasto display. Low calorie dishes are also featured on the menu. Sunday brunch is a always festive occasion, with some lively Italian music. Closed for lunch on Saturday. Reservations are required.
AE, D, DC, MC, V. **$$$**

Andrew Jaeger's House of Seafood
622 Conti St
Tel: 522 4964
Fax: 522 5873
Needless to say, the emphasis here is on critters from the sea – Gulf fish (blackened, pan-seared – however you like it), oysters in

various costumes, shrimp and catfish all appear on the lengthy menu. There are also foods for landlubbers, such as steak and chicken dishes. Casual dress is acceptable. Reservations are recommended.
AE, D, DC, MC, V. **$$$**

Romantic Riverboats

From its second-floor perch in French Market Place, **Bella Luna** offers dazzling views through floor-to-ceiling windows of illuminated riverboats on the Mississippi. Chef Horst Pfeiffer marries Italian and Southwestern influences in his imaginative menu; particularly good are the quesadillas stuffed with shrimp and goat cheese. The desserts are also excellent. Dinner only; reservations recommended.
914 N. Peters Street
Tel: 529 1583
Fax: 522 4858
AE, DC, MC, V. $$$

Bacco
310 Chartres St
Tel: 522 2426
Fax: 587 9047
Ralph and Cindy Brennan's Italian restaurant turns out wood-fired pizzas and homemade pastas in the large dining room with Venetian chandeliers and Baroque paintings on the high ceilings. The menu is lengthy and includes a sensational pork tenderloin. Portions are enormous. The place can be found off the lobby of the Hotel de la Poste. Open daily. Reservations are recommended.
AE, D, DC, MC, V. **$$$**

Brigtsen's
723 Dante St, Uptown
Tel: 861 7610
Fax: 866 7397
This small, informal, and popular restaurant has a changing menu that features a blending of Cajun and Creole specialties. Dinner only. Closed on Sunday and Monday. Reservations are required.
AE, MC, V. **$$$**

Broussard's
819 Conti St
Tel: 581 3866 or (800) 248 5423
Fax: 581 3873
Situated one block from Bourbon Street, this romantic old-world French Creole restaurant has several dining rooms and a courtyard. The sauces here are superb, notably those for rack of lamb and braised quail. Indulge yourself in one of the lavish desserts. Dinner only. Reservations and jackets are required.
AE, D, DC, MC, V. **$$$**

Café Degas
3127 Esplanade Ave
Tel: 945 5635
Fax: 943 5255
Across the street from the Degas House bed-and-breakfast, and near City Park and the Fair Grounds, this is a *trés intime* French bistro. Dining is done in a tin-roofed pavilion, so it can get a little noisy when there is a hard rain or heavy traffic on Esplanade. The menu includes onion soup, crepes, salads and steaks. The dress is casual, Reservations are recommended.
AE, MC, V. **$$$**

Café Giovanni
117 Decatur St
Tel: 529 2154
Fax: 528 9265
Email: www.cafegiovanni.com
Chef Duke LoCicero calls his cuisine New World Italian, and his presentations are as appealing to the eye as to the palate. Specialties include a prosciutto pinwheel and veal parmesan. Dinner nightly. Closed for lunch on Saturday, Sunday, and Monday. Jackets and reservations are recommended.
AE, D, DC, MC, V. **$$$**

Café Rue Bourbon
241 Bourbon St
Tel: 524 0114
Fax: 524 0146
Email: joabbott@cajun.net
Classic Creole and Cajun foods are served in the several attractive rooms of this 19th century townhouse. There is also balcony dining overlooking Bourbon Street. Among the favourites are Oysters Rockefeller, shrimp Creole, and crawfish and shrimp étouffées.

Reservations are recommended.
AE, DC, MC, V. **$$$**

Caribbean Room
Pontchartrain Hotel, 2031
St. Charles Ave, Garden District
Tel: 524 0581
Luxurious hotel dining room serving
innovative French Creole dishes
with a focus on seafood. Mile-High
Pie is the dessert extravaganza.
Reservations are recommended.
AE, D, DC, MC, V **$$$**

Christian's
3835 Iberville St
Tel: 482 4924
This popular Mid-City neighborhood
restaurant, set in an old church with
stained glass windows and pews,
serves up classic Creole cuisine,
with local favorites such as
bouillabaisse, gumbo, and fresh
Gulf fish served in a hearty wine
sauce. Closed on Sunday. and for
lunch on Saturday.
AE, DC, MC, V. **$$$**

Gabrielle
3201 Esplanade Ave
Tel: 948 6233
Reservations are not only required,
they are essentials here, as this
tiny, triangular restaurant is almost
always jammed to the rafters, such
is its popularity. The recipes are
straight out of Cajun Country,

Celebrity Chef

K-Paul's Louisiana Kitchen is the
bastion of Cajun celebrity chef
Paul Prudhomme. The menu
changes daily, but expect to find
his famed blackened fish dishes,
as well as other delectable
creations like classic crawfish
etouffée, blackened beef tenders
and sweet potato pecan pie. The
restaurant was recently
renovated to create a handsome
upstairs dining room.
Reservations are not accepted
for lunch, so there is often a line
of people waiting to get in. Be
sure to book for dinner.
Closed Sunday and Monday.
416 Chartres St, French Quarter
Tel: 524 7394
Fax: 943 2935
AE, DC, MC, V. **$$$**

courtesy of chef and owner Greg
Sonnier. His wife Mary turns out
superb desserts, such as carrot
cake and cobblers. There are
imaginative renditions of duck,
rabbit, and alligator, some
wonderful sausage dishes, and
roast chicken served with rice and
pan gravy. Be sure to leave room for
dessert. Dinner only. Closed on
Sunday and Monday.
AE, D, DC, MC, V. **$$$**

Mike's on the Avenue
628 St Charles Ave
Tel: 523 1709
Fax: 523 7327
Chef and owner Mike Fennelly's
classy restaurant presents a fusion
of Pacific Rim, American Southwest,
and Creole New Orleans touches.
Among his popular offerings are
Chinese dumplings, crawfish-filled
spring rolls, and grilled oysters in a
Korean barbecue sauce. The venue
is in the Lafayette Hotel. Closed for
lunch on Saturday and Sunday.
Reservations are recommended.
AE, D, DC, MC, V. **$$$**

Mr B's Bistro
201 Royal St, French Quarter
Tel: 523 2078
Fax: 521 8304
This well-established restaurant
with a large, handsome dining room
that has etched glass and mahogany paneling, offers excellent Creole
and New American cuisine.
Seafood, pasta, and steaks feature
on the menu and desserts are
exotic, especially any of the ones
involving chocolate. Dress is smart
casual. Reservations are
recommended.
AE, D, DC, MC, V. **$$$**

Mosca's
4137 US Highway 90 W.
Tel: 436 9942
An out-of-the-way Italian restaurant
worth traveling for. Try the oysters
in bread crumbs or the superb
roasted chicken. Dinner only.
Closed on Sunday and Monday.
Reservations are recommended.
No credit cards. **$$$**

Pelican Club
615 Bienville St/312 Exchange
Alley
Tel: 523 1504
Fax: 522 2331

The atmosphere here is hushed and
sophisticated, with romantic lighting
and white tablecloths. Specialties
including seafood and pasta dishes,
duck and poultry, and excellent
steaks. Reservations are
recommended. Open for lunch
Monday to Friday.
AE, D, DC, MC, V. **$$$**

Peristyle
1041 Dumaine St
Tel: 593 9535
Chef and owner Anne Kearney calls
her cooking "American bistro-
style," and demonstrates it with
the likes of grilled sea bass with
lemon vinaigrette, steamed
mussels, and pan-roasted squab
served with polenta triangles.
Peristyle is a tiny spot on the
fringe of the Quarter and is usually
crowded. Reservations are
recommended. Closed on Sunday
and Monday and for lunch on
Tuesday, Wednesday, Thursday and
Saturday.
MC, V. **$$$**

Rib Room
Omni Royal Orleans Hotel,
621 St. Louis St, French Quarter
Tel: 529 7045
Fax: 529 7016
Old-brick walls and a sizzling rotis-
serie create a cozy atmosphere.
Huge windows overlook the Royal
Street scene. Beef, game, fowl, and
seafood are all featured on the
menu. The oyster po-boys at lunch
are very good. A champagne brunch
is offered on Sunday. Reservations
are recommended.
AE, D, DC, MC, V. **$$$**

Moderate

Alex Patout's
221 Royal St, French Quarter
Tel: 525 7788
Fax 525 7809
The chef and owner comes from
a long line of Cajun culinary artists
in South Louisiana. His stylish
restaurant showcases seafoods
enhanced by exotic sauces and
seasonings. There are fixed-price
menus for lunch and dinner. Jackets
and reservations are recommended
for dinner. Closed for lunch on
weekends.
AE, D, DC, MC, V. **$$**

Bizou
701 St. Charles Ave
Tel: 524 4114
Fax: 522 1679
Bizou (meaning 'kiss') is a small, chic restaurant run by French chef Daniel Bonnot. Steak au poivre is usually on the changing menu. Recommended are roast duckling with ginger and orange sauce, and the oysters.
AE, D, MC, V. **$$**

Chef's Table
2100 St Charles Ave
Tel: 525 2433
Fax: 525 2455
Specialties in this casual bistro are fried green tomatoes, lobster bisque, gumbo, and barbecue shrimp. There is a piano bar in the evening, an on-site bakery and take-out deli. Dinner reservations are recommended. Closed on Sunday.

Price Guide

$$$$	Over $35 (deluxe)
$$$	$25 –35 (expensive)
$$	$20–25 (moderate)
$	Under $20 (inexpensive)

Price categories are for one three-course dinner, not including beverages, gratuities, and a 9.5 percent tax.

AE, D, DC, MC, V. **$$**

Dooky Chase
2301 Orleans Ave, Treme
Tel: 821 2294
Artworks by local black artists decorate the walls of this stylish restaurant, where soul Creole appears in the form of pork chops, stewed okra, sweet potatoes, and apple pie. Got to be the only one of its kind; if not, certainly the best.
AE, MC, V. **$$**

Gautreau's
1728 Soniat St, Uptown
Tel: 899 7397
Situated in a former pharmacy, this small, casual neighborhood eatery is a great local favorite, serving steaks, fish, and veal dishes. Dinner only. Reservations required. Closed on Sunday.
AE, D, DC, MC, V. **$$**

Nola
534 St. Louis St, French Quarter
Tel: 522 6652
Fax: 524 6178
Another local restaurant of well-known chef Emeril Lagasse. Expect homemade everything, from andouille and Worcestershire sauce to delicious ice cream. Reservations are recommended.
AE, DC, MC, V. **$$**

Palace Café
605 Canal St, Central Business District
Tel: 523 1661
Fax: 523 1633
The Palace is New Orleans' version of a grand Parisian café. The menu features meat, fowl and seafood, plus sinfully delicious desserts. There also is a regular Sunday Blues Brunch.
AE, D, DC, MC, V. **$$**

Ralph & Kacoo's
519 Toulouse St, French Quarter
Tel: 522 5226
Fax: 522 5253
Seafood (and huge portions of it) is the specialty in this casual place. A complimentary serving of yummy, mouth-watering hush puppies (potatoes) comes with each meal.
AE, D, DC, MC, V. **$$**

Red Fish Grill
115 Bourbon St
Tel: 598 1200
Fax: 598 1211
Ralph Brennan's seafood restaurant in the Chateau Sonesta hotel serves heavenly specialties, such as sweet potato catfish and crawfish fettuccine. Although fish is definitely the meat of the matter, there are also pasta dishes, hickory grilled steak and chicken offerings. A steel band plays for the Sunday brunch, which features eye-openers such as a drink called the Red Fish Grill Poinsettia – a blend of champagne and cranberry juice. Open daily for lunch and dinner. Dress is casual. Reservations are not required.
AE, D, DC, MC, V. **$$**

Tujaque's
823 Decatur St, French Quarter
Tel: 525 8676
Fax: 525 8785
The city's second oldest restaurant,

in business since 1856, is in an atmospheric building across from the French Market. A six-course, fixed-price meal is served nightly; the entrée specialty is brisket of beef. Dress is casual.
AE. D. DC, MC. V. **$$**

Upperline
1413 Upperline St, Uptown
Tel: 891 9822
Fax: 897 3477
This intimate café displays art by Louisiana artists and plays taped local jazz. The cuisine is New Orleans and continental dishes. Closed on Monday evenings. Reservations are recommended.
AE, DC, MC, V. **$$**

Inexpensive

Acme Oyster House
724 Iberville St, French Quarter
Tel: 522 5973
Fax: 524 1595
Oysters are the specialty at this simple venue that has been going strong since around the turn of the century. There is a large marble oyster bar and table seating. Salads and sandwiches are available.
AE, DC, MC, V. A. **$**

Bozo's
3117 21st, Metairie
Tel: 831 8666
This is a popular place for gumbo and seafood dishes. It is situated across Causeway Boulevard from Lakeside Mall.
MC, V. **$**

Bruning's
1924 West End Pkwy.
Tel: 288 4521
Located at Lake Pontchartrain, the view whets the appetite for the terrific selection of seafood.
AE, MC, V. **$**

Camellia Grill
626 S. Carrollton Ave, Uptown
Tel: 866 9573
The customers of this extremely popular diner are sometimes seen lined up outside. Virtually a New Orleans institution, the Camellia is famed for its burgers, waffles, chilli, and delicious homemade pastries. No credit cards. **$**

Dunbar's
4927 Freret, Uptown
Tel: 899 0734

Drinking in New Orleans

New Orleans is certainly a hard-drinking town, which is reflected in the fact that it is the only city in the US in which the go-cup is used. The go-cup, as the name suggests, is a cup intended for drinks 'to go.' Carrying a glass of beer or an open beer can is an illegal offense, punishable by a stiff fine, thus, virtually every drinking hole in town provides its customers with go-cups.

Packaged liquor, beer, and wine can be purchased 24 hours a day, seven days a week in New Orleans from grocery and convenience stores, even pharmacies. The legal drinking age is 21.

For a true taste of New Orleans, visitors can try any of the several indigenous alcoholic concoctions. The ubiquitous Hurricane, which originated at Pat O'Brien's, is a potent libation made with dark rum and fruit juices. Another local favorite, the Sazerac, is definitely not for the faint of heart. It is claimed that this drink is the world's first cocktail. It is made with bourbon and bitters and served in a glass that's first swirled with a light coating of ersatz absinthe. (In the original version of the drink, real absinthe was used; this is now illegal in the US). Other cocktails include the rich Ramos gin fizz, made with gin, egg white, soda, cream, and orange flower water. The legendary mint julep contains bourbon, quinine, and mint.

For a list of bars, dance halls and clubs where drinking has been known to take place, see 'Nightlife' on page 292.

This is a very downhome place serving the likes of lip-smackin' fried chicken, red beans and rice, and po-boys.
MC, V. **$**

Gumbo Shop
630 St Peter St, French Quarter
Tel: 525 1486,
toll-free (800) 55GUMBO
Fax: 897 3454
Email: www.gumboshop.com
The Gumbo offers traditional Creole fare in an informal room with an adjoining patio. Their combination platter of red beans and rice, shrimp Creole, and jambalaya is a good introduction to local cuisine.
AE, DC, MC, V. **$**

La Madeleine
547 St Ann St, French Quarter
Tel: 568 9950
Fax: 525 1680
Open for breakfast, lunch, and light dinners, this small, simple restaurant in Jackson Square is almost always packed solid. Salads, sandwiches, and quiches are served, but the main attraction is the selection of breads and pastries. Breads are baked in a wood-burning oven, and the delicious aroma wafts out into the square. Closes daily at 9pm.
AE. DC, MC, V. **$**

Liuzza's
3636 Bienville St
Tel: 482 9120
An old neighborhood institution in Mid-City, Liuzza's is an informal family-style Italian restaurant. You'll find familiar entrées such as lasagna, fettuccine Alfredo, and Italian sausage with pasta. There is a good line-up of salads, seafood dishes, pizza, and sandwiches. Liuzza's sandwich specialty is the 'Frenchuletta,' which is akin to the muffuletta. Closed on Sunday.
No credit cards. **$**

Mother's
401 Poydras St, Central Business District
Tel: 523 9656
Fax: 525 7671
This small, funky eatery opens at 5am for breakfast, which features delicious homemade biscuits, ham and eggs, and grits. The place has been a local favourite for more than 50 years. Superb po-boys, Creole and Cajun dishes, and fried seafood are available for both lunch and dinner. Closed on Sunday and Monday.
No credit cards. **$**

Old Dog New Trick
307 Exchange Alley
Tel: 522 4569
Fax: 949 2936
A restaurant dedicated solely to vegetarian food seems masochistic in the cholesterol capital of the world, but here it is, and doing very well indeed. An all-natural menu, from grains to sweeteners, is the 'Trick', so to speak. They serve grilled vegetables, pizzas, burgers, salads, soups, and desserts. The restaurant is in an ancient passageway between Conti and Bienville streets in the Quarter.
No credit cards. **$**

Poppy's Grill
717 St Peter St
Tel: 524 3287
Fax: 566 1835
This classic 24-hour diner, situated across the street from Preservation Hall and Pat O'Briens, has a jukebox and a bright neon sign. Hearty breakfasts and big burgers are the specialties. The atmosphere is very laid-back, so reservations are not required.
AE, MC, V. **$**

Praline Connection
542 Frenchmen St,
Faubourg Marigny
Tel: 943 3934
Fax: 524 6927
This casual neighborhood restaurant opens for breakfast, lunch and dinner and stays open late on weekends. The menu features wonderful Southern cooking – cornbread, barbecue pork, turnip greens, blackeyed peas and fried chicken. The name of the place comes from the sweet-shop adjacent to the main dining room, where many delectations involving chocolate are served.
Praline Connection II in the Warehouse District (907 St Peters St, tel: 523 3973), has the same fine fare, and gospel music as well.
AE, D, DC, MC, V **$**

Remoulade
309 Bourbon St
Tel: 523 0377
Fax: 581 7908
Owned and operated by Arnaud's, which is just around the corner – and with which it shares a kitchen – Remoulade is a very casual eatery that serves continuously from 11.30am until midnight. Favorites are jambalaya, po-boys, burgers, and barbecue babyback ribs.
AE, D, DC, MC, V. **$**

Sid-Mar's
1824 Orpheum St
Tel: 831 9541
This super-casual local favorite in Bucktown near Lake Pontchartrain serves fresh seafood – boiled, broiled, fried and stuffed.
MC, V. **$**

Snacks and Ice Cream

Café Beignet
334-B Royal St
Tel: 524 5530
There is outdoor seating to manage the overflow of customers in this tiny, usually crowded spot that is a combination of café, art gallery, and concierge service. There are rich pastries and gourmet coffees, as well as light lunch and supper items. You can also make reservations here for restaurant and riverboat cruises. Open daily. No credit cards.

Café du Monde
813 Decatur St, French Quarter
Tel: 581 2914
Fax: 587 0847,
toll-free (800) 772 2927
Email: www.cafedumonde.com
Almost always packed with locals and tourists, this famous and casual 24-hour haven serves only coffee (regular and café au lait, laced with chicory), orange juice, and beignets dusted with powdered sugar. This is a great spot for people-watching, as it's right on Jackson Square and is the traditional last stop after a night on the town. There are branches of the coffeehouse in Riverwalk, New Orleans Centre, and the Esplanade Mall as well as in Atlanta and Japan. No credit cards.

Café Havana
842 Royal St
Tel: 569 9006, (800) 860 2988
Fax: 569 9007
Anyone who likes the aroma of cigars will be in hog-heaven here. This cozy cigar bar has a walk-in humidor, cigars and cigar paraphernalia for sale, plus rocking chairs and espresso and cappuccino, and a limited selection of sweets.
AE. MC. V.

Café Maspero
601 Decatur St, French Quarter
Tel: 523 6250
There's almost always a long line of locals as well as tourists waiting to get in for the famous oversized sandwiches and thick-cut French fries served here. Dress is very casual. Credit cards not accepted.

Croissant d'Or
617 Ursulines St
Tel: 524 4663
This is the place to go for the best croissants and French pastries in town. You can expect long lines for breakfast, especially during special events.
La Marquise, its sister patisserie, (625 Chartres St, tel: 524 0420) also bakes excellent pastries.
V, MC.

Kaldi's
941 Decatur St
Tel: 586 8989
Although it is set in an early 19th century bank building, Kaldi's atmosphere is a throwback to the 1960s. Pastries and gourmet coffees are on offer, but passing the time of day is a major pursuit, with folks huddled over chess, newspapers and crossword puzzles.
AE. D. MC, V.

Napoleon House/Girod Bistro
500 Chartres St, French Quarter
Tel: 524 9752
A popular spot, the Napoleon has peeling sepia walls, pictures of the Little Corporal, taped classical music, and wonderful muffulettas, salads, sandwiches, and desserts. There is outside seating in a pretty courtyard adjoining the bar. Adjacent to the bar is the Bistro, which serves classic Creole cuisine.
AE, MC, V.

Culture

Art Galleries

For centuries, the greatest concentration of art galleries in New Orleans was to be found in the French Quarter. However, the revitalization of the Warehouse District has seen the opening of a profusion of galleries, so much so that the area has been referred to by some as the 'Soho of the South.' The **Contemporary Arts Center** (900 Camp St) has long been the center for avant-garde visual arts in the area, and it continues to be the focal point of the Warehouse District contemporary arts scene. Each fall, the visual arts season kicks off with 'Arts for Art's Sake', an evening of formal gallery openings followed by a gala celebration at the center.

Below is a list of art galleries to be found around town:

Arthur Roger Gallery
432 Julia St, Warehouse District.
Houses an extensive selection of contemporary paintings and sculpture , made by local and regional artists.

Bryant Galleries
524 Royal St, French Quarter.
Concentrates on Haitian, European, and American art, showing sculptures, graphics, glass, and primitives.

Carol Robinson Gallery
4537 Magazine St, Uptown.
Shows contemporary paintings, sculpture, and graphic art.

Dyansen Gallery
433 Royal St, French Quarter.
The collection includes a selection of Erté sculptures, lithographs, seriographs and gouache paintings.

Downtown Gallery
1330 St Charles Ave,
Warehouse District.

Degas in Nola

The French Impressionist painter Edgar Degas (1834-1917) came to New Orleans in October 1872 and returned to Paris in March 1873, a visit which coincided with two exotic holidays, All Saints Day and Mardi Gras. The artist was very taken with New Orleans and its strange, other worldly quality. Degas' ties with the city were significant: his mother, Celestine Musson De Gas, was born into a local French-Creole family; his father purchased a house in the city; and his two younger brothers, René and Achille, lived in New Orleans. René later married his first cousin, Estelle Musson, one of the women Degas found most sympathetic to paint. Degas created hundreds of drawings, pastels and paintings while in New Orleans and also back in Paris, and his family featured widely in these intimate portraits. In 1999, the New Orleans Museum of Art assembled a large body of this work, tracked down from collections around the world, to present the exhibition 'Degas Comes Home'.

Features contemporary works by local and regional artists.
Galerie Simonne Stern
518 Julia St, Warehouse District
Shows the works of regional artists, including paintings, drawings, sculpture, works in glass, and ceramic art.
Hanson Galleries
229 Royal St, French Quarter.
Shows the work of internationally acclaimed contemporary artists such as Peter Max and Leroy Neiman.
Le Mieux Galleries, 332 Julia St, Warehouse District.
Holds monthly exhibitions of aspiring and nationally known Louisiana artists working in various media.
Miriam Walmsley Gallery
201 N. Peters, French Quarter.
Shows the works of local and regional artists, including paintings,

drawings, sculptures, ceramic art, and lots of very good crafts.
Nahan Galleries
540 Royal St, French Quarter.
Features top-quality contemporary paintings and sculptures by nationally known artists.
Rodrigue Gallery
721 Royal St, French Quarter.
Concentrates on the paintings and prints of internationally renowned Louisana artist George Rodrigue.
St Charles Gallery
541 Julia St, Warehouse District.
Features Old Master drawings, 19th-century French and English paintings, fine watercolors and antique maps and prints.
Kurt E. Schon Ltd
510 St Louis St.
Shows traditional 19th-century English and French paintings – salon works and paintings by Impressionists and Victorian artists.
Tilden-Foley Gallery
4119 Magazine St, Uptown.
Exhibits paintings and sculptures by contemporary artists as well as 19th- and early 20th-century American paintings.

Concerts

Classical concerts are occasionally performed at several of the city's churches, notably **St Louis Cathedral** (Jackson Square, tel: 525 9585); **St Charles Avenue Presbyterian Church** (1545 State St, tel: 897 0101); and **Trinity Episcopal Church** (1329 Jackson Ave, tel: 522 0277). The universities, among them **Tulane** (tel: 865-5000); **Loyola** (tel: 861 2011); **Dillard** (tel: 283 8822); and the **University of New Orleans**, known as **UNO** (tel: 286 6000), also present concerts during the year.

In order for visitors to hear some excellent modern music, all they have to do is stroll down **Bourbon Street**, stop by **Jackson Square**, or rest on **Moonwalk**. Street musicians often perform all over the French Quarter. There are also free jazz concerts in **Dutch Alley** in the French Market. Schedules from the Dutch Alley kiosk (at the foot of St Philip Street in the French Market.)

Major rock concerts are often held in the **Louisiana Superdome** (Sugar Bowl Drive, Box Office, tel: 587 3800). The UNO **Lakefront Arena** (6801 Franklin Ave, Box Office tel: 286 7222) is another popular venue for nationally renowned performers. *For music clubs see 'Nightlife', page 292.*

Ballet

The New Orleans Ballet Association (tel: 522 0996) presents contemporary and classical dance at the **Theatre of the Performing Arts** in Armstrong Park. The company usually mounts four productions between September and May.

Opera

The New Orleans Opera Association mounts four productions annually between October and March. They are held at the **Mahalia Jackson Theatre for the Performing Arts** in Armstrong Park. Tickets are available through the New Orleans Opera Association (tel: 529 2278).

Theater

Touring Broadway shows and top-name entertainers appear at the **Saenger Performing Arts Center** (143 N. Rampart St, Box Office tel: 524 2490). New Orleans also has first-rate community theaters.
Le Petit Théâtre du Vieux Carré (616 St Peter St, tel: 522 2081), the oldest community theater in the country, presents a season of plays and musicals between September and June; the **Children's Corner** presents plays geared for children aged three and up.

The **Contemporary Arts Center** (900 Camp St, tel: 522 0122) showcases the talents of new playwrights and mounts avant-garde productions. **Southern Rep** (1437 S. Carrollton Ave, tel: 861 8163) presents plays by Southern playwrights at its theater in Canal Place.
Summer Lyric Theatre (Tulane University, St Charles Ave, tel: 865 5269) offers musical productions throughout the summer season.

Tours

Guided Tours

Friends of the Cabildo
Tel: 523 3939
Fax: 524 9130
Email: Cabildo@gnofn.org;
www.gnofn.org.cabildo
This group conducts walking tours of the French Quarter each week from Tuesday to Saturday at 9.30am and 1.30pm, and on Sunday at 1.30 only. The group gathers in front of the Presbytère, and the tour price includes admission to a minimum of two Louisiana State Museum buildings.

Heritage Tours
Tel: 949 9805
A noted authority on Southern writers conducts walking tours through the French Quarter to the homes and haunts of internationally known authors such as Tennessee Williams, William Faulkner, and Sherwood Anderson.

Jean Lafitte National Historical Park
Tel: 589 2636
Park Rangers conduct free tours through various locations, including the French Quarter and the Garden District. (Reservations are required for the Garden District tour, and you must purchase your own streetcar fare.) Tours are conducted daily, come rain or shine, except on Christmas Day, New Year's Day, and during Mardi Gras. The tours begin at the Folk Life Center, (916–18 N. Peter's St in the French Market).

Le Ob's Tours
Tel: 288 3478, (800) 827 0932
Fax: 288 8517

This organization conducts city and plantation tours that focus on the African-American experience in New Orleans and environs.

Magic Walking Tours
Tel: 588 9693
Fax 522 8523
Haunted houses and the New Orleans Cemetery No.1 are among the fascinating tours of the French Quarter and Garden District.

Preservation Resource Center
Tel: 581 7032
This organization is actively involved in preserving the historical areas in the city. The PRC occasionally conducts informative walking tours with a focus on architecture.

Save Our Cemeteries
Tel: 525 3377; (888) 721 7493
Fax: 525 677
Save Our Cemeteries is a local group that conducts walking tours of St Louis Cemetery No. 1 each Sunday at 10am. The group meets at the Royal Blend Coffeehouse, 623 Royal Street. Reservations are recommended for the 90-minute walk, and a security guard accompanies the group.

Travel Packages

There are several companies that offer attractive packages for travelers who would rather not go it alone in or out of the city:

American Express Vacations
Box 5014, Atlanta, GA 30302
Tel: (800) 241 1700; in
GA (800) 282 0800

Domenico Tours
751 Broadway, Bayonne, NJ
Tel: (800) 554-TOUR.

Maupintour
Box 807, Lawrence, KS
Tel: (800) 255 4266

Tours by Andrea
2838 Touro St, New Orleans, LA 70122
Tel: 944 0253; (800) 553 4895

Tour Operators

Gray Line
Tel: (800) 535 7786
Fax: 587 0742
Email: www.graylineofneorleans.com
Gray Line offers city tours, plantation country tours, riverboat/city tours, and nightclub tours.

McGee's Landing
Tel: (318) 228 2384
Tours of the exotic 800,000-acre Atchafalaya Basin are given on a pontoon boat which can be caught from a location that is a one-and-a-half hours' drive west of New Orleans.

New Orleans Tours
Tel: 592 0562; (800) 543 6332
Fax: 592 0549
This operator offers city tours, plantation country tours, and combination riverboat/city tours.

Tours by Isabelle
Tel: 391 3544; (888) 223 2093
Fax: 391 3564
Email: www.toursbvisabelle.com
Multilingual guides in small minivans give city tours, bayou tours (which include a visit to a Cajun alligator hunter), plantation tours and also a Grand Tour, which is the bayou tour with lunch and a visit to Oak Alley plantation.

Websites

The Internet is a good resource for tourists. These sites are worth scanning for excellent background information and contacts:
- **New Orleans Metropolitan Convention & Visitors' Bureau:**
  www.nawlins.com
- **New Orleans Welcome Center:**
  www.neworleansvb.com
- **Louisana Office of Tourism:**
  www.louisianatravel.com

Many local attractions now have websites that can be consulted for tourist information. Below is a selection of some of the websites worth visiting:
- **Audubon Zoo:**
  www.auduboninstitute.org
- **Bally's Casino:**
  www.ballys.com
- **Children's Museum:**
  www.lcm.org

- **Contemporary Arts Center:**
  www.cacno.org
- **Delta Queen Steamboat Company:**
  www.deltaqueen.com
- **Longue Vue House:**
  www.longuevue.com
- **Mardi Gras World:**
  www.mardigrasworld.com
- **New Orleans Museum of Art:**
  www.noma.org

Festivals

Mardi Gras

The city's all-out party is, of course, **Mardi Gras**, which occurs annually in **February** or **March**. (Because it occurs 46 days before Easter, the date varies from year to year.) Carnival season begins on Twelfth Night (January 6), gradually gathers steam, and ends with a big bash on Mardi Gras. The literal translation of Mardi Gras is Fat (or Shrove) Tuesday, which is the big day, but the last two weeks of Carnival are also known as Mardi Gras.

During the last four days before Fat Tuesday there are parades every day and every night, and the streets of the Central Business District are awash with fantastic floats, marching bands, and highly enthusiastic spectators. On the night of Lundi Gras (Fat Monday, the night before Fat Tuesday), the city hosts a huge free-to-the-public masked ball in Spanish Plaza, replete with live music and fireworks. Fat Tuesday is given over entirely to parades and about a million masked and costumed revelers. At midnight on Fat Tuesday the celebration officially ends and Ash Wednesday marks the beginning of Lent.

Jazz and Heritage Festival

This festival is second only to Mardi Gras, and is commonly known as the **Jazz Fest**. A celebration of music, food, and crafts, it begins on the last weekend of **April** and continues through the first weekend of **May**. This internationally acclaimed event brings thousands of visitors to the city, including top-name musicians from all over the world.

During the two weekends the main venue for the festivities is the Fair Grounds; in between there are all-night jam sessions in many bars and nightclubs around the city. In addition to Mardi Gras and the Jazz Fest, there are more than 75 other festivals, many of them involving a great deal of food.

City Festivals

The following is a listing of some of the other major annual festivals:
February: The always-worth-visiting **Black Heritage Festival** features plenty of jazz and gospel music, as well as a mock jazz funeral.
March: The **Tennessee Williams/New Orleans Literary Festival** is a weekend of plays, symposia, parties, and leisurely French Quarter walking tours.
Mid-March: in a city that loves parades, there are at least two **St Patrick's day** parades each year. On **St Joseph's Day** the city's Italian community decorates altars with food and celebrates with a parade that brings out the Mardi Gras Indians for their only appearance other than on Fat Tuesday.
Early April: The well-attended and colorful **French Quarter Festival** is a full weekend of food, music and fireworks displays.
April: **Spring Fiesta**, which takes place the weekend after Easter, features a parade through the French Quarter and tours of private homes and courtyards.
June: The **Great French Market Tomato Festival** is another great excuse for food, music, and festivities.
Late June/Early July:
The **New Orleans Food & Wine Experience** features tastings from the city's finest restaurants.
Early July: **Go 4th on the River** is the city's big Independence Day celebration on the Riverfront.
September: The always interesting **New Orleans Writers' Conference** brings together aspiring writers and nationally known editors, agents,

and publishers, who give talks and lectures on writing.
October: The **Swamp Fest**, at the Louisiana Swamp Exhibit in Audubon Zoo, is a great music-cum-food celebration of the Cajun culture.
Late October: **Halloween**, rapidly becoming a major event, includes much masking and eye-popping costumes, as well as a Witches Run and tours of haunted houses.
December: The highly seasonal **A New Orleans Christmas** lasts the whole month and features Christmas tree lightings, caroling, Christmas teas, parades, and 'open house' at historic homes.

Regional Festivals

As Louisiana's music and food becomes more popular, some discerning visitors are frequenting the numbers of local fairs and festivals which are held throughout the year in the countryside outside New Orleans. These have colorful names like the **Zachary Sausage Festival** (Zachary), the **Gonzales Jambalaya Festival** (Sorrento), the **Franklin Cajun Fest** (Franklin), the **Cajun French Music and Food Festival** (Lake Charles), the **Festival International de Louisiane** (Lafayette), and the fun-filled **Festival Acadiens** (Lafayette).

The best way to find out about these local fairs is to consult the *Louisiana Fairs and Festivals Guide*, a pamphlet available from the New Orleans or Louisiana Tourist Boards. Next to each event listing is a telephone number which can be called to obtain more specific information.

Other Events

January 1: The Sugar Bowl Classic, played in the Superdome, is one of the nation's oldest college bowl games, and attracts thousands of ardent football fans. Under the umbrella of the Sugar Bowl Classic are tennis, basketball, and sailing match-ups.
Mid-April: The Crescent City Classic, a popular 10K road race, begins in

Jackson Square and ends with much hoopla at the Audubon Zoo.
Late April: The Freeport-McMoRan Golf Classic, which takes place at the English Turn Country club, is a prestigious PGA golf tournament that attracts golfers from around the globe.
May: The Zoo-To-Do, a major social event, is the largest nonmedical fund-raiser in the country.
November 1: All Saints Day is a local memorial day when graveyard tombs are banked with flowers and New Orleanians flock to the cemeteries for candlelight vigils.
November: The Bayou Classic is an annual 'shoot-out' between the Southern University and Grambling University football teams.
December: Celebration in the Oaks, when City Park's majestic trees are festooned with Christmas lights.
December 24: Bonfires on the Levee is an ages-old Christmas Eve tradition in the parishes to the west of the city, where gigantic bonfires on both sides of the Mississippi are torched to light the way for Papa Noel. As part of Creole Christmas there are river-boat excursions from Jackson Square to see the lightings.
December 31: The Countdown in Jackson Square is the New Orleans version of the New Year's Eve cele-bration in New York's Times Square.

Temperature Tip

The city's hot, humid summers are not to be underestimated, especially if you plan to be at an outdoor festival all day. The locals take the weather seriously and so should you; the gay Pride Fest was moved from June to September specifically because of the heat. Wear a hat to shield your head from the sun, and sunscreen for your skin. You may want to cover up bare arms and legs with light-weight clothing. Drink plenty of water and go easy on the booze. Salt tablets, which make the rounds at Jazz Fest and are available at pharmacies, replace body salt lost through perspiration.

Nightlife

New Orleans is a 24-hour town, which means there are no legal closing hours. There are clubs and bars that stay open around the clock; others that don't become animated until midnight or later; and still others that close down around 1am or 2am, or whenever business slacks off. Because there are few rules regarding closing time, it's best to call your destination to see if it is still open before heading out bar-hopping at 4am. (Bar-hopping at 4am is not uncommon in The Big Easy).

Don't be shy to ask about prices and policy before entering. Many nightclubs and discos have a cover charge; if in doubt, call in advance to find out. Although closing hours are somewhat loose, you can usually count on a two-drink minimum rule, especially in bars that feature music.

The terms 'pub,' 'bar,' and 'night-club' tend to blur in this town. There are bars with great music, and great bars with no music at all. A nightclub can be anything from a funky dive to a sleek club.

Bars

Bayou Bar
Pontchartrain Hotel, 2031 St Charles Avenue, Garden District
Tel: 524 0581
Sophisticated, up-market piano bar for soothing sounds.

Checkpoint Charlie's
501 Esplanade Ave
Tel: 947 0979
This bar made its film debut in the film *The Pelican Brief*, when Julia Roberts did her laundry here. It does have a laundromat, as well as very loud, very late blues and rock, a pool table, and a lending library.

Esplanade Lounge
621 St Louis St
Tel: 529 5333
Held in the lobby lounge of the Royal Orleans hotel, where romantic piano music is played nightly. Pastries, liqueurs, and coffee can be bought.

544 Club
544 Bourbon St, French Quarter
Tel: 523 6611
R&B saxophonist Gary Brown and his band have long played great Top 40 hits and soul classics here.

The F&M Patio Bar
4841 Tchoupitoulas
Tel: 895 6784
A great favorite of locals, with a jukebox, a late-night menu, and a pool table.

Fourth Quarter Sports Bar
309 Decatur St
Tel: 525–PLAY
The longest bar in New Orleans serves up beer and burgers. The venue also offers billiards, big-screen TVs and a great crowd.

Jimmy's Club
8200 Willow, Uptown
Tel: 861 8200
College kids and young rockers flock in here for loud, live rock.

Lafitte's Blacksmith Shop
941 Bourbon St, French Quarter
Tel: 523 0066
This ancient bar is an ages-old favorite of artists and writers.

Napoleon House
500 Chartres St, French Quarter
Tel: 524 9752
Wildly popular with local and visiting artists and writers, this bar offers taped classical music and a great atmosphere.

Pat O'Brien's
718 St Peter St, French Quarter
Tel: 525 4823
One of the world's best-known places, Pat's has three bars, including a raucous piano bar and a courtyard. This is where the cocktail the Hurricane originated.

The Polo Lounge
300 Gravier St
Tel: 523 3000
An up-market piano bar in the sumptuous Windsor Court Hotel that is a meeting place for the city's local elite.

The Red Room Bar
2040 St Charles Ave.
Tel: 528 9759
A super-lush supper club that has a bar menu for those more intent on listening (and cigar–smoking) than dining.

Sazerac Bar
Fairmont Hotel, Central Business District
A handsome up-market bar that has been a favorite watering hole of local politicians and high-rollers since the 1930s.

Clubs

Chris Owens Club
Corner of Bourbon and St Louis Streets, French Quarter
Tel: 523 6400
Virtually a New Orleans icon in herself, the classy Ms Owens does a sexy Las Vegas-style show in a sophisticated supper club.

Donna's
800 N. Rampart St.
Tel: 596 6914
This small, somewhat squashed club features barbecue and live brass bands.

Funky Butt
714 N. Rampart St
Tel: 558 0872
Named after a 19th-century jazz hall, this very popular venue has art deco flourishes, both a jazz and a dance floor, and a menu of Creole, Middle Eastern, and Mediterranean delights.

House of Blues
225 Decatur St
Tel: 529-BLUES
This live music venue is another in a blues chain co-founded by Isaac Tigrett, who also co-founded the Hard Rock cafés with Dan Aykroyd, and other celebrities. House of Blues is a large rambling place with several rooms and hearty fare as well as hard-driving blues.

Jimmy Buffett's Margaritaville
1104 Decatur St, French Quarter
Tel: 592 2565
The New Orleans hang-out for Parrot Heads is a big sprawling venue where live music of the mixed-bag variety is played nightly. When he's in town, Buffett himself likes to

take the stage. An adjacent shop sells Parrot Head paraphernalia.

Maple Leaf Bar
8316 Oak St, Uptown
Tel: 866-9359; 24-hour concert line: 866-LEAF
Popular with all ages for its live music and casual, friendly crowd. Good every night, but the Cajun night dances (usually on Thursday) are not to be missed.

Nightlife Note

If you hear of a 'great little place' off-the-beaten track that dishes up 'killer drinks, spicy food and music the devil would die for', then chances are it's true: New Orleans is that kind of town. Unfortunately, the best clubs are often in the worst areas. Don't set off into the unknown with just a scrap of paper giving the address; try to arrange with your tipster to meet up beforehand and go together. Failing that, take a taxi straight to the destination, and, when you're ready to leave again, call a cab from the club.

Michaul's
840 St Charles Ave, Central Business District
Tel: 522 5517
A great place for live Cajun music and dancing.

Mid-City Lanes & Sports Palace
4133 S. Carrollton Ave, Mid-City
Tel: 482-3133
This combination bowling alley and dance hall features 'rock and bowl' to live music every Friday night.

Mulate's
201 Julia St, Warehouse District
Tel: 522 1492
Live Cajun music, food, and dancing in the New Orleans branch of a popular club headquartered in the heart of Cajun Country.

Palm Court Jazz Café
1204 Decatur St, French Quarter
Tel: 525 0200
Traditional jazz played by some of the city's best musicians, is showcased in this handsome café that became an overnight sensation after its opening in 1989. It is

always crowded, and serves moderately priced Creole and Cajun food.

Pete Fountain's Club
Hilton Hotel, 2 Poydras St
Tel: 523 4374
This sophisticated club on the third floor of the Hilton is the home base of New Orleans native and clarinetist Pete Fountain. The famed musician is often out on tour, so call before visiting if hoping to catch a performance.

Preservation Hall
726 St Peter St, French Quarter
Tel: 522 2238 (day), 523 8939 (night). In a class by itself, the Hall is neither pub, nightclub, nor bar. Internationally renowned, it is virtually a shrine (albeit a funky one) to the preservation of traditional jazz. This seedy spot is where all the old-time jazz legends play. Not to be missed, but don't expect creature comforts. There isn't a bar, but you can get a go-cup next door at Pat O'Brien's and bring it in.

Snug Harbor
626 Frenchmen St, Faubourg Marigny
Tel: 949 0696
Local and nationally acclaimed artists play jazz, R&B, blues, and you-name-it in this long-time favorite of the young and the not-so-young. Good steaks and burgers are served in the adjoining café. Dress is very casual.

Storyville District
125 Bourbon St, French Quarter
Tel: 410 1000
Not a club exactly – more a musical way of life – the Storyville is an entertainment and dining complex set up by Jazz Fest supremos in conjunction with a noted restaurateur. Music from noon until 1am, most of it live.

Tipitina's
501 Napoleon Ave, Uptown
Tel: 897 3943 or 895-TIPS
Oozing with atmosphere, this laid-back club is the place for classic New Orleans-style rhythm and blues, as well as traditional jazz, Cajun, rock, and zydeco. Local artists and nationally known touring performers play Tip's. This is where the Neville Brothers perform when

they're in town. This popular place has bars and dance floors upstairs and down. Stiff competition in the form of the House of Blues has forced Tip's to air condition the Uptown club and open two additional venues: **Tipitina's Big Room** (310 Howard Ave) occupies more than one big room of the former City Lights. **Tipitina's French Quarter** (223 N. Peters St) is located right around the corner from House of Blues.

Gambling

Casino gambling floated into New Orleans in 1994 in the form of 19th-century style riverboats with gingerbread trim and large red paddlewheels. The boats have not had an easy ride.

State law requires that riverboats cruise for 90 minutes every three hours, but the law has repeatedly been flouted since the boats' operators find it more lucrative to remain dockside. At the time of going to press, three gambling riverboats remained afloat in New Orleans, all of them simply aslosh with slot machines, gaming tables, video poker, buffets, and entertainment. The riverboats are: **Bally's *Casino Lakefront Resort*** (1 Stars & Stripes Blvd, tel: 248 3200 or (800) 572 2559), on Lake Pontchartrain near the Lakefront Airport; the ***Treasure Chest*** (5050 Williams Blvd, Kenner, tel: 443 8000 or (800) 298 0711) also on Lake Pontchartrain; and the ***Boomtown Belle*** (4132 Peters Rd, Harvey, tel: 366 7711), on the West Bank, docking in the Harvey Canal.

After years of false starts and lawsuits, the long-awaited land-based casino at the foot of Canal Street, **Harrah's Casino**, opens. With 2,840 slot machines and 114 gaming tables, the casino has five themes – the Jazz Court, Mardi Gras Court, Court of the Mansion, Smuggler's Court, and a Court of Good Fortune. Some kinks still remain, but it seems that by and large, New Orleans finally has a gambling den on dry land.

Shopping

What to Buy

Few visitors to New Orleans leave town without at least one box of **pralines** – gift boxes can be found in candy and souvenir shops all over town: Southern Candymakers at 334 Decatur Street is among the best, for, as well as having won the 'Best Candy' award at the Atlanta, Georgia, Gourmet Show, they make the sweet stuff right in the shop for all to see.

Chicory coffee, **beignet mix**, and **spices** are also widely available. New Orleans and south Louisiana **cookbooks** are popular and make wonderful gifts. There are several places that ship **New Orleans food**. One shop – Bayou to Go – can be found at the airport, where you can pick up your alligator along with your plane. The New Orleans School of Cooking, which has a retail shop in the Jax (Jackson) Brewery, also ships local foods and spices.

Souvenirs to Go

Popular souvenirs from the city include **Carnival masks**, which are prominently featured in many gift shops. These range from small ceramic decorative wall masks to garish and elaborate face masks made of leather, feathers, sequins and beads. **Mardi Gras beads** themselves – those small ropes of gaudy glitter thrown from the floats to the scrambling crowds below – also make good trinkets to carry home, especially if purchased in the Mardi Gras colors of green and purple. **Mardi Gras posters** are for sale all the year round, just in case you missed the real event.

Jazz Fest posters are also hot items for tourist shopping; first editions are now collectors' items. The city is known for its many **antique stores**, which range from chic and expensive to little poke-around places. **Jazz records** and tapes, **second-line parasols**, **Panama hats**, and **bisque dolls** dressed in frilly antebellum garb are also popular.

Let's Go Antiquing (tel: 899 3027) is a shopping service whose expert on antiques provides customized shopping tours and helpful advice.

Shopping Areas

The Central Business District has several posh shopping malls on Poydras and Canal streets. There are 40 or so stores and boutiques in **Canal Place** (333 Canal St) including Saks Fifth Ave, F.A.O. Schwarz, Gucci, Godiva Chocolatiers, Benetton, and Esprit. On the third level there is a health club, a barber and beauty salons, a food court and four first-run cinemas. The **New Orleans Centre** (1400 Poydras St) has Lord & Taylor, Macy's, Ann Taylor, Gentlemen's Quarter Ltd, Rapp's Luggage, and Sam Goody Records & Tapes, as well as a host of other shops and several restaurants. **Riverwalk** (foot of Poydras Street at the Mississippi River) has more than 140 shops, including The Sharper Image, Abercrombie & Fitch, Banana Republic, The Gap, and Victoria's Secret, as well as the shops of 60 or so local merchants, a large food court, and several upscale restaurants. The Central Business District's rapidly expanding **Warehouse District** is noted for art galleries, most of them specializing in contemporary works by regional artists; **Julia Street** is known as Gallery Row. When you visit it you'll find out why.

The **French Quarter** is awash with shops, ranging from those housed in tiny hole-in-the-wall places to handsome Creole townhouses to the Jackson Brewery Corporation's three malls – The

Jackson Brewery, the Millhouse, and the Marketplace, all three of which contain a vast array of boutiques and restaurants. In the **Jax Brewery** most shops have moved to make room for the opening of Planet Hollywood, but one fixture that remains is the New Orleans School of Cooking.

Adjacent to the Brewery, the **Millhouse** also has a slew of shops, including Aca Joe's, The Limited, Benetton, Fudge Time, and Bergen Galleries. A short walk away, the **Marketplace** is home to, among others, Bookstar, Tower Video, the Hard Rock Café, and Chico's Clothing. A block downriver of the Jax Brewery, the **French Market**, anchored at the upriver corner by Café du Monde on Jackson Square, has within its arcades and colonnades an assortment of specialty boutiques, candy stores, ice-cream parlors, and open-air cafés with Dixieland bands holding forth. (There are frequent free jazz concerts in Dutch Alley in the French Market.)

Just downriver from the French Market are the open sheds of the **Farmer's Market**, where farmers have been bringing their produce to town for more than 160 years. Rows of bins are loaded with pecans and fresh produce. On weekends, a huge flea market is spread out around the Farmer's Market; locals and tourists love to poke through and look for 'junque.'

Royal Street is famed for exclusive and expensive antique stores, many of which carry exquisite 17th-, 18th-, and 19th-century furniture, jewelry, and decorative pieces. Notable among the stores are Rothchild's, Henry Stern, Dixon & Dixon, M.S. Rau, Keil's, Manheim, and Waldhorn's. These can be found between Canal and St Ann streets. **Chartres Street** also has a fine selection of up-market antique stores, including Lucullus, Charles Cooper, Blackmoor, and Boyer Antiques & Doll Shop.

Magazine Street has scores of antique stores housed in once-grand Victorian mansions and little Creole cottages. The Magazine Street Merchants Association publishes a handy guide, available at the New Orleans Welcome Center, that details six miles of stores, boutiques, and restaurants.

Uptown, away from the Quarter, **Riverbend** is popular for shopping sprees. It contains many fascinating shops and boutiques of mainly local merchants. **East New Orleans**, the **Lakefront area**, and **Metairie** have sprawling concrete malls with major department stores, such as Sears Roebuck & Co, Dillard's, and J.C. Penney.

Shopping Hours

Most downtown department stores are open Monday–Saturday 9.45 or 10am–5.30 or 6pm; some open Sunday 1–5pm. Some shopping malls in town are open daily 10am–10pm or 9am–9pm. Hours vary greatly in the French Quarter; many establishments are open all seven days of the week. As a general rule they are open 9am–5.30 or 6pm.

Export Procedures

The up-market shops and department stores will arrange for goods to be mailed and shipped abroad.

Louisiana Tax Free Shopping (LTFS), based on Europe's VAT, provides refunds of Louisiana State tax and, in some cases, local sales tax, to international visitors on items purchased in Louisiana from participating retailers. Only those merchants displaying the LTFS sticker participate in the program. International visitors with a valid passport and a roundtrip international travel ticket of less than 90 days' duration qualify for sales tax refund. It works as follows: When making a purchase, visitors show their passports and request a receipt and tax refund voucher. They then pay the full price, including sales tax, for the purchase and receive a receipt along with the voucher. At the LTFS

refund center located at the airport, the vouchers can be redeemed upon presentation of the voucher, receipt, passport, and travel ticket. Refunds of up to $500 will be made in cash; larger refunds will be issued by check and mailed to visitors at their home address. If purchases are made by credit card, a visitor may elect to apply the tax refund as credit on his or her card.

Complaints Procedures

If you wish to make a complaint, it should be filed with the Better Business Bureau (1539 Jackson Ave, tel: 581 6222) or with the Chamber of Commerce (301 Camp St, tel: 527 6900).

Clothes Chart

Men		Women	
Suits		**Suits/Dresses**	
US	Metric	US	Metric
34	44	8	36
36	46	10	38
38	48	12	40
40	50	14	42
42	52	16	44

Shirts		**Blouses/Sweaters**	
US	Metric	US	Metric
14	36	32	40
14.5	37	34	42
15	38	36	44
15.5	39	38	46
16	40	40	48
16.5	41	42	50

Shoes			
US	Metric	US	Metric
7	39	5	35
7.5	40	5.5	35
8	41	6	36
8.5	42	6.5	37
9	43	7	38
9.5	43	7.5	38
10	44	8	39
10.5	44	8.5	39

Sport

Participant Sports

A number of participant sports can be enjoyed in New Orleans:

Bicycling
During the day, some of the French Quarter streets are closed off to motor traffic to allow for pedestrians and cyclists. City and Audubon Parks are ideal places for cycling. Bikes can be hired at French Quarter Bicycle & Stroller Rental (410 Dauphine St, tel: 522 3101), Bicycle Michael's (618 Frenchmen St, tel: 945 9505), and the City Park Casino (tel: 483 9371).

Boating
Canoes and paddle boats can be rented at the Casino (tel: 483 9371) for easy boating on the pretty lagoons of City Park. Sailing on Lake Pontchartrain is a favorite summertime activity. A Pierson 26 can be rented from Tim Murray Sailboats (tel: 283 2507). North of Lake Pontchartrain, the Bogue Chitto and Tangipahoa Rivers are great places for canoeing and tubing. For information about rentals in the area, contact the St Tammany Parish Tourist & Convention Commission (tel: (800) 634 9443).

Golf
The city has many fine public golf courses. Among them is an 18-hole course at Audubon Park (473 Walnut St, tel: 865 8260), four 18-hole courses, plus a 100-tee double-decker driving range at City Park (1040 Filmore Ave, tel: 483 9396); and an 18-hole course at the Joe Bartholomew Municipal Golf Course (6514 Congress Dr. Pontchartrain Park, tel: 288 0928).

Hiking
Backpacking hikes are organized from time to time by the Louisiana Nature and Science Center (tel: 246 5672).

Horseback Riding
Organized trail rides are arranged at Cascade Stables in Audubon Park (tel: 891 2246).

Jogging
Audubon Park has a 2-mile jogging track that runs beneath a canopy of oak trees; there are 18 exercise stations along the way. Other popular jogging places are the Mississippi River levee, especially Uptown at the great river bend, and in City Park.

Tennis
The Audubon Park Tennis Center (Tchoupitoulas at Audubon Park, tel: 895 1042) has 10 tennis courts. City Park Wisner Tennis Center (Victory Ave, tel: 483 9383) has 39 courts. The Joe Brown Tennis Center (5603 Read Blvd, tel: 246 7414) has 12 courts. The Rivercenter Tennis & Racquetball Club (New Orleans Hilton Riverside & Towers, 2 Poydras St, tel: 587 7242) has 8 courts.

Spectator Sports

Baseball
The city has no major league franchise; however, the New Orleans Zephyrs, an AAA team affiliated with the Houston Astros, play home games at Zephyr Stadium in Jefferson Parish (tel: 734 5155). Locals also turn out to cheer the teams of Tulane University and the University of New Orleans.

Basketball
During the week preceding the annual Sugar Bowl shootout, the Superdome is the venue for the Sugar Bowl Basketball Tournament. The Dome also hosts the men's NCAA Final Four when it's played in New Orleans. The women's NCAA Final Four is played at UNO Lakefront Arena. Colleges and universities that play home games in gyms and fieldhouses around town include Delgado Junior College, Dillard, Xavier, Southern University, Tulane University, and the University of New Orleans.

Football
The main venue is the Louisiana Superdome. The New Orleans Saints of the National Football League play home games in the Superdome on Sunday afternoons and the occasional Monday night. The season begins in September and runs through December, culminating in January with the Super Bowl. New Orleans has hosted more Super Bowl games than any other city in the US.

On Saturday afternoons the Tulane Green Wave plays home games in the Superdome. In November, the Bayou Classic pits Grambling University against Southern University in a tough annual grudge match.

On New Year's Day, the annual Sugar Bowl Classic features top-flight collegiate teams slugging it out in the Superdome (see box).

Golf
In the spring the English Turn Country Club (Hwy 406, East Canal, Westbank, tel: 831 4653) hosts the Entergy Classic, a PGA event that attracts top professional golfers from around the world.

Horse Racing
The season at the Fair Grounds (1751 Gentilly Blvd, tel: 943 2200), the nation's third oldest track, opens Thanksgiving Day and runs to mid-April.

Running
Thousands compete each April in the Crescent City Classic, which begins in Jackson Square and ends in Audubon Park. Other organized runs include the Mississippi River Bridge Run (August); the Witches Run (October); the Thanksgiving Day Classic (November); and the Corporate Run (December). For information, contact the Greater New Orleans Runners Association (tel: 454 8247 or 340 7223).

Ice Hockey

The New Orleans Brass (1201 St. Peter St, tel: 522-7825) of the East Coast Hockey League played their first two seasons in the Municipal Auditorium; the team is moving to the New Orleans Arena, behind the Superdome. Their season runs from mid-October till the first of April.

Soccer

The New Orleans Storm (6000 Airline Hwy, tel: 734-5155), an A Minor League affiliate of the Dallas Burn, plays at Zephyr Stadium. The season runs from April till August

The Sugar Bowl

The annual college-football Sugar Bowl Classic on New Year's Day is a big event in the sports calendar, watched on TV by households all over America.

The idea of a mid-winter championship was first discussed in 1927 by James M. Thomson, publisher of the *New Orleans Item*, and sports editor Fred Digby, who coined the name 'Sugar Bowl.' It was only in 1934 that plans were realized: 300 guarantors were approached to put up $100 each to raise the $30,000 needed to launch the game. Although America was still suffering the effects of the Great Depression, investors were interested. They were given the choice of having the $100 paid back in cash or in football tickets: without exception they chose the tickets.Today, this agreement is still honored, with families of the investors guaranteed the right to buy 20 tickets to the heavily subscribed Bowl, the equivalent in dollars of the original investment.

The first game was an unqualified success. It was played between New Orleans' Tulane University, unbeaten in the South, and the Temple Owls, unbeaten in the North. In an exhilarating, nail-biting finish, Tulane won.

Further Reading

Recommended Books

Thousands of books have been written about New Orleans. For the discerning reader, here is a hand-picked list of books we think captures the essence of the city:

Fiction

The Moviegoer by Walker Percy (1961 Random House, reissued in 1998 in paperback by Vintage Press). Winner of the 1961 National Book Award, this story follows Binx Bollinger – the title character – during Mardi Gras week in New Orleans. Ironic and witty, the book captures the mood and spirit of the city and of Carnival.

All Saints by Karen Palmer (1997 Soho Press). This author's debut novel begins with the release from prison of a Cajun, Harlan Desonnier, who was incarcerated for eight years for the accidental killing of his wife. Set in the 1950s, the story is a tale of Harlan's spiritual redemption, and vividly depicts the character, landscapes, and lifestyles of New Orleans and, more importantly, the culture and attitudes of Cajun Country.

A Confederacy of Dunces by John Kennedy Toole (1987 Grove Press, republished in 1995 by Random House). Winner of the 1987 Pulitzer Prize, this rollicking romp through New Orleans tells of the outrageous escapades of the impossible Ignatius J. Reilly. The plot is richly-woven and wildly funny. No book better captures New Orleans dialects better than this. Sadly, Toole took his own life in 1980, in part because he was unable to find a publisher for this book. After his death, his mother, Thelma, persevered, finally persuading the writer Walker Percy to read the manuscript. He not only read it, but wrote the book's introduction.

Non-fiction

Prism of the Night: A Biography of Anne Rice by Katharine Ramsland (1994 Plume). Rutgers University professor Katharine Ramsland explores Rice's life, combining psychological interpretations with a philosophical theme. The section on the death of Rice's daughter as it relates to *Interview with the Vampire* is particularly moving. Ramsland is also the author of *The Vampire Companion: The Official Guide to Anne Rice's The Vampire Chronicles* (1995, Ballantine) and other Rice-related books.

Haunted City: An Unauthorized Guide to the Magical, Magnificent World of Anne Rice by Joy Dickenson (1995 Citadel Press). This delightful book takes the reader on a tour of the French Quarter, the Garden District, and the plantation sights visited by characters in Rice's novels.

Hail Babylon: In Search of the American City at the End of the Millennium by Andrei Codrescu (1998 St Martin's Press). Essays and sketches by National Public Radio commentator, artist, and documentary filmmaker Andrei Codrescu, a transplanted Transylvanian who makes his home in the Crescent City. In this collection, he provides atmospheric and often wickedly funny sketches of New Orleans as well as Oxford, Mississippi, Little Rock, Arkansas, and Park City, Utah.

The Muse is Always Half-Dressed in New Orleans by Andrei Codrescu (1995 Picador USA Press). In this collection of essays, Codrescu reflects on the contrast between the moods of Transylvania and New Orleans. The book includes an ode to baseball; an interview with Robert Duvall and a review of a movie, "that hardly anyone has ever seen."

New Orleans Stories: Great Writers on the City, edited by John Miller, illustrated by Andrei Codrescu (1992 Chronicle Books). A collection of trenchant, often hilarious essays on New Orleans by Walker Percy, Tennessee Williams, Truman Capote, William

Faulkner, and Louis Armstrong, among others.

Fabulous New Orleans by Lyle Saxon (1989 Pelican). This book was first published in 1928 before the evolution of today's Vieux Carré. Noted Louisiana writer Saxon recalls visits to the French Quarter when it was a decaying neighborhood, overgrown with weeds. Romantics will love reading this book in a setting such as Kaldi's or the Napoleon House and reflecting on the sea changes that have occurred in the Quarter since the book was written.

Mardi Gras: New Orleans by Henri Schindler (1997, Abbeville Press). This is a definitive history of Carnival and Mardi Gras, by a well-known New Orleans historian.

Lords of Misrule: Mardi Gras and the Politics of Race in New Orleans by James Gill (1997 University of Mississippi Press). New Orleans *Times-Picayune* columnist James Gill documents the debate that began with the 1991 city council's order that all Carnival krewes must sign an oath that their clubs be fully desegregated.

Architecture

New Orleans: Life in the Cities of the Dead, photographed by Mason and Robert Florence, edited by Ann Cahn, (1997 Batture) and *Elysium: A Gathering of Souls: New Orleans Cemeteries* (1997, LSU Press). Both of these beautiful coffee-table books show haunting photographs of the mausoleums, monuments, statuary and tombs of New Orleans' famed above-ground cemeteries.

New Orleans Architecture: Vol. VIII, The University Sector by Friends of the Cabildo (1997 Pelican Publishing). This is the eighth in a series of books on New Orleans architecture that has been compiled and published since the early 1970s. The books are thoroughly researched, with detailed descriptions of the city's architecture. Earlier books in the series have covered the American Sector; the Creole Faubourgs; Faubourg Treme and Bayou Road; and the Cemeteries. At the time of going to press, the highly anticipated volumes on the French Quarter and the Garden District are still in the works.

Art

Art in the American South: Works from the Ogden Collection by Randolph Delehanty (1996, LSU Press). Delehanty, former curator of the Ogden Collection of Southern Art, has compiled 237 full-color reproductions culled from the collection of Roger Houston Ogden, New Orleans attorney and entrepreneur. The Ogden Collection is one of the most comprehensive collections of Southern art in the world. In this handsome book Delehanty has divided the artworks into categories, among them landscapes, rivers, and seaboards; Ssouthern flora and fauna; and portraits of Southerners.

Queen of the Vampires

Anne Rice is New Orleans' most famous contemporary writer, so here's a list of some of her best books. Signed editions are sometimes available from Rice's local bookshop:
Garden District Bookshop
2727 Prytania Street
New Orleans, LA 70130
Tel: 504 895 2266
Fax: 504 895 0111
Email: Betbooks@aol.com

Interview with the Vampire (1976, Knopf) As told in his own words, the mortal and immortal life of Louis the Vampire. The book that started the whole thing off.
Feast of All Saints (1979, Random House) Historical novel set in 1840s New Orleans.
Vampire Lestat (1985, Knopf) Louis revisited. A more sympathetic vampire this time around, Louis reveals himself to the world and becomes a famous rock musician.

The Witching Hour (1990, Knopf) The first in the Mayfair Witches series tells the tale of a tightly knit family of Nola-based witches.
Violin (1997, Knopf). A Gothic romance whose protagonist, Triana Becker, lives in New Orleans and mourns a dead daughter, all the while experiencing uncanny visions in which she sees the ghost Stefan, formerly a Russian prince, who feeds on her grief in order to perform on his Stradivarius. Some reviewers have noted auto-biographical threads in this novel.
Memnoch the Devil (1997, Ballantine, paperback). In the fifth of the Vampire Chronicles, Lestat is in New York stalking a big-time cocaine dealer and religious-art smuggler, when he realizes he himself is being stalked. His stalker is Memnoch the Devil, with whom Lestat has debates about God and Man and flaps off on a tour of heaven, hell, and all of history.

The Vampire Armand (1998, Knopf). In this sequel to *Memnoch the Devil,* the book opens with Armand hovering over Lestat, who is lying on the floor of a cathedral. Armand, who first appeared at the Theatres des Vampires in *Interview with the Vampire* narrates this totally absorbing tale, relating just how he was 'recruited' by Marius, who will later induct Lestat into the vampire world.
Pandora (1998, Knopf). Further vampire chronicles. Pandora is the daughter of a senator in the time of Augustus Caesar who flees to Antioch, where she discovers the Egyptian and Oriental cults and encounters the sexy and handsome Vampire Marius. This is the story of how a Roman girl becomes a vampire in modern Paris.
Vittorio The Vampire: New Tales of the Vampires (1999, Knopf). Independent of the Lestat series, Rice calls this her vampire version of *Romeo and Juliet.*

History and General

Encyclopedia of Witches and Witchcraft, by Rosemary Ellen Guilley (Facts on File, New York/Oxford, 1989).

Gumbo Ya-Ya (A Collection of Louisiana Folk Tales), compiled by Lyle Saxon, Edward Dreyer, and Robert Tallant (Pelican Publishing, Gretna, La, 1987).

A History of Louisiana, by Harriet Magruder (D.C. Heath & Co, Boston, 1911).

History of New Orleans, by John Smith Kendall (Lewis Publishing Co, Chicago, two volumes, 1922).

Huey Long's Louisiana Hayride, The American Rehearsal for Dictatorship, 1928-40, by Harnett T. Kane (Pelican Publishing Co, Gretna, La, 1941).

In and Around the old St Louis Cathedral of New Orleans, by C.M Chambon (Philippe's Printery, New Orleans, 1908).

In the Land of Dreamy Dreams, by Ellen Gilchrist (University of Arkansas Press, 1981).

Lives of the Saints, by Nancy Lemann (Knopf, New York, 1985).

Louisiana, A Narrative History by Edwin Adams Davis (Claitor's Publishing Division, Baton Rouge, third edition, 1971).

My Tears Spoiled My Aim and Other Reflections on Southern Culture. by John Shelton Reed (University of Missouri Press, Columbia, Missouri, 1993).

New Orleans City Guide, written and compiled by the Federal Writers' Project of the Works Progress Administration for the city of New Orleans (Houghton Mifflin Co., Boston, 1938).

New Orleans Unmasqued, by S. Frederick Starr (Edition Dedeaux, 1985).

New Orleans Yesterday and Today, by Walter G. Cowan, John C. Chase, Charles L. Dufour, O.K LeBlanc, and John Wilds (Louisiana State University Press, Baton Rouge, 1983).

Southern by the Grace of God, by Michael Andrew Grissom (Pelican, Gretna, La, 1988).

A Southern Collection by Estill Curtis Pennington (Morris

Communications Corporation, Augusta, Georgia, 1992).

Storyville, New Orleans, Being an Authentic, Illustrated Account of the Notorious Red-Light District, by Al Rose (University of Alabama Press, 1974).

The Streetcars of New Orleans by Louis C. Kennick and E. Harper Charlton (Pelican Publishing Co, Gretna, La, 1975).

Voodoo in New Orleans, by Robert Tallant (Pelican Publishing Co, Gretna, La, 1983).

Other Insight Guides

Nearly 200 books in the *Insight Guides* series cover every continent and include 40 titles devoted to the United States, from Alaska to Atlanta, Seattle to Miami.

Destinations in this particular region include:

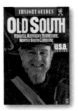

Insight Guide: Old South
A local team of writers and photographers offers a revealing look into the fascinating history, culture, people and places of five 'Northern' Southern states.

Insight Guide: Atlanta
In this beautiful, fully illustrated book, the 'capital of the New South' and Olympic-host city is explained and explored by local writers and an award-winning photographer.

Insight Pocket Guides and Insight Compact Guides

Insight Guides publishes two other series for visitors with limited time:

Insight Pocket Guides act as a 'substitute host' to a destination. A local writer presents a selection of timed, hand-picked itineraries and personal recommendations. Pocket Guides also include a large, fold-out map to the region.

Insight Compact Guides are slim, easy-to-carry books. They are similar to miniature travel encyclopedias for on-the-spot reference.

ART & PHOTO CREDITS

All color photography by
PING AMRANAND except for:
British Film Institute 95
Syndey Byrd 6/7, 8/9, 23, 31, 63, 70/71, 72/73, 74, 75, 77, 78, 79, 84, 98, 99, 100, 148, 149, 170/171, 215, 224, 225, 232T, 234T, 236
Jan Butchofsky-Houser 240, 246, 250
Ron Calamia 220/221, 264
Alex Demyan 1, 2/3, 4/5,16, 62, 76, 82L, 82R, 86, 91, 121, 123, 126, 127, 131, 142T, 153, 154, 154T, 155, 162, 166L, 175T, 176T, 177, 180/181, 184, 186, 188, 197, 198/199, 202T, 203T, 204, 204T, 205, 206T, 212, 214T, 216, 217, 224T, 226, 228/229, 231, 248L, 248T, all small cover pictures except front flap below
Brian A Gauvin 241, 252/253, 254, 255, 256, 256T, 257, 258L, 258T, 259, 260, 260T, 261, 262, 262T, 263, front flap below
Historic New Orleans Collection 18/19, 25, 34, 37, 38, 40, 41, 42/43, 47, 48/49, 50, 51,5 4/55, 56, 61, 64, 103
Dave G Houser 3B, 175, 178, 230, 233, 235, 238/239, 242T, 244T, 245, 247, 249, 251
Louisiana Office of Tourism 97, 243T
Louisiana State Museum 52
New Orleans Jazz & Heritage Festival/ProCreations 101
Tony Perrottet 104L, 104R, 105, 218/219
ProCreations Publishing Company 96
Rex Features 94
Topham Picturepoint 39, 66, 67
Archives and Manuscripts, Earl K. Long Library, University of New Orleans 20, 22, 23, 24, 26, 27, 30, 32, 33, 46, 57

Picture Spreads

Pages 88/89
All photography:
Brian A Gauvin

Pages 158/159
Top row left to right:
Brian A Gauvin, Syndey Byrd, Alex Demyan/courtesy Louisiana State Museum/Gallier House
Center row:
all photography Brian A Gauvin
bottom row:
all photography Brian A Gauvin

Pages 208/209
Top row left to right:
Alex Demyan, Syndey Byrd, Louisiana Tourist Office, Alex Demyan
Bottom row left to right:
Louisiana Tourist Office, Alex Demyan, Alex Demyan, Alex Demyan, Louisiana Tourist Office

Map Production
Gar Bowes Design
© 1999 Apa Publications GmbH & Co.
    Verlag KG, Singapore

Cartographic Editor **Zoë Goodwin**
Production **Stuart A Everitt**
Design Consultants
Carlotta Junger, Graham Mitchener
Picture Research
Hilary Genin, Monica Allende

Index

*Numbers in italics refer to
photographs*

fences 144, 196
Fencing Masters' House 140
Ferrér, Cayetano 53
ferries 205, 223
festivals 15, 95, *208–9*, 248, 262
  see **Mardi Gras;** *also* **Travel Tips**
  Jazz Fest 15, *100*, 101
  Tennessee Williams Literary
    Festival 91, 94
  filles à la cassette 20, 25
films *see* movies
Firehouse 207
fires 17, 29–30, 125, 158, 206
First Skyscraper 142–3
fish 83–5
fishing 214
Flea Market 134
Flower, Mayor Walter C. 52
food 81–9
  see also **restaurants; shopping**
  bread pudding 85, *197*
  Cajun 16, 244
  crawfish 81, 84–5, 249
  festivals 208, 209
  king cakes 76
  Mile High Pie *194*
  pastry shops 126
football 187
Fort St John 216
Foster, Governor 244
Fountain, Pete 175
Franklin 243–4, *245*
Fred's Lounge 250
French 20, 23–7, 33–4
  Bayou St John 215–16
  Cajun Country 16, 241
  cemeteries 165
  immigration 37–8
  Mardi Gras 75, 78
French Louisiana 208, 209, 241–51
French Market 58, 86, 131, 132,
  134, 135
French Quarter 17, 34, 61, 115, *127*
  architecture *158–9*
  Bourbon Street 149–51
  festivals 209
  Jackson Square 121–30
  preservation 57–8, 60
  Riverfront to French Market 131–5
  Royal Street 139–44
  tours 94, 133
  Upper and Lower Quarter 153–6
Freret, James 195
Freret, William 201
Friedman, Patty 92

g

Gaines, Myra Clark 167
Gallery Row 176

Gallier, James, Jr 144, 159, 193, 196
Gallier, James, Sr 144, 159, 193
  Boston Club 183–4
  Gallier Hall 188
  Pontalba Buildings 126
  St Patrick's Cathedral 189
  tomb 168
Gallier Hall 40–1, 159, *188*
Gallier House 144, *159*
gambling *see* casinos
Garden District 133, *193*, 193–7,
  209
gardens
  Jungle Gardens 246
  Rip Van Winkle Gardens *250,
  251*
Gelderman, Carol 94
Germans 37, 45, 98, 205
ghosts 124, 144, 236
Gilchrist, Ellen 92
Girod, Nicholas 156, 167
Girod Street 183
Golden Age 193
golf courses 204, 216
Gone With The Wind 202
Goodrich-Stanley Place 205
Gottschalk, Louis Moreau 97
Grand Derangement, Le 241, 248
Gravier, Bernard 183
Great River Road 231–4
Greek Revival
  see also **Architecture**
  Algiers 201, 206
  Boston Club 183–4
  Custom House 179
  Gallier Hall *188*
  Garden District 193, 195, 196
  Oaklawn Manor 244
  plantations 232–3, 234–5
  tombs 168
Green, Roger 177
Grevemberg House 244
gris-gris 103, 106
Guidry, Black 259–60, *261*
Gum Bayou 256–7
gumbo 82–3, 209
Guste, Bernard *88*

h

Hackberry 262
Halloween 208
Harrah's 173
Harris, Joel Chandler 233
Haughery, Margaret Gaffney 205
Haunted House 144
Heine, Alice 144
Hellman, Lillian 92
Hermann-Grima House 150–1

Historic New Orleans Collection
  141, 141–2
hockey 188
Holly Beach 262
Holy Name Church 203
Holy Name of Mary Church 207
Honey Island Swamp 255–7, *256*
Honey Island Swamp Tours 255–7,
  258
Hood, A. Baldwin 57
Hooker, John Lee 106
hotels 40, 61–2, *140*
  see **bed and breakfast;** *also*
  Travel Tips
  Bourbon Orleans Hotel 143
  Columns Hotel *201*, 201–2
  Hilton 175
  Omni Royal Orleans Hotel 139–40
  Pontchartrain Hotel *194*
  Royal Sonesta 150
  St Charles 40, *57*, 159
Houma 209, 242
Houmas House 234
housing projects 68–9, 205
Howard, Henry 126, 193–4, 196,
  234, 235
hurricanes 20, 24, 262–3
Hush...Hush, Sweet Charlotte 234

i

Iberville, Pierre le Moyne, Sieur d'
  20, 23, 215
ice hockey 62
IMAX Theatre 178, 189
immortelles 165
Indians
  Chicksaws 25–6
  Chitimacha 244–5
  Choctaw 215
  Natchez 25
Interview with the Vampire 62, 91
Irish 15, 37, 38, 189, 205
Irish Channel *200*, 205, 209
islands 246
Italians 15
  French Quarter 58, 121
  muffuletta 8
  music 98
  Piazza d'Italia 178
  St Joseph's Day *208*

j

Jackson, General Andrew 34–5,
  153, 179, 236
  and Lafitte 123, 133
  statue 122
Jackson Avenue 194–5